ACCLA...

"if it's cutting edge you want in a city that teeters between conservative and revolutionary, this is the book to buy."
—Toronto Sun

"Slangy and wired, yet so explicit and well-written that it makes a good read."
—Prague Post

"No other guide captures so completely and viscerally what it feels like to be inside the city."
—San Francisco Bay Guardian

"Sharp writing and a thrilling layout make it a guidebook you can read from cover to cover without a yawn, a fascinating introduction to all that makes the city exciting and extreme."
—San Francisco Examiner

"For travelers who've outgrown the shoestring budget of their college days, there's Avant- Guide, a new series from itinerant genius Dan Levine."
—Elle

"IT'S HIP TO BE THERE... All the usual topics from history to hotels to shopping but with a welcome cutting-edge spin."
—Chicago Sun-Times

"This book understands..."
—Chicago Tribune

"Brutally honest insiders give you the straight scoop on where to be seen so you don't feel or look like a tourist."
—Fitness Magazine

"The brash, Euro-cover girl speaks visual volumes about the hipster tone of this guide."
—The Oregonian

fiercely
independent!

Each Avant•Guide is created by
independent experts who never
accept discounts or payments in
exchange for positive coverage.

¶

Our visits to restaurants, clubs and
other establishments are anonymous,
and expenses are paid by Avant•Guide.

¶

FEW OTHER GUIDEBOOKS
CAN MAKE THIS CLAIM.

〜〜〜〜〜〜〜〜〜〜〜

AVANT GUIDE

San Francisco

!
E
MP
IRE
PRESS

Empire ~ New York

Empire Press
Empire State Building
350 Fifth Avenue., Ste. 7814
New York, NY 10118

E-mail: editor@avantguide.com
Web: www.avantguide.com

Editor-in-Chief: Dan Levine
Photo Editor: Sharka Worthington

Demo Design: deMo wshe (li6® & mig²⁵) www.mowshe.cz

Writer/Researchers: Michelle Goldberg, Sara Kimberlin,
Victoria Maitland-Lewis, Michael Stabile,
H. Victor Thomas, Grant Young.

Copy Editor: Jeannette Vota
Additional Research: Honza Žaboch, Ivana Nosková

Photography: Kristoff Halversham, SFCVB,
Casey Mahon (Chap 8/Dining),
Liz Steger (146, 155)
Cover: SFCVB, Kristoff Halversham; Allphoto
Digital Imaging by Li6oreK
Back Cover Photo: Michael Benabib

Digital Cartography: Copyright © Empire Press
Cover Films: Mousehouse 2H & Robko

Web Design: [ ] Lundegaard -> www.lundegaard.cz

Very Special Thanks:
Lori Armstrong, Tunisha Grant, Michael Benabib, Pluto, Deborah Brady,
Sarah Date, Chronic, The Scott Bros., Jonathan Pontell, Dr. Shedivka,
Silkworm, Marilyn Wood and Sheri Wiggins.

ISBN: 1-891603-03-5
First Edition
All contents copyright ©Empire Press 2000. All rights reserved.
Printed in USA by Bind-Rite Graphics/Command Web
Distributed in North America by Publishers Group West

ALSO FROM AVANT✳GUIDE
Avant✳Guide New York City
Avant✳Guide London
Avant✳Guide New Orleans
Avant✳Guide Prague

COMING SOON...
Avant✳Guide Cuba
Avant✳Guide Disney World
Avant✳Guide Paris
Avant✳Guide Italy

CONTENTS

ENGAGING
SAN fRANCiSCO
dEFOGgEd

It's just so "klee-shay" how absolutely everybody rhapsodizes about San Francisco's beauty, yet we can't help but nod our proverbial heads in agreement. Architect Frank Lloyd Wright summed it up by saying, "What I like best about San Francisco is San Francisco." The hills and views are what enraptures the aesthetes; its position on the tip of a 46.6 square-mile peninsula makes San Francisco one of the most beautiful little cities on Earth. The City by the Bay is defined by the surrounding water—one of the world's finest land-locked harbors—and its close proximity to nature. One never feels far removed from fresh air, even in the corporate canyons of the Financial District. A 500-square-mile cleft in the California coastline, the Bay is the region's most important resource for both work and fun. It's at once a major center for water-borne commerce and the perfect excuse to go out and play. So, while many residents are primarily drawn here for business, most stay on for pleasure. Although a steady stream of container ships and freighters are always gliding through the Golden Gate, you'll almost always find a regatta's worth of sailboats bobbing around them.

San Francisco's history is a mixture of Spanish colonialism and rowdy American romanticism. The first European settlement on the peninsula was established in 1776 by Spanish Colonel Juan Bautista de Anza and christened "Yerba Buena," or Good Herb, a prescient appellation that's not lost on modern-day tokers. Following the 1848 discovery of gold at Sutter's Mill, 140 miles east, Yankees arrived en masse, swelling the population from less than 800 to over 40,000 in just two years.

Born from the mid-19th-century Gold Rush, the city is so young that only a few years ago it was hard to find anyone who was actually born here. Even today the majority of the city's residents seem to be transplants from somewhere else.

The largest group of "locals" are whitebread liberals from California suburbs and the American Midwest who, despite short haircuts and Financial District prudence, pride themselves on their sociological progressiveness and tolerance of other cultures. The most progressive San Franciscans are the ones who didn't grow up here. The city's famously broad-minded politics has become a self-fulfilling prophesy in that it attracts like-minded liberals. And so the city's famously progressive social atmosphere progresses.

The result is a generally happy city. People live in San Francisco because they want to, not by default or accident of birth. San Francisco does, indeed, feel more cheerful than most urban centers.

The city's liberal politics have earned it ridicule from the rest of the country, along with lots of praise from the nation's outcasts and vagabonds. Homelessness, coupled with a rise in panhandling, is epidemic in San Francisco. Not only is this a beautiful place for the penniless, it's also extremely hospitable, offering loads of social benefits for the financially-challenged. The abundance of homeless in San Francisco is proof-positive that this problem must be solved at a national, not local, level.

Of course, the Eddie-Bauer-wearing, "Dharma and Greg" version of the city only tells half the story. In addition to the blonde-haired liberal transplants, there are several other demographic phenomena on the cultural landscape.

Mexicans and Mexican-Americans have been a major part of the city's ethnic mix from the get-go. African-Americans make up more than ten-percent of the population; and almost a third of the city is ethnically Chinese, a thriving community that's still drawing new immigrants. Southeast Asians are also migrating here by the planeload; their emerging presence is most visible to the casual observer via dozens of new Philippine, Thai, Malay and Indonesian restaurants that are popping up in the Tenderloin, and around the rest of the city.

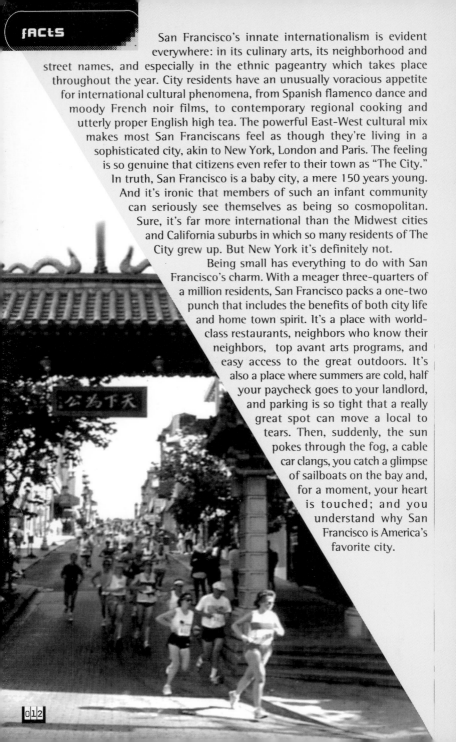

San Francisco's innate internationalism is evident everywhere: in its culinary arts, its neighborhood and street names, and especially in the ethnic pageantry which takes place throughout the year. City residents have an unusually voracious appetite for international cultural phenomena, from Spanish flamenco dance and moody French noir films, to contemporary regional cooking and utterly proper English high tea. The powerful East-West cultural mix makes most San Franciscans feel as though they're living in a sophisticated city, akin to New York, London and Paris. The feeling is so genuine that citizens even refer to their town as "The City." In truth, San Francisco is a baby city, a mere 150 years young. And it's ironic that members of such an infant community can seriously see themselves as being so cosmopolitan. Sure, it's far more international than the Midwest cities and California suburbs in which so many residents of The City grew up. But New York it's definitely not.

Being small has everything to do with San Francisco's charm. With a meager three-quarters of a million residents, San Francisco packs a one-two punch that includes the benefits of both city life and home town spirit. It's a place with world-class restaurants, neighbors who know their neighbors, top avant arts programs, and easy access to the great outdoors. It's also a place where summers are cold, half your paycheck goes to your landlord, and parking is so tight that a really great spot can move a local to tears. Then, suddenly, the sun pokes through the fog, a cable car clangs, you catch a glimpse of sailboats on the bay and, for a moment, your heart is touched; and you understand why San Francisco is America's favorite city.

StUPid fACtS

961	Licensed Taxis (5,000 Drivers)
9,600,000	Yearly Cable Car Riders
8.5	Length Of San Francisco-Oakland Bay Bridge (In Miles)
9.5	Speed Of Cable Cars (Miles Per Hour)
26	Fog Signals Around San Francisco Bay
39	Cable Cars
46.38	Total Area In Square Miles
90	Legitimate Theaters
496	Square Miles In San Francisco Bay
2,325	Gallons Of Paint Used Annually On The GG Bridge
14,000	Victorian Houses

POPULAtiON

San Francisco	723,959
Greater Bay Area	6,931,300

EthNiCiTY

White	46.6 percent
Chinese	28.4 percent
Hispanic	13.9 percent
African-American	10.5 percent
Filipino	4.4 percent
Japanese	1.6 percent
American Indian	0.4 percent
Other	32.8 percent

hiSTORY iN A hURRY

10,000 BC	Miwok and Ohlone (Costanoan) Indians begin to settle in the Bay Area.
1542	Juan Cabrillo enters San Diego Bay in the first documented European visit to California.
1579	Explorer Sir Francis Drake claims California for England and names it "New Albion."
1769	Father Junípero Serra begins an expedition that will eventually settle missions throughout the California coast. An advance party scouts San Francisco Bay.
1775	The *San Carlos* is the first ship to sail into San Francisco Bay.
1776	Spain claims the San Francisco Bay and establishes a fort; Father Junípero establishes Mission Dolores to convert the Ohlone to Christianity.
1791	Los Angeles founded.
1804	Spain divides its territory into Alta and Baja (Lower and Upper) California.
1821	Mexico declares independence from Spain and annexes Alta California.
1828	Fur trapper Jed Smith is the first ethnic European to reach California across the Sierra Nevada Mountains.
1835	William Richardson founds "Yerba Buena" on the peninsula that is now San Francisco.
1846	United States captures California in Mexican-American War.
1847	Yerba Buena is renamed San Francisco; it has 800 residents.
1848	Gold discovered in the low Sierras near Sacramento; first Chinese arrive in San Francisco; bank and post office established.
1849	Gold Rush swells city's population to 25,000; San Jose named state capital; Tadich Grill, San Francisco's oldest restaurant, opens.
1850	California becomes the 31st State of the US; City of San Francisco is incorporated.
1851	Lawlessness abounds; vigilante committee hangs four men in Portsmouth Square; first Chinese laundry opens.
1852	Zion M.E. Church established by African-American Methodists; Chinese Theater opens.
1854	State capital relocated to Sacramento; streets lighted with gaslamps; Alcatraz lighthouse established.
1856	Maguire's Opera House opens.
1857	US Army headquarters at Presidio established.
1859	"Comstock Lode" discovered in western Nevada triggering Silver Rush.
1860	Three mile railroad completed, from foot of Market Street to the Mission; Telegraph line opened between San Francisco and Los Angeles; Pony Express arrives with mail from New York; the martini is invented in either San Francisco or nearby Martinez—the debate continues.
1861	California remains largely untouched by US Civil War.
1862	Telegraph line opened between San Francisco and New York.

1863 – Iratabe, Mojave Indian Chief, visits; fortifications built on Angel Island; Cliff House opens; railroad and ferry connections to Oakland begun; San Francisco and San Jose Railroad opens.

1865 – Earthquake strikes city; James Cooke performs a tightrope walk from Cliff House to Seal Rocks.

1866 – Sutter Street's Emanuel Synagogue consecrated.

1867 – Anti-Chinese riots ravage city; Bank of California opens.

1868 – University of California established in Berkeley; earthquake destroys parts of city.

1869 – Transcontinental Railroad reaches San Francisco; the first carload of freight brings boots and shoes from Boston.

1870 – Golden Gate Park established.

1871 – City Hall begun.

1872 – California Stock Exchange begun; Woman's Suffrage Convention meets.

1873 – San Francisco gets first cable car on Clay Street

1875 – Palace Hotel opens on Market Street.

1876 – Chinese petition Board of Supervisors for protection, which fails to materialize.

1877 – "Sandlot Riots" against Chinese.

1878 – Baseball championship won by the Athletics; B'Nai Brith lays cornerstone of new Eddy Street building.

1879 – Seawall construction begins; public library opens.

1881 – Los Angeles Times begins publication.
1882 – British playwright Oscar Wilde visits.
1886 – Fior d'Italia, one of America's oldest Italian restaurants, opens.
1887 – Snow covers San Francisco in February; Orpheum Theater opens.
1891 – Stanford University opens.
1892 – First buffalo born in Golden Gate Park.
1896 – Sutro Baths opens.
1900 – Cioppino is invented in San Francisco; bubonic plague strikes; law prohibits burials within city limits.
1903 – First automobile crosses country from New York to San Francisco in 63-days.
1904 – Bank of Italy (later Bank of America) established; plague subsides.
1905 – Nearby Yosemite named first National Park; Oakland's Frank Epperson invents the Popsicle.
1906 – The Great Earthquake strikes, followed by four days of fires that destroy the city.
1907 – Fairmont Hotel opens on Nob Hill; Mayor Eugene Schmitz sentenced to five years in prison for corruption; bubonic plague strikes again; Cliff House destroyed by fire.
1909 – Seawall completed; San Francisco Symphony Orchestra founded.
1912 – Muni railroad service begun on Geary Street.
1913 – Final trip of horse-drawn car from the ferry to 8th Street.
1914 – Board of Supervisors votes to remove all city cemeteries; Crab Louis is invented at Solari's Restaurant.
1915 – San Francisco celebrates opening of Panama Canal with the Panama-Pacific Exposition.
1921 – DeYoung Museum in Golden Gate Park opens.
1923 – US President Warren G. Harding dies in San Francisco's Palace Hotel.
1924 – First transcontinental airmail flight arrives from New York; Palace of Legion of Honor dedicated.
1930 – Communists parade up Market Street.
1932 – San Francisco Opera House opens.
1933 – Construction begun on Golden Gate Bridge; Coit Tower dedicated; Alcatraz Island becomes a Federal prison.
1934 – Police open fire on striking longshoremen killing two, and prompting a three-day strike that brings the city to a standstill.
1936 – Bay Bridge completed; The "Clipper" begins regular passenger flights between San Francisco and Honolulu.
1937 – Golden Gate Bridge opens.
1938 – Herb Caen inaugurates his column for the San Francisco Chronicle.
1939 – Johnny Kan's Chinese Kitchen begins America's first Chinese-food delivery service.
1942 – Japanese-Americans sent to internment camps after the bombing of Pearl Harbor.

- "Trader Vic" Bergeron invents the Mai Tai in San Francisco.
- World War II ends; fifty nations meet at San Francisco Opera House to sign the United Nations Charter.
- 1946 – Prison revolt on Alcatraz results in the deaths of three prisoners and two guards; Yamato, the oldest Japanese restaurant in the US, opens in San Francisco.
- 1951 – General Douglas MacArthur visits; Prime Minister Yoshida of Japan signs treaty at Opera House ending World War II.
- 1952 – Irish Coffee is invented at Buena Vista Cafe.
- 1954 – San Francisco International Airport opens.
- 1955 – Allen Ginsberg reads *Howl* at the Six Gallery.
- 1956 – First Black & White Ball held at the Palace, Mark Hopkins, Fairmont and St. Francis hotels.
- 1958 – Union Square consecrated as a historical landmark.
- 1961 – UC Berkeley students stage a peace rally in Golden Gate Park.
- 1962 – Baseball World Series played in San Francisco between Giants and Yankees (Yankees win); President John F. Kennedy visits; huge "Be-In" takes over Golden Gate Park; three men escape from Alcatraz.

1963 – California becomes most populated state in the US; Alcatraz decommissioned as a prison.

1964 – Student unrest grows as the Civil Rights and anti-Vietnam War movements gain momentum; Sioux Indians lay claim to Alcatraz Island; John Steinbeck receives Nobel Prize for literature.

1966 – César Chavez organizes United Farm Workers in Northern California; Black Panther party founded; Sutro Baths destroyed by fire.

1967 – Human "Be-In" marks the beginning of San Francisco's Summer of Love.

1968 – GIs and vets march for peace from Golden Gate Park to Civic Center.

1970 – First bicycles permitted to cross Golden Gate Bridge; first fern bar, Henry Africa, opens in San Francisco.

1971 – Standard Oil freighters collide beneath Golden Gate Bridge releasing millions of gallons of crude into the Bay; US marshals recapture Alcatraz Island from protesting Indians; Alice Waters invents "California Cuisine" at Chez Panisse in Berkeley.

1972 – The Bay Area Rapid Transit (BART) system opens; Transamerica Pyramid completed.

1973 — National Park Service begins tours of Alcatraz Island.
1974 — Symbionese Liberation Army kidnaps local publishing heiress Patricia Hearst.
1975 — Steve Wozniak and Steve Jobs found Apple Computer Inc. in nearby, newly-named Silicon Valley.
1977 — Eight earthquakes jostle Bay Area; first double-death dive off Golden Gate Bridge.
1978 — Supervisor Harvey Milk and Mayor George Moscone are shot dead in City Hall by former supervisor Dan White; Dianne Feinstein becomes Mayor.
1980 — BART riders trapped in tube by power outage; two earthquakes hit Bay Area.
1981 — First AIDS cases are recorded.
1982 — San Francisco 49ers win Super Bowl.
1983 — Davies Symphony Hall opens.
1984 — AIDS begins to ravage the city's Gay community.
1985 — 49ers win another Super Bowl; former supervisor Dan White kills himself.

1989 – Huge earthquake, measuring 7.1 on the Richter scale, strikes San Francisco causing 63 deaths and $6 billion in property damage; Anti-AIDS protesters close Golden Gate Bridge; Oakland A's defeat San Francisco Giants in World Series.

1990 – Board of Supervisors votes to demolish quake-damaged Embarcadero Freeway; Soviet President Mikhail Gorbachev visits.

1991 – Huge urban wildfires in Berkeley and Oakland.

1993 – Board of Supervisors bans smoking in offices.

1994 – The Presidio becomes a National Park.

1995 – City elects Willie Brown, its first African-American mayor; San Francisco Museum of Modern Art opens; The Grateful Dead's Jerry Garcia dies.

1997 – Herb Caen, longtime columnist for the Chronicle, dies at 80.

1998 – Macy's West flagship store unveils a new facade and grand entrance on Union Square.

2000 – A new stadium, Pacific Bell Park, opens on the Giants' opening day; San Francisco Airport adds a new International Terminal.

2001 – Airport Rail Transit (ART) opens, connecting SFO with downtown San Francisco.

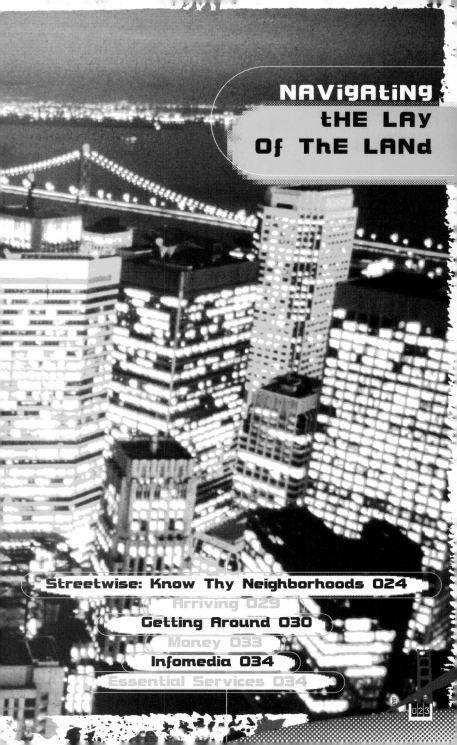

NAViGATiNG tHE LAy Of THE LANd

023

StREEtWiSE: kNOW ThY NEiGhbORHOOdS

Like every city, San Francisco is a conglomeration of neighborhoods, each with its own unique history and characteristics.

See Chapter 5/Exploring for in-depth information on all of the city's neighborhoods.

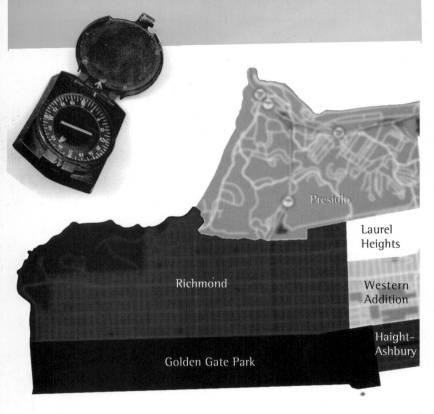

Presidio

Laurel Heights

Richmond

Western Addition

Haight-Ashbury

Golden Gate Park

Sunset

Twin Peaks

The Financial District – A sea of suits by day and becalmed by night, these corporate canyons are the closest San Francisco comes to New York. Begun with the '49ers when gold was discovered in the Sierra Nevadas, the District is now the West Coast hub for oil, telecommunications, insurance and banking.

Union Square – Once the site of brutal Unionist rallies during the Civil War, Union Square has become an eclectic mix of business lunchers, fire-and-brimstone preachers, foreign shoppers, conventioneers and the homeless. Most of the city's hotels and theaters are located close by, as are the majority of the city's high-end shops.

>>>

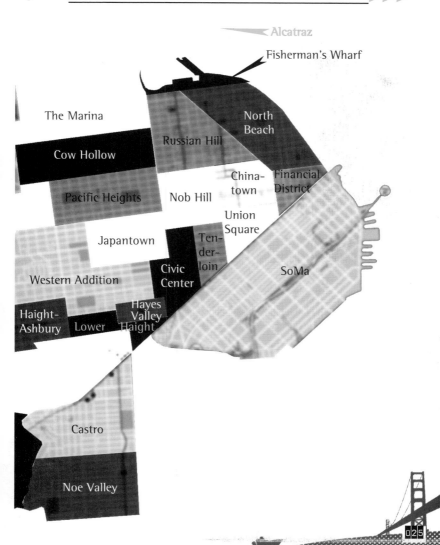

The Tenderloin is San Francisco's Times Square; the old Times Square, with its crime, street people, drug dealers, prostitution and seedy residential hotels. The encroachment of good restaurants, nightspots and coffeeshops are slowly converting the neighborhood into the "trendyloin."

The Civic Center, home to City Hall, the opera house, Davies Symphony Hall and San Francisco's main library, is also the city's hub of homelessness.

Chinatown, one of the largest in the West, single-handedly bestows cultural integrity into a city that otherwise might be mistaken for the whitebread towns of Portland and Seattle. Authentic bustling fish markets and herbalist shops, along with great restaurants, make Chinatown significant for locals and visitors alike.

North Beach is best known for its Italian roots and Beat-generation adolescence. It's also the city's best neighborhood for restaurants.

SoMa – Huge warehouse space, cheap rents and flexible zoning has changed the character of South of Market from industrial neighborhood to dance club district. San Francisco's Party Central is also a transport hub and home to Multimedia Gulch, headquarters of the city's software industrialists.

The largely Hispanic **Mission District** is named for San Francisco's oldest building— Mission Dolores, established in 1776. Low rents have also attracted edgy young things who pack the area's numerous burrito joints and avant bars.

Haight-Ashbury, made famous by hippies and Deadheads, is still the stomping ground for those who turn-on, tune-in and drop out. And a nonstop strip of retro and contemporary fashion stores continues to make Haight Street one of the city's most spirited. The **Lower Haight**, both less modish and more menacing than its alta neighbor, has a plethora of great dive bars, alterna-shops and budget restaurants.

The Castro, synonymous with gay life since the 1970s, is as much a theme park as it is a residential haven. A huge rainbow flag hangs at the corner of Market and Castro streets signaling the entrance to a gay Zion.

Noe Valley, which neighbors the Mission and the Castro, is very much an amalgam of those two worlds. Mexican immigrants and gay men co-exist peacefully in a tight-knit community that works hard to keep gentrification at bay.

Twin Peaks is more than just a tourist vista, it's a small neighborhood of older, affluent whities and a haven for hikers and nature lovers. Several steep stairway walks are rewarded with some of the city's last remaining wilderness.

Fisherman's Wharf, the city's most touristed area, is a lengthy waterfront shopping mall, and a little bit of Peoria right in the heart of San Francisco.

The Presidio's 1,500 acres of forests, grasslands and beaches recently passed from US military occupation to public recreation area.

The Marina's close proximity to both the Bay and downtown make it one of the city's most scenic and desirable neighborhoods. Its reputation is as a haven for rich young things who shuttle to their veal-fattening pens each morning and live for weekends. Excellent coffee shops, good restaurants and decent shops cater to these locals.

Pacific Heights is amongst the toniest of neighborhoods, built with gorgeous mansions and beautiful parks that have long been the choice of the city's media elite and society folk.

Japantown is something of a sushi Disneyland, now that less than five percent of San Francisco's Japanese-American population resides there. Most city-dwellers only know the neighborhood for its Spring Cherry Blossom Festival and Kabuki 8 movie theater, but it's still very much a Japanese cultural center.

The Western Addition, a large swath of land in the geographical center of the city, is something of a microcosm of San Francisco. European, African, gay, straight, rich, poor... everyone lives side-by-side in a cluster of tiny neighborhoods. Visitors know it best for Alamo Square's picture-postcard row of Victorian "painted ladies."

Hayes Valley is the city's newest up-and-comer, packed with cool restaurants and hip boutiques catering to yupsters and working-class folks alike.

The Richmond is home to San Francisco's second largest population of ethnic Chinese, and much of the consumer industry is geared toward their culture. The closer one gets to the Pacific Ocean, the more this area—also known as The Avenues—resembles a Northern Californian beach town, with a plethora of seafood shacks and an odd assortment of ramshackle surfer abodes.

The Sunset District, south of Golden Gate Park at the western edge of the city, is primarily a residential area with broad streets that slope toward the sea. **The Inner Sunset,** east of 19th Avenue, is heavily influenced by San Francisco State University and UC-San Francisco, both of which are nearby.

San Francisco International Airport (SFO)
Tel. 650/876-7809 or 800/SFO-2008.

Miles from San Francisco:	About 14
Average Car Travel Time:	About 25 minutes
Shuttle:	$10–$13 + tip (15%)
Taxi (metered):	$30–$40 + tip (15%)
Limousine:	$45 + tip (15%)
SamTrans Bus:	$1

SFO, the seventh busiest airport in the world, is a great place to land. The airport is modern, facilities are good, and it's relatively cheap and easy to get into the city, providing you don't travel during rush hour. And life is getting even better as the airport authority completes a five-level rental-car facility and 26-gate International Terminal. Now if they could just do something about the food....

In 2001, a new **Airport Rail Transit (ART)** system will debut at SFO, connecting it with downtown San Francisco in just under 30 minutes. In the meantime, here are your transport options:

By Shuttle – Shuttles are 8-passenger vans offering door-to-door service between the airport and the city. Lots of competition between companies means frequent service and low prices. If you arrive between 7am and 11pm, you don't need a reservation, just head to the upper level of whichever terminal you arrive at and take any van from the well-marked, curbside pick-up point. Rides cost $10 to $13, and most companies offer discounts for two or more people traveling together. You'll need a reservation for late arrivals and the way back: **Bay Shuttle** (tel. 415/564-3400), **Quake City Shuttle** (tel. 415/255-4899), **Lorrie's Airport Shuttle** (415/334-9000) and **SuperShuttle** (415/558-8500).

By Taxi – The fastest way to the city is by cab. Metered taxis line up at the upper level of each terminal. If two or more are traveling together in a cab, so much the better—in San Francisco there are no extra charges for additional passengers (up to a limit of 4 in most cabs), or for baggage placed in the trunk. The fare will be between $30 and $40, and a 15% tip is customary.

By Limousine – You can cruise into town in late-model stretch luxury for just a few bucks more than a tattered cab. Contact **Steve Kay and Jerry** (tel. 415/309-0726; www.mrlimo.com) or **Empresso** (tel. 415/576-1779; www.empresso.com). Reservations required.

By Bus – It is theoretically possible to get from the airport to San Francisco by city bus, although, to be honest, we don't know anyone who has ever done it. Here's the deal: **SamTrans** bus 7F departs every 30 to 60 minutes from the upper level of each terminal, costs just $1 and takes about an hour to the Transbay Terminal at First and Mission streets.

Oakland International Airport (OAK)

Tel. 510/577-4245.

Miles from San Francisco: About 20
Average Car Travel Time: About 30 minutes
AirBART to BART: $2 + $3
Shuttle: $30 + tip (15%)
Taxi (metered): $40–$50 + tip (15%)
Limousine: $60 + tip (15%)

Many locals swear by Oakland International Airport, preferring it to the far busier SFO. It was also the preference of Amelia Earhart, who launched her ill-fated round-the-world voyage from this airport's North Field. You can get to and from the airport via shuttle, taxi or limousine (see SFO above), but the quickest and cheapest option is via Bay Area Rapid Transit and the AirBART Shuttle connection to Oakland's Coliseum Station on the Fremont line. The AirBART Shuttle costs $2 each way and runs about every 10 minutes.

Arriving By Bus

You may have to travel for days squeezed between Charles Manson and the Elephant Man, but **Greyhound/Trailways** (tel. 800/231-2222) is relatively cheap and can get you here from almost anywhere. Round-trip fares vary depending on your point of origin, but few, if any, ever exceed $200. Several money-saving multiday passes are also on offer. The main San Francisco bus station is the Transbay Terminal at First and Mission streets.

Arriving By Train

Amtrak (tel. 800/872-7245) trains don't go to San Francisco; Oakland is as close as they get. Bay Area-bound trains depart daily from New York passing through Chicago and Denver. The journey takes about three and a half days and seats fill up quickly. The lowest round-trip fare—about $350 from New York, and $279 from Chicago—is good for 45 days and allows up to three stops along the way. The Oakland terminus is in Jack London Square, at Broadway and 2nd Street. Amtrak buses meet each arrival and ferry passengers to San Francisco's Ferry Building, Pier 39 and Fisherman's Wharf.

GETTING AROUND

Public transportation in the city is operated by the **San Francisco Municipal Railway**, better known as **Muni** (tel. 415/673-6864), which operates the cable cars, historic streetcars (trams), the metro, buses and trolley buses.

Muni operates Mon-Fri 530am-1230am, Sat 6am-1230am, and Sun 730am-1230am. Limited night service is offered on some lines.

The fare for Cable Cars is $2. Buy your ticket on board (the conductor will make change).

The fare for Bus, Streetcar and Metro is $1—in exact change. Metro faregates do not accept dollar bills.

Muni offers discount transit passes for one, three and seven days of unlimited travel. They cost $6, $10 and $15, respectively, and can be purchased at the **Visitor Information Center** at 900 Market Street, downstairs from the Powell/Market cable car terminal. When you pay your fare on buses, streetcars and metro lines, a slip is provided which allows for two transfers onto any of these carriers. No transfers are given or accepted on cable cars; single fares must be paid each time you board.

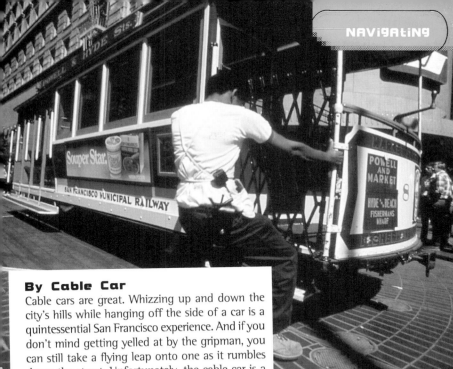

By Cable Car

Cable cars are great. Whizzing up and down the city's hills while hanging off the side of a car is a quintessential San Francisco experience. And if you don't mind getting yelled at by the gripman, you can still take a flying leap onto one as it rumbles down the street. Unfortunately, the cable car is a victim of its own popularity. Because they are perpetually packed with tourists, these mobile landmarks can rarely be counted on for timely transportation.

There are three cable car routes in San Francisco. Two of them, the **Powell-Hyde** and the **Powell-Mason** lines, begin at the corner of Powell and Market streets (near Union Square) and run across Nob Hill to Fisherman's Wharf. The Powell-Hyde line terminates at Hyde and Beach streets; the Powell-Mason goes to Bay and Taylor streets.

The **California Line** runs east-west on California Street between Market Street and Van Ness Avenue, serving the Financial District, Chinatown and Nob Hill. This line tends to be the least crowded.

Theoretically, cable cars can be boarded at any designated stop along the way. However, during busy summer months when they are jam-packed, it's all but impossible to get on anywhere but at the start of each route. That translates into a Disneylandish wait at the departure point of up to an hour, and sometimes more.

By Historic Streetcar

The introduction of historic trams in 1995 was a colorful addition to the San Francisco cityscape. Each car in this international collection has been painted in its original style, be it from Boston, Chicago or Milan. Collectively known as the F-Market line, these beautiful streetcars run along the center of Market Street, between downtown's Transbay Terminal and the Castro District.

By Metro

Beginning downtown, at Embarcadero Station, the Muni metro's five underground streetcar lines (J-Church, K-Ingleside, L-Taraval, M-Ocean View and N-Judah) take you under Market Street to various points in the western and southwestern regions of the city. The J and N lines branch off after the Van Ness station, after which they operate on the surface; and the K, L and M continue underground to West Portal Station before splitting into their own separate surface lines.

By Bus and Trolley Bus

Muni's buses and trolley buses (electric buses powered by overhead lines) cover every corner of the city. Each route has a number and name (i.e., 5-Fulton, 24-Divisadero, 42-Downtown Loop) which, along with the destination, is prominently displayed on the front and side of each bus. Some routes, such as the 38L-Geary Limited or 14L-Mission Limited, only make some stops.

Buses usually run every five to 20 minutes. Routes can be complicated. If you plan on busing a lot, purchase a Muni map ($2) from the San Francisco Convention & Visitors Bureau's Visitor Information Center.

By Taxi

San Francisco's taxis suck. The problem is in getting one, as there just aren't enough of them on the roads. Try flagging down a taxi at dinnertime, when you're late for a meeting, or if it's raining, and they're as scarce as a cop in an emergency. And repeated attempts to allow more cabs on city streets have been thwarted by the taxi lobby. Theoretically it's possible to hail cabs in the street. When the roof light is lit, the car is available for hire. Better yet, phone for a cab (or ask the restaurant to call for you) and they'll pick you up. Major taxicab companies include City Wide Dispatch (tel. 415/920-0700), De Soto (tel. 415/673-1414), Luxor (tel. 415/282-4141) and Yellow (tel. 415/626-2345).

The meter starts at $1.70 and hikes up $1.50 with each mile. The average fare is $7 to $10, and cabbies expect a 15% tip. Drivers will furnish receipts upon request.

On Foot

San Francisco is not for windshield tourists. Walking is the best way to get around, and you'll quickly learn how to play chicken with cars like a native. There are plenty of hills, of course, but there are also plenty of roads around them. It takes about an hour to walk from Union Square to Fisherman's Wharf, depending on how many slow-walking "Meanderthals" are in your way.

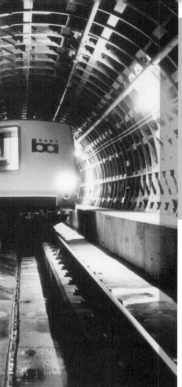

By BART

Completed in 1972, Bay Area Rapid Transit (BART) connects San Francisco with South San Francisco and the East Bay. Its four lines run from 4am to midnight on weekdays, and from 8am to midnight on weekends. A $1 Billion expansion is extending the line to San Francisco International Airport. Trains run beneath Market Street at the Embarcadero, Montgomery Street, Powell Street and Civic Center. Fares range between $2.20 and $4.50, depending on how far you go. Call 650/992-2278 for fare and schedule information.

By Car

Don't do it. You don't need a car in San Francisco. Parking is difficult and expensive (at least $20/day) and public transport and taxis can get you everywhere. If money is no object, by all means get behind the wheel. The city is bigger then it initially looks, and flying over the hills is a gas—especially in a rental. If you're planning a trip to the Wine Country, or elsewhere outside the peninsula, then a car is almost mandatory. *See* Cars & Driving in Chapter 11 for rental information.

MONEY

There is absolutely no need to carry a bundle of cash when traveling to San Francisco, or any other major American city for that matter. In fact, you can travel here without a penny in your pocket and obtain all the dough you need from hundreds of ATMs that work seamlessly with banks around the globe. Your bank will charge between $1 and $3 for each withdrawal.

Credit cards are widely accepted in San Francisco's restaurants, hotels and shops. Cash advances from Visa and MasterCard can be obtained from most banks, and most ATMs will also accept them, as long as you have a Personal Identification Number (PIN).

Foreigners should see Chapter 11 (Before You Go/Dollars and Don'ts) for more information regarding money and exchange.

Travelers Cheques

Travelers Cheques are obsolete. You don't use them at home, so why embarrass yourself with these clumsy dinosaurs when you're away? Any company claiming their travelers cheques are as good as cash is lying: Even the tellers at American Express may refuse to exchange their own cheques without your picture ID in tow. Stick to ATMs and credit cards.

The www.avantguide.com *CyberSupplement* is the best source for happenings in San Francisco during your stay.

Once in the city, head to the nearest newsstand (*see* Chapter 7/Shopping), check out the metropolis' mediascape, and stock-up on the city's listings magazines . The **San Francisco Bay Guardian** is an excellent weekly arts tabloid for theater, film, music and club listings. **SF Weekly**, its thinner rival, also offers entertainment listings. Both are available free from sidewalk boxes. **San Francisco Metropolitan**, a very cool weekly magazine, is the best publication in the city for nightlife and alternative happenings. It's distributed free at cafes and clubs. **San Francisco** magazine is a fine glossy with good restaurant listings and updates on club openings. The city's two daily newspapers combine on Sundays to create the hefty **San Francisco Examiner and Chronicle,** which contains a great Datebook supplement of entertainment listings and reviews. **Bay Area Reporter** and **Bay Times** have good listings of gay and lesbian happenings. Both are available free at many downtown clubs, restaurants and clothing stores.

The San Francisco Convention & Visitors Bureau's **Visitor Information Center** is located on the lower level of Hallidie Plaza, at Market and Powell streets (tel. 415/391-2000). They offer a wide range of free literature about sites and events in the city and have a helpful multilingual staff. They're open Mon-Fri 9am-5pm, Sat-Sun 9am-3pm. The Bureau also operates information hotlines listing current events in five languages: **English** (tel. 415/391-2001), **Deutsch** (tel. 415/391-2004), **Français** (tel. 415/391-2003), **Español** (tel. 415/391-2122) and **Japanese** (tel. 415/391-2101).

ESSENtiAL SERViCES

COMPUTERS/INTERNET – If you have trouble jacking-in visit **Internet Alfredo,** 790A Brannan St (at Seventh; tel. 415/437-3140; www.ina.com), a cyber spot with Web access that's the choice of SFs digerati. They've got 18 terminals and are open 24/seven. In a pinch? Rent a laptop at **Computown**, 720 Market St (at 3rd; tel. 415/982-8324).

CREDIT CARDS – **American Express/Optima** (tel. 800/528-4800); **MasterCard/EuroCard** (tel. 800/307-7309); **Visa** (tel. 800/336-8472).

CURRENCY EXCHANGE – Most change places are clustered around Union Square and Fisherman's Wharf. Established companies include **Foreign Exchange Limited,** 415 Stockton St (btw Bush/Sutter; tel. 415/677-5100) and **American Express,** in The Anchorage Mall, 333 Jefferson St (at Jones; tel. 415/775-0240).

EMERGENCIES – Police/Fire/Ambulance (tel. 911)

EYEWEAR/CONTACT LENSES – **Urban Eyes**, 2253 Market St (btw Noe/Sanchez; tel. 415/863-1818) is one of the coolest places in the city for Oliver Peoples, LA Eyeworks, Kata and other dandy frames. Replacement contacts in a hurry? Go to **City Optix**, 2154 Chestnut St (btw Pierce/Steiner; tel. 415/921-1188) for immediate, inexpensive replacements.

FILM PROCESSING/PHOTOGRAPHY – **Fox Photo**, 455 Powell St (btw Sutter/Post; tel. 415/421-8033), is the city's largest chain of one-hour developing spots with locations all over town. Check the Yellow Pages for branches. For professional developing, head to **Adolf Gasser**, 181 Second St (btw Mission/Howard; tel. 415/982-4946). See Chapter 7/Shopping for info on buying camera equipment.

LAUNDRY/DRY CLEANING – In some neighborhoods you'll find launderers and dry cleaners on almost every block. Ask at your hotel or check the *Yellow Pages* under "Cleaners." **La Post Cleaners**, 612 Post St (at Taylor; tel. 415/474-8183) turns things around in a single day.

LOST PROPERTY – If you lost it in San Francisco, it's probably gone forever. Try calling the **Property Control Office**, 850 Bryant St (btw Sixth/Seventh; tel. 415/553-1377). It's open Mon-Fri 8am-430pm. If you lost it in on **Muni** public transit, phone their lost-and-found office (tel. 415/923-6168).

LUGGAGE STORAGE – San Francisco's airports have luggage storage facilities that are open nonstop. You can also leave luggage at almost any hotel. At an average cost of $2 per item, your bags can stay at the Palace, even if you can't.

PHARMACIES – **Walgreens** fills prescriptions 'round the clock at 3201 Divisadero St (at Lombard; tel. 415/931-6417); and 498 Castro St (at 18th; tel. 415/861-6276). They have lots of other stores around town too. Check the *Yellow Pages*.

POSTAL SERVICES/EXPRESS MAIL – The **main post office**, at the Civic Center, 101 Hyde St., San Francisco, CA 94142 (tel. 800/275-8777) is open 24/seven. **DHL** (tel. 800/225-5345), **Federal Express** (tel. 800/463-3339) and **UPS** (tel. 800/742-5877) are all well represented in San Francisco.

TAXES – In San Francisco, the combined city and state sales taxes amount to 8.5%. Local hotel-occupancy tax is 14%.

TELECOMMUNICATIONS – Local calls from pay phones cost 25¢ for three minutes; directory assistance (tel. 411) is free. Examine the handset for crud before putting it anywhere near your face. Only about 50% of sidewalk payphones seem to be working at any given time, so listen for a dial tone before depositing money. You may still lose your quarter.

VIDEO – NTSC is the video standard. Tapes and multi-format machines can be rented from any Blockbuster Video store. Check the phonebook for the nearest location.

¶
¶
#03

SLEEPiNG: WhERE tO STAY

If ever there was a time to own a hotel in San Francisco, this is it. Business is booming, occupancy rates are at a 15-year high and, according to law of supply and demand, so are prices. Not surprisingly, several new properties are sprouting up, the majority of which are of the "boutique" variety—small (usually 125 rooms or less), design-driven hotspots that offer a personalized alternative to the major chains. Dominated by three main players: Kimpton Hotels, Joie de Vivre Hospitality and Personality Hotels— that operate nearly 35 stylish small hotels between them—San Francisco has long been one of the world's liveliest boutique hotel markets. That's a boon for avant travelers who shy away from corporate, group-oriented hotels in favor of more intimate, stylish experiences.

Alas, boutique hotels are becoming chainified. Behemoths Hilton and Sheraton are hustling to get into the haute-hostelry biz while Starwood Hotels and Resorts (which own Westin and Sheraton) is behind W, a brand new San Francisco hotel that is part of their first attempt at creating a boutique chain. Nearby, Toronto-based Four Seasons is opening a Market Street tower hotel that will be one of the very best places to stay in the city.

Finding a great hotel here doesn't take much effort. The city is packed with wonderful places to stay—in all price ranges. Quality ranges from Spartan to spectacular and is usually—but not always— reflected by price. All the hotels listed below share one thing in common: an enviable location; and are within walking distance to major sights. Hotels far from the action, or difficult to reach by public transportation, are not listed below—we wouldn't want to stay in them. Every establishment listed meets our strict criteria for service, facilities and value.

The hotels in this guide represent the very best in each price category that San Francisco has to offer. The rates quoted below *do not* include 14% tax. Weekend rates are usually lower than mid-week.

The "rack" is the highest rate that a hotel charges for its rooms. These are the prices printed on the hotels' rate cards, and is the price usually quoted when you simply phone and ask "how much do you charge?" Because of travel agent commissions, discount reservations services (see below), and corporate and club discounts, most hotel rooms are sold for substantially less than rack. The best way to reserve a hotel room is to phone, fax or e-mail and ask for their "best corporate rate." To compare prices and save time, contact several hotels and then immediately cancel the ones that don't work for you.

Discount Reservations

Several agencies offer discounted hotel rooms in the city. These companies negotiate bulk rates with specific hotels and act as a kind of clearing house for last-minute reservations. The result is often steep discounts on quality lodgings, including many options for under $100.

Hotel Reservation Network (tel. 800/964-6835; www.180096hotel.com) offers rates as low as $75 per night for economy class accommodations, and features discounts at many San Francisco hotel chains (including Marriott, Sheraton and Hyatt) and independent properties.

Accommodations Xpress (tel. 800/444-7666; www.accommodationsxpress.com) is another nationwide accommodations service with hotel listings in San Francisco and other US cities. Reservation information and requests are handled entirely on the Web.

Apartment Rentals

Bed and Breakfast International (tel. 650/696-1690 or 800/872-4500; www.bbintl.com) rents apartments to short-term visitors when their owners are away. These range from corporate-owned flats to highly-personalized places belonging to vacationing locals. Amenities vary, but every apartment is carefully pre-screened and priced far below a comparable hotel room. Expect to pay between $75 to $200 per night.

hOTELS bY AREA

The cost (**$**)
reflects the average price of a double room.

> **$** = Under $100; **$$** = $100–$140;
> **$$$** = $140-$200; **$$$$** = Over $200

UNiON SQUARE		page
Allison Hotel	$	054
Amsterdam Hotel	$$	049
Hotel Beresford	$$	049
Clift Hotel	$$$$	041
Cornell Hotel de France	$$	054
Hotel Diva	$$$	046
Grant Plaza Hotel	$	055
Kensington Park	$$$	047
Marines' Memorial Club and Hotel	$$	051
Maxwell Hotel	$$$	048
Hotel Metropolis	$$	051
Hotel Monaco	$$$$	043
Hotel Nikko	$$$$	044
Hotel Rex	$$$$	044
Hotel Triton	$$$	048
Hotel Union Square	$$	052
Sheehan Hotel	$$	052
Sheraton Palace Hotel	$$$$	045
Westin St. Francis	$$$$	045
tENdERLOiN		
Andrews Hotel	$$	049
Brady Acres	$	054
Commodore Hotel	$$	050
Fitzgerald Hotel	$	055
Hotel Beresford Arms	$$	049
CiViC CENTER		
Abigail Hotel	$	053
Inn at the Opera	$$$	047
Phoenix Hotel	$	056
NOb HiLL		
Huntington Hotel	$$$$	042
Mark Hopkins Inter-Continental	$$$$	043
Ritz-Carlton	$$$$	044
NORtH bEACH		
Hotel Boheme	$$$	046
San Remo Hotel	$	057
PACiFiC hEiGHtS		
El Drisco Hotel	$$$$	041
fiNANCiAL diStRiCt		
Hotel Griffon	$$$$	041

tOP ENd hOTELS

Clift Hotel

495 Geary St (at Taylor). Tel. 415/775-4700 or 800/658-5492. Fax 415/331-7542. www.travelbase.com/destinations/san-francisco/clift. $205-$305; suites from $360. Valet parking $25. AE, MC, V.

Perhaps the grandest dame in the pantheon of San Francisco's elegant old hotels, the Clift is best known for its soaring lobbies and reception rooms that speak of another era. That's not to say the bedrooms aren't nice; they are. Recently renovated, the guest quarters are predictably comfortable affairs, with faux-opulent furnishings and marble-clad baths. And while the suites aren't cheap, they're much larger than prices would suggest. Everyone loves the Clift's lobby-level Redwood Room, an art deco lounge so wonderful it maintains a refined elegance despite its immense popularity with camera-wielding tourists (see Chapter 9/Bars & Lounges).

326 Rooms: Air conditioning, cable TV, telephone, dataports, hairdryer, minibar, radio, room service (24 hours), concierge, restaurant, bar, business center, fitness center, wheelchair access.

El Drisco Hotel

2901 Pacific Ave (btw Broderick/Baker). Tel. 415/346-2880 or 800/634-7277. Fax 415/567-5537. www.eldriscohotel.com. $220 single/double; suites from $325. AE, MC, V.

Far from the madness of Union Square, but only a short walk from the Union Street shops, El Drisco is something of a lavish retreat atop a Pacific Heights ridge. Unknown to tour groups, this unique hotel is designed for individuals who prefer to live like the natives—the flush ones. Rooms are luxuriously simple, filled with old European furnishings and contemporary American amenities that include 2-line phones, VCRs, CD players and plush bathrobes. But as nice as this may be, it pales in comparison to the spectacular views of gorgeous neighborhood mansions in the foreground and the Golden Gate Bridge and entire bay in the distance. Continental breakfast is included, as is 24-hour coffee and tea service.

43 Rooms: Cable TV, VCR, telephone, dataports, hairdryer, minibar, radio, concierge, fitness center, wheelchair access.

SLEEPiNg

Hotel Griffon

155 Steuart St (btw Harrison/Folsom). Tel. 415/495-2100 or 800/321-2201. Fax 415/495-3522. $215-$260 single/double; suites from $315. Parking $15. AE, MC, V.

Sleek, contemporary furnishings, excellent amenities and a dynamite location in the heart of the Financial District makes the Griffon perfect for business travelers who aren't enamored by the corporate mind. There's a neo-New York energy here, created by lofty ceilings, sandblasted brick walls, and functionally stylish mahogany furnishings. Desks and lighting are made for working; and double-paned windows keep the city out. The best rooms have unobstructed water views. Guests enjoy full access to the ultra-modern YMCA next door and can walk to some of the city's best restaurants.

62 Rooms: Air conditioning, cable TV, telephone, dataports, hairdryer, minibar, radio, room service (Mon-Fri 1130am-9pm, Sat-Sun 530-930pm), concierge, restaurant, bar, wheelchair access.

Huntington Hotel

1075 California St (at Taylor). Tel. 415/474-5400 or 800/227-4683 (US), 800/652-1539 (California). Fax 415/474-6227. $230-$375 single/double; suites from $425. Parking $19.50. AE, MC, V.

Members of the New Guard looking for privacy, and those from the Establishment who don't want to encroach on friends, hole up at the Huntington, long the bastion of privilege. This is luxury's lap; where kings stay, along with A-list celebs looking for opulent anonymity. Built with Old World style, the 12-story brick hotel is at once elegant and upbeat. Each individually decorated guestroom is like a mini-apartment, fitted with European antiques and signature artwork, and fully-loaded with all the requisite top-hotel trimmings. The Nob Hill location translates into impressive views of Huntington Park and Grace Cathedral in the foreground, and all of San Francisco beyond. Well-off neighbors can often be found in the clubby, wood and brass Big Four Restaurant on the ground floor.

140 Rooms: Air conditioning, cable TV, telephone, dataports, fax, hairdryer, minibar, radio, room service (6am-1130pm), concierge, restaurant, bar.

Mark Hopkins Inter-Continental

1 Nob Hill (at California/Mason). Tel. 415/392-3434 or 800/327-0200. Fax 415/421-3302. sanfrancisco@interconti.com; www.interconti.com. $260-$320 single/double; suites from $475. Valet parking $25. AE, MC, V.

When money is no object and pampering is a priority, the "Mark" Hopkins is sure to hit the proverbial... well, you know. Once a magnate for millionaires, celebs and those who hunt them, the Spanish Renaissance-style skyscraper has settled down to become just another top business hotel. What earns its mention here is the excellent Nob Hill location and spectacular views—perhaps the best in the city. While guestrooms will win no avant-style awards, each is classically elegant, designed with muted colors and marble-clad bathrooms. In-room printer/fax/copiers, dataport phones and specially-designed desks attest to the hotel's corporate orientations. The glass-wrapped Top of the Mark restaurant and lounge is one of the most sensational spots in the city. An elegant interior and awesome 360-degree views made it the choice of World War II servicemen who stopped in for a last drink with loved ones before heading off to the Pacific; and it remains one of the city's most romantic rooms.

390 Rooms: Air conditioning, cable TV, telephone, hairdryer, minibar, radio, room service (6am-1am), concierge, 2 restaurants, 2 bars, business center, fitness center, wheelchair access.

Hotel Monaco

501 Geary St (at Taylor). Tel. 415/292-0100 or 800/214-4220. Fax 415/292-0111. $195-$265 single/double. $14-$16. AE, MC, V.

The Monaco is the jewel in the Kimpton crown; a large, lush hotel that straddles the fence between massive proportion and individualized personality. Based on this property's success, the company is extending its Monaco brand to Chicago and other American cities. The formula? Small, well-styled rooms and personal service that appeals to self-important style fiends. It's a luxurious place designed with multinational influences and packed with conveniences. Suites with their Jacuzzi tubs and magnificent city views are particularly special.

201 rooms: Air conditioning, cable TV, telephone, radio, concierge, restaurant, business center, fitness center, wheelchair access.

Hotel Nikko

222 Mason St (at O'Farrell). Tel. 415/394-1111 or 800/645-5687. Fax 415/421-0455. $270 single/double; suites from $525. Valet parking $27. AE, MC, V.

A deep bow to post-contemporary corporate life, Hotel Nikko is the choice of visiting celebs, globobosses and entertainment-industry *arrivistes*. The huge hotel happily flaunts its wealth of space which is, of course, downtown San Francisco's most precious commodity. The enormous clean lined, white marble lobby is built with particular attention to the senses that's just oh so Japanese. High-speed Mitsubishi elevators whisk guests to chic-simple rooms with emperor-sized beds and fantastic floor-to-ceiling windows that offer decadent views from the top floors.

Bathrooms are particularly large and contain separate showers and baths. Two $1,000+ per night Japanese Suites are some of the finest accommodations we've seen anywhere. Each unites a Western-style living room with a traditional tatami room, in which silk covered futons are unrolled each night. There's a space for performing the tea ceremony, and a small rock garden overlooking all of San Francisco. All guests are welcome to use the hotel's rooftop lap pool and fitness center, a glass-covered extravagance that has become one of the greatest places for a swim in the city.

523 Rooms: Air conditioning, cable TV, telephone, dataports, fax, hairdryer, minibar, radio, room service (24 hours), concierge, restaurant, bar, business center, fitness center and swimming pool, wheelchair access.

Hotel Rex

562 Sutter St (btw Powell/Mason). Tel. 415/433-4434 or 800/433-4434. Fax 415/433-3695. www.sftrips.com. $185-$235 single/double. Parking $16. AE, MC, V.

Dedicated to figures such as Jack London and Mark Twain who put SF on the literary map, Hotel Rex is an upscale, stylish place for people who love old books. Thousands of them cram the enchanting lobby, along with dozens of colorful portraits by pre-war California artists. The hotel's design is meant to mimic a 1930s literary salon as nostalgics imagine it must have been. Accordingly, each room is a mini-salon of its own, shaped by local artisans and furnished with period pieces hand-picked from thrift and antique shops. But there is nothing musty about the amenities which include voicemail phones, writing desks and comfortable reading chairs. The hotel regularly sponsors readings, book signings and literary roundtables. Deluxe continental breakfasts and evening wine hours are included in the rates.

94 rooms: Cable TV, telephone, dataports, hairdryer, minibar, radio, concierge, wheelchair access.

Ritz-Carlton

600 Stockton St (at California). Tel. 415/296-7465 or 800/241-3333. Fax 415/296-8559. www.ritzcarlton.com. $365-$550 single/double; suites from $525. Valet parking $30. AE, MC, V.

The RC is the swankiest chain-hotel in San Francisco. The colossal, columned, neo-classical building is as spectacular as its abfab location, on the eastern slope of Nob Hill. An elegant polished-marble lobby with crystal chandeliers, plush furnishings and museum-quality art, gives way to equally rich guestrooms, many of which have wonderful views of the city and Bay. The hotel is one of the few in the city that regularly attracts locals, most of whom come for afternoon tea in The Lobby Lounge or food and drinks on The Terrace, one of the city's largest and prettiest outdoor restaurants (see Chapter 8/Dining).

336 Rooms: Air conditioning, cable TV, VCR, telephone, dataports, hairdryer, minibar, radio, room service (24 hours), concierge, 3 restaurants, 3 bars, business center, fitness center and swimming pool, wheelchair access.

Sheraton Palace Hotel

2 New Montgomery St (at Market). Tel. 415/512-1111 or 800/325-3535. Fax 415/243-8062. www.sfpalace.com. $250-$420 single/double; suites from $475. Valet parking $22. AE, MC, V.
No San Francisco hotel has a longer, more illustrious history than the Palace. Built in 1875, the original building withstood the great earthquake of 1906 only to succumb to fire two days later. After extensive reconstruction, the hotel reopened as the city's finest; complete with a stained glass-covered Garden Court that remains one of the most awe-inspiring rooms in all of California (see Chapter 8/Afternoon Teas). The adjacent Maxfield's Restaurant is a wood-paneled club room named for the original Maxfield Parrish painting that hangs over the bar. Taken as a whole, the Palace is a beautiful, well-run hotel that is geared for serious business, yet mixed with plenty of pleasures. Each executive-sized guestroom has a large, firm bed, office quality desk, good lighting and mahogany reproduction antiques. And there's a loaded onsite health club with an exquisite greenhouse-topped swimming pool.

550 Rooms: Air conditioning, cable TV, telephone, dataports, hairdryer, radio, room service (24 hours), concierge, 3 restaurants, 3 bars, business center, fitness center and swimming pool, wheelchair access.

Westin St. Francis

335 Powell St (on Union Square). Tel. 415/397-7000 or 800/937-8461. Fax 415/774-0124. $229-$405 single/double; suites from $450. Valet parking $26. AE, MC, V.
A landmark since 1904, the St. Francis is both blessed and beleaguered by its ground zero location, directly on Union Square. Now Westin-owned and catering to corporate-types and conventions, this toast of the last century feels a bit soggy by today's standards. Though it's no longer a trend setter, the hotel still offers plenty to coo about, including a spectacular rosewood-paneled lobby and clubby Compass Rose bar—both of which have been meticulously restored to their turn-of-the-century heyday. Upstairs you'll find sizable rooms with good accouterments, bad plumbing and plenty of quiet. Although the staff is pleasant, the place is just too large to provide speedy or personal service. The hotel is actually two separate buildings: the original main structure with traditional rooms and suites, and the newer, more modern 32-story tower, which offers awesome city views from the upper floors. A ride to the top of the tower, in the exterior glass elevator, is an exhilarating scenic experience in its own right.

1189 Rooms: Air conditioning, cable TV, VCR, telephone, dataports, hairdryer, minibar, radio, room service (24 hours), concierge, 2 restaurants, 3 bars, business center, fitness center, wheelchair access.

Hotel Boheme

444 Columbus Ave (btw Green/Vallejo). Tel. 415/433-9111. Fax 415/362-6292. mail@ hotelboheme.com; www.hotelboheme.com. $129-$149 single/double. Parking $23. AE, MC, V.
Perched above a café in the heart of North Beach, Boheme is a something of a Beat-era theme hotel done in high style. Each of the 15 rooms in this bay-windowed Victorian hotel are impeccably dressed with warm earth tones, brass or canopy beds, bistro tables and antique cherry-wood wardrobes in which you can hang your beret. Hallways are decorated with Bohemian memorabilia that includes Allen Ginsberg's poetry, and light fixtures made from collages of 1950s jazz sheet music. Although rooms are small, they feel cozy rather than cramped. A friendly staff and complimentary sherry each evening help make the Boheme a nearly perfect little boutique hotel. Paradoxically, no smoking is allowed.
15 Rooms: Cable TV, telephone, dataports, hairdryer, radio.

Hotel Diva

440 Geary St (btw Mason/Taylor). Tel 415/885-0200 or 800/553-1900. Fax 415/885-3268. www.personalityhotels.com. $149-$179 single/double; suites from $199. Valet parking $22. AE, MC, V.
The Diva emerged from a recent facelift with a sophisticated, streamlined deco design that's proving popular with hip New York and L.A. types for its show-biz flair. In the lobby cool blues, cold steel and curvaceous lines evoke ocean swells. It's calmer upstairs, where spacious rooms are fitted with Le Corbusier chairs, sconce lighting and a wealth of electronic accessories. True to its name, the Diva is ideally located for theater-goers: It's literally across the street from the Geary and Curran, and within walking distance to numerous other playhouses. Continental breakfast, included, is delivered to your door each morning.
111 Rooms: Air conditioning, VCR, telephone, dataports, hairdryer, minibar, radio, room service (11am-11pm), concierge, restaurant, business center, fitness center, wheelchair access.

Inn at the Opera

333 Fulton St (btw Franklin/Gough). Tel. 415/863-8400 or 800/325-2708. Fax 415/861-0821. $140-$215 single/double; suites from $215. Valet parking $22. AE, MC, V.

Inn at the Opera is a super-luxurious boutique hotel for cash-rich travelers looking for a more personal experience than the Ritz-Carlton or the Four Seasons. Plush from the carpeting up, the inn is decorated with tasteful, hand-painted antiques and Oriental rugs. The opulence extends to guestrooms, where overstuffed pillows and armfuls of towels are combined with virtually every known convenience and pleasure, right down to twin phone lines, fresh fruit and flowers. The inn is also the most service-intensive spot in the city, with bellmen, concierges and room service personnel who greet each guest by name. Ironically, the hotel has chosen to name itself after its location, which is actually the single drawback to this wonderful place. Situated virtually across the street from the Opera House's stage door, this Civic Center spot is both dull and slightly dangerous at night. Take a limo.

48 Rooms: Cable TV, VCR, telephone, dataports, hairdryer, minibar, radio, room service (5-10pm), concierge, restaurant, bar, wheelchair access.

Kensington Park

450 Post St (btw Powell/Mason). Tel. 415/788-6400 or 800/553-1900. Fax 415/399-9484. www. kensingtonparkhotel.com. $150-205 single/double; suites from $350. Valet parking $22. AE, MC, V.

Kensington Park is a midscale Union Square charmer; a quiet neighborhood spot and reliable standby that always feels comfortable to come home to. Built at the turn-of-the-century and tinged with a neo-Victorian character, the hotel has quaintly ornate public areas and charming rooms, all of which are fitted with mahogany furnishings and baths adorned in marble and brass. There's even a chaise lounge in the elevator. Guestrooms start on the fifth floor so each has a little bit of a view, and a few get a peek at Union Square itself. Complimentary coffee and croissants are served every morning, and tea and sherry are poured each afternoon. The hotel shares its building with the respected Theater on the Square (see Chapter 9/Nightlife) and the outstanding seafood restaurant Farallon (see Chapter 8/The Restaurant Scene).

87 Rooms: Telephone, dataports, hairdryer, radio, concierge, restaurant, fitness center, wheelchair access.

Maxwell Hotel

386 Geary St (at Mason). Tel. 415/986-2000 or 888/734-6299. Fax 415/397-2447. www.sftrips.com. $135-$155 single/double. Parking $15. AE, MC, V.

The Maxwell is yet another old pile of bricks that has been given a new lease on life by the trendy Joie de Vivre group. Its a beautiful boutique property renovated in 1930s style, complete with brocade upholstered furnishings and earth-toned velvet curtains. The result is an ultra-modern designer hotel attracting in-the-know guests with fresh rooms, personal service and a good location close to Union Square. Its perfect mix of contemporary and classical fashions includes mahogany chairs, colorful hand-painted lampshades and plush gentleman's-club carpeting. Two penthouse suites come with private roof decks and stunning citywide views.

153 rooms: Cable TV, telephone, dataports, hairdryer, minibar, radio, concierge, restaurant, business center.

Hotel Triton

342 Grant Ave (at Bush). Tel. 415/394-0500 or 800/433-6611. Fax 415/394-0555. www.hotel-tritonsf.com. $135-$185 single/double. $14-$16. AE, MC, V.

Bill Kimpton, whose name is now synonymous with stylish San Francisco hotels, opened this modish youth magnet in the early 1990s before the word "trendy" ever preceded "hotel." The hook is excessive design, high-quality and moderate prices—hey, even the hip need a reasonably-priced place to stay. The hotel wows, if not inspires. The mind-altering decor crams lots of over-the-top elements into painfully undersized rooms, most of which are individually designed by local artisans. The hotel, adjacent to the Chinatown Gate, incorporates the trendy European-style Cafe de la Presse which serves espresso drinks along with international newspapers and magazines.

140 rooms: Air conditioning, cable TV, telephone, radio, concierge, restaurant, business center, fitness center, wheelchair access.

Amsterdam Hotel

749 Taylor St (btw Sutter/Bush). Tel. 415/673-3277 or 800/637-3444. Fax 415/673-0453. info@amsterdamhotel.com; www.amsterdamhotel.com. $89-$139 single/double. Parking $13. AE, MC, V.

The Amsterdam is a thoroughly recommendable moderately-priced hotel offering large rooms filled with curvaceous modern furnishings. While the schizophrenic decorating will never make the pages of Wallpaper magazine, rooms are quiet, accommodations are pleasant and everything is spotlessly clean. The sleek marble-clad bathrooms are particularly nice for the price; those at the top of the range are fitted with televisions and Whirlpool tubs.

34 rooms: Cable TV, telephone, dataports, hairdryer.

Andrews Hotel

624 Post St (btw Taylor/Jones). Tel. 415/563-6877 or 800/926-3739. Fax 415/928-6919. andrewsh@flash.net; www.andrewshotel.com. $92-$132 single/double; suites from $142. Parking $15. AE, MC, V.

A turn-of-the-century Turkish bath and gentlemen's club, the Andrews has gracefully aged into a turn-of-the-millennium mid-priced hotel. Victorian architecture means narrow halls, steep staircases and intimate rooms. Modern touches include modem-capable phones, clock-radios and well-lit writing desks, as well as fresh flowers and white lace curtains in each room. The location is great but, ultimately, it's the management's keen eye for detail that separates Andrews from the chaff.

48 rooms: Telephone, dataports, radio, restaurant.

Hotel Beresford

635 Sutter St (btw Mason/Taylor). Tel. 415/673-9900 or 800/533-6533. Fax 415/474-1317 or 800/533-5349. beresfordsfo@delphi.com; www.beresford.com. $109-$119 single/double. Parking $16. AE, MC, V.

Almost identical in style and price to its Beresford sister (below), this hotel represents another great value in the area. The look is Victorian traditional, with Old World decor unified by heavy carpeting, floral wallpaper, soft lighting and subdued framed prints. The lobby parlor is a comfortable place to lounge; and complimentary continental breakfasts are served in the adjacent White Horse Tavern, an "olde Englishe" theme pub.

114 Rooms: Telephone, dataports, minibar, radio, restaurant, bar, wheelchair access.

Hotel Beresford Arms

701 Post St (btw Jones/Leavenworth). Tel 415/673-2600 or 800/533-6533. Fax 415/474-0449 or 800/533-5349. beresfordsfo@delphi.com; www.beresford.com. $109-$119 single/double; suites from $140. Valet parking $16; self parking $13. AE, MC, V.

Old-fashioned in spirit and up-to-date in substance, the Beresford Arms is a terrific mid-priced downtowner featuring over-sized rooms and an enviable location (three blocks from Union Square). A fine Victorian wood-and-marble entrance leads to less-intensively detailed bedrooms, some of which contain Whirlpool baths and VCRs; and most suites have kitchenettes. Complimentary continental breakfasts, and wine and cheese each afternoon are served in the elegant lobby.

102 Rooms: Cable TV, telephone, dataports, radio, wheelchair access.

Commodore Hotel

825 Sutter St (btw Jones/Leavenworth).
Tel. 415/923-6800 or 800/338-6848.
Fax 415/923-6804. www.sftrips.com.
$99-$129 single/double. Parking $14-
$16. AE, MC, V.

The Commodore is one of the best-priced
offerings from the design-conscious Joie de
Vivre Hotels, owner of several stylish Bay Area
properties known for mod decor, personal service
and good value. Popular with working creatives
and black-clad wannabes, the hotel welcomes
you with whimsical 1920s luxury liner detailing and
playful custom furnishings. Guest rooms are large
and relatively simple affairs filled with all the
necessities and few indulgences. The lobby-level Red
Room bar is one of the funkiest hotspots in town,
filled nightly with all manner of jet-lagged waifs,
advertising urchins, design brats and other hip folk.

114 rooms: Cable TV, concierge, telephone,
dataports, radio, coffee shop.

Marines' Memorial Club and Hotel
609 Sutter St (btw Mason/Taylor). Tel. 415/673-6672
or 800/562-7463. Fax 415/441-3649. marineclub
@msn.com; www.marineclub.com. $100-$115
single/double; suites from $150. Parking $15. AE, MC,
V.
One of the most unique places to lodge in San Francisco,
Marines' Memorial was originally created for ex-military
personnel at the close of WWII. Accordingly, the hotel is
decorated with military memorabilia (including Douglas
MacArthur's corncob pipe) and the typical guest is an octogenarian
weekender hitting the city with his wife in tow. The rigorous staff
is excellent and welcomes civilians with the same attentive,
professional service you'd expect at the Ritz-Carlton. Really. The
best thing about this reasonably-priced find is that it feels like
something much more expensive. Rooms are rather plain, but well-
sized. And many of the suites are truly enormous, with two-story
vaulted ceilings, full kitchens and even the occasional walk-in closet.
137 rooms: cable TV, telephone, dataports, hairdryer, radio, room
service, concierge, restaurant, bar, fitness center and swimming pool,
wheelchair access.

Hotel Metropolis
25 Mason St (at Turk). Tel. 415/775-4600 or 800/553-1900. Fax
415/775-4606. www.hotelmetropolis.com. $129-$159 single/double;
suites from $175. Parking $19. AE, MC, V.
A comfortably chic boutique hotel that has become intensely popular with
traveling creatives, the Metropolis is a style-maven's paradise complete
with a two-story waterfall that gently cascades behind the check-in desk.
Each ample guestroom is furnished in a post-ironic yin/yang scheme
lifted from the four elements: Earth, fire, wind and water. The Zen
even reaches onto the night-table (where an alarm clock has soothing
wake-up noises like rain and crashing waves), into the minibar
(where you'll find ginseng tea) and to a communal Holistic Well-
Being Room (complete with meditative music, tatami mats and a
miniature rock garden). The latter might seem a bit over the top
when you peek in, until you find yourself sitting there for an
hour. Temporal matters are catered to with two-line dataport
phones, a business center with free internet access, and in-room
Super Nintendo systems. Rates include continental breakfast,
and biscotti and lattes each afternoon. Hotel Metropolis is one
of our favorite places to stay in San Francisco.
105 Rooms: Cable TV, telephone, dataports, hairdryer,
minibar, radio, concierge, restaurant, bar, business
center, fitness center, wheelchair access.

Sheehan Hotel

620 Sutter St (btw Mason/Taylor). Tel. 415/775-6500 or 800/848-1529. Fax 415/775-3271. sheehot@aol.com; www.citysearch.com/sfo/sheehanhotel.com. $89-$159 single/double. Parking $16. AE, MC, V.

It's hard to tell the difference between the many mid-range hotels packed into this corner of Union Square, but the Sheehan offers some special touches that make it stand out. Rooms, which are neutral in tone and character, offer writing desks and good lighting. Public areas are brightened with fresh flowers, and continental breakfasts are served gratis in an ample, comfortable lobby. Built by the YWCA, the building boasts a terrific indoor swimming pool and fitness center (a rarity for a hotel of this caliber) with complimentary access for guests. The Sheehan also shares the building with the tiny Lorraine Hansberry Theater, where guests can see performances for half-price.

65 rooms: Cable TV, telephone, dataports, hairdryer, radio, bar, fitness center and swimming pool, wheelchair access.

Hotel Union Square

114 Powell St (btw Ellis/O'Farrell). Tel. 415/397-3000 or 800/553-1900. Fax 415/399-1874. www.hotelunionsquare.com. $125-$139 single/double; suites from $189. Valet parking $19. AE, MC, V.

Funny thing is, that despite its uninspired name, this hotel is not even located directly on Union Square. It's actually situated a couple of blocks away, at the foot of the Powell Street cable car turnaround, where throngs of tourists line-up daily for the trip to Fisherman's Wharf. Inside, however, it's surprisingly pleasant for the price, offering neo-deco rooms with lofty ceilings, large windows and sleek, blond wood furnishings. Penthouse suites are, uh, tops, as they come with small garden patios. Standard rooms enjoy voicemail service, Super Nintendo games and complimentary continental breakfast buffets.

131 Rooms: Cable TV, telephone, dataports, hairdryer, minibar, radio, concierge, wheelchair access.

Abigail Hotel

246 McAllister St (btw Hyde/Larkin). Tel. 415/861-9728 or 800/243-6510. Fax 415/861-5848. $89-$99 single/double. Valet parking $15. AE, MC, V. The Abigail has hosted travelers since 1925—and looks it. Although a relatively small place, it's designed with a tad more style than the average mid-range hotel. Antique Victorian furnishings, down comforters and window seats overlooking City Hall all get our thumb's up. But an aging paint job and other minor decorative lapses sometimes make us wonder where the management's thumbs are. The Civic Center location is a bonus for serious music lovers, though the evening stroll home will remind you of the The Beggar's Opera.

62 rooms: Cable TV, telephone, dataports, radio, restaurant.

Allison Hotel

417 Stockton St (at Sutter). Tel. 415/986-8737 or 800/628-6456. Fax 415/392-0850. info@allisonhotel. com; www.citysearch.com/sfo/allisonhotel. $89-$109 single/double; suites from $139. Parking $17. AE, MC, V.

Decent prices and a dynamite location tell the whole story at this low-end hotel. Unspectacular yet functional rooms, dressed with modern wood furnishings and colorful spreads, offer just enough space to swing a cat. Front rooms are brighter but noisier, since they overlook the entrance to the Broadway Tunnel. Did we mention that they offer decent prices and a dynamite location?

87 rooms: Cable TV, telephone, dataports.

Brady Acres

649 Jones St (btw Geary/Post). Tel. 415/929-8033 or 800/627-2396. Fax 415/441-8033. staff@bradyacres.com; www.bradyacres.com. $65-95 single/double. Parking $14-$16. MC, V.

This cozy little guesthouse crams all the pluses of a five-star hotel into rooms that aren't much larger than a walk-in closet. Like a clown-filled circus car, each accommodation is stuffed to the gills with goodies ranging from coffeemakers, refrigerators and answering machines to toasters, microwaves, cookware and cassette players. There are complimentary chocolates, shampoo and conditioner too. You may not be able to turn around in the pint-sized bathroom, but you'll be charmed by its sparkling clean clawfoot tub. There are even ironing boards, vacuums and a coin-operated laundry with free soap in the basement. All in all, Brady Acres is one of San Francisco's best values.

25 rooms: Cable TV, telephone, dataports, hairdryer, radio.

Cornell Hotel de France

715 Bush St (btw Powell/Mason). Tel. 415/421-3154 or 800/232-9698. Fax 415/399-1442. reservations@cornell. com; www.cornellhotel.com. $65-$115 single/double. Parking $13. AE, MC, V.

French in name only (they don't even allow pets!), the Cornell also plays against type by being both clean and friendly. An over-decorated lobby gives way to standard mid-class rooms with cedar-lined closets and voicemail phones. Rates include a huge complimentary breakfast buffet that's worth waking up for, served in the hotel's chaotically tapestried Jeanne D'Arc Restaurant.

55 rooms: Cable TV, telephone, dataports, hairdryer, restaurant.

Fitzgerald Hotel

620 Post St (btw Taylor/Jones). Tel. 415/775-8100 or 800/33-HOTEL. Fax 415/775-1278. $75-$155 single/double. Parking $12-$16. AE, MC, V.

A solid performer in San Francisco's portfolio of moderate class hotels, the Fitzgerald is a reliable choice smack-dab in the city center. Tastefully decorated guestrooms all have decent amenities, lounge chairs and writing desks. Queen-bedded rooms are best for size; and those in the front of the house have decent urban views. Rates include continental breakfast and use of the nearby Sheehan Hotel's indoor lap pool and fitness center. Overall, a very reasonable place to stay.

47 rooms: Cable TV, telephone, dataports, hairdryer, radio.

Grant Plaza Hotel

465 Grant Ave (btw Pine/California). Tel. 415/434-3883 or 800/472-6899. Fax 415/434-3886. grantplaza@ worldnet.att.net; www.grantplaza.com. $52-$95 single/double. Parking $15. AE, MC, V.

This budget inn is one of the best values in the city for tightwads. Despite its buzzing ground-zero location near the Chinatown Gate, guestrooms are sparkling clean and relatively quiet. And although they're remarkably unstylish, rooms do include extras not often seen in low-end hotels such as voicemail phones, satellite TV, electronic keycards, hairdryers and plenty of towels. Corner rooms on the higher floors are both larger and brighter; while those in back are quietest.

72 rooms: cable TV, telephone, dataports, hairdryer.

Phoenix Hotel

601 Eddy St (btw Larkin/Polk). Tel. 415/776-1380 or
800/248-9466. Fax 415/885-3109. $89-$109
single/double. Free parking. AE, MC, V.

An urban motor inn turned chic, the Phoenix was one of
the city's first designer hotels. While it has long since been
eclipsed by far trendier places, the motel holds its own
with second-tier rock stars, B-filmmakers and anyone else
looking for stylish digs at reasonable rates. Located on a
hardscrabble Civic Center block, the interior is something
of an urban oasis; featuring a 1950s tropical bungalow
decor with island furnishings and original art in every room.
It's a funky place, to say the least, complete with a modern
sculpture garden, and heated outdoor swimming pool
painted with a Francis Forlenza mural. The hotel's
exclusive closed-circuit TV channel features films made
in San Francisco. Rates include continental breakfast.
44 rooms: Cable TV, telephone, dataports, restaurant, bar,
wheelchair access.

San Remo Hotel

2237 Mason St (btw Chestnut/Francisco). Tel. 415/776-8688 or
800/352-REMO. Fax 415/776-2811. lara@sanremohotel.com;
www.sanremohotel.com. $60-$80 single/double; $125 suite.
Parking $10-$12. AE, MC, V.

San Remo's personable staff, bargain prices and convenient location
make it one of the city's best finds. Tucked into a quiet neighborhood between North Beach and Fisherman's Wharf, the three-story
restored Italiante Victorian is the epitome of hominess. Turn-of-the
century furnishings are augmented by original leaded windows and
lots of climbing plants that enliven the public areas. Though small,
the guestrooms are comfortably furnished and individually decorated.
Most contain wrought-iron beds and antique wooden armoires. All
rooms, except the sole suite, share bathrooms, all of which are kept
spotlessly clean. If you do manage to snag the wonderful
top floor suite, you may never want
to leave.

62 rooms: Hairdryer, bar.

¶
¶
#04

SiGhtSEEiNg
SAN fRANCiSCO'S GREAtEST hitS

Alcatraz Island

Tel. 415/705-5555 (tickets), 415/773-1188 (recorded info). Open daily 830am-5pm; sometimes later in summer. Blue & Gold Ferries depart every half-hour from Pier 41, Fisherman's Wharf. Admission $7.75; $11 with audio tour.

A visit to Isla de los Alcatraces (Isle of the Pelicans) as it was originally called, includes a great boat ride, awesome views and even some wilderness; but the main draw, of course, is the legend of "Hellcatraz," the infamous former prison in tide-ripped San Francisco Bay. It's the contrasts that make Alcatraz so cruel and unusual: the contrast between the natural beauty of the Bay and The Rock's image as a dreaded, escape-proof citadel; the contrast between the exciting sights and sounds of the city, and the soulless, bleak aspects of incarceration where prisoners could practically smell the Ghirardelli chocolate from their maximum security cells. Alcatraz was America's toughest federal penitentiary from 1934 to 1963, home to such notorious lifers as George "Machine Gun" Kelly, Al Capone and Robert Stroud, the "Birdman of Alcatraz." Much of the prison is intact, including the main prison block with its steel bars, claustrophobic (9 x 5-foot) cells, mess hall, library and "dark holes," where recalcitrants languished in inky blackness. The windswept exercise yard, with its concrete bleachers and towering

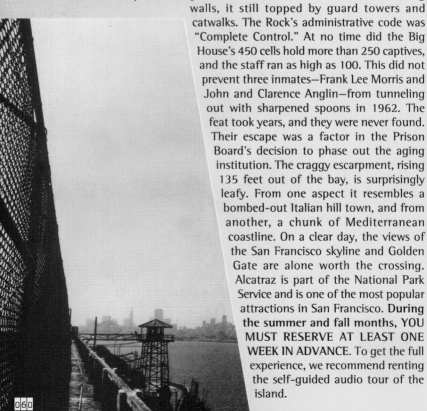

walls, it still topped by guard towers and catwalks. The Rock's administrative code was "Complete Control." At no time did the Big House's 450 cells hold more than 250 captives, and the staff ran as high as 100. This did not prevent three inmates—Frank Lee Morris and John and Clarence Anglin—from tunneling out with sharpened spoons in 1962. The feat took years, and they were never found. Their escape was a factor in the Prison Board's decision to phase out the aging institution. The craggy escarpment, rising 135 feet out of the bay, is surprisingly leafy. From one aspect it resembles a bombed-out Italian hill town, and from another, a chunk of Mediterranean coastline. On a clear day, the views of the San Francisco skyline and Golden Gate are alone worth the crossing. Alcatraz is part of the National Park Service and is one of the most popular attractions in San Francisco. **During the summer and fall months, YOU MUST RESERVE AT LEAST ONE WEEK IN ADVANCE.** To get the full experience, we recommend renting the self-guided audio tour of the island.

Cable Cars

Tel. 415/673-6864 or 415/474-1887. Operate daily 6am–125am.

It's great fun whizzing up the city's hills "halfway to the stars," as Tony Bennett sang, while hanging off the side of a cable car. Because they are perpetually packed with tourists, these mobile National Historic Landmarks operate more as a theme park ride than reliable transportation: there are only three lines—a total of 8.8 miles of track—and a whopping 10 million riders annually. Refurbished in the 1980s, San Francisco's cable cars still operate much as they did on August 2, 1873, when their inventor, wire rope manufacturer Andrew Hallidie, guided the first car down Clay Street. The cars have no motors and are towed up and down hills by cables that run beneath the streets. The drivers, known as gripmen or grips, operate what is essentially a two-ton pair of pliers which clamp onto cables that move at a steady rate of 9.5 miles-per-hour.

In their heyday, eight cable car lines ran on 112 miles of track. The fact is, however, that cable propulsion is very inefficient. Of the energy produced to run the system, only an estimated 4% actually moves the cars. Gripmen (and they're all men) are something of an elite bunch of attention-loving hams who enjoy interacting with their public. Don't be surprised if you hear a grip leading his passengers in song while rumbling down the city's streets. Conductors, the other members of the crew, tend to the passengers, collect fares and occasionally help out with the cars' breaks. The first car is out of the Cable Car Barn and Museum (see below) at 6am and returns at 130am. The fare is $2. See Chapter 2/Getting Around for complete information.

Coit Tower

Telegraph Hill (near Filbert/Kearny). Tel. 415/362-0808. Open daily 10am–630pm. Admission free; $3 to the top.

The lower slopes of that home-grown Matterhorn, Telegraph Hill, has long been part of the local pasta belt, home to such venerable North Beach landmarks as Caffe Trieste, Figoni Hardware, Italian & French Baking Co., Panama Canal Ravioli Factory and the Savoy-Tivoli. The neighborhood often looks as if there's a street fair in progress, whether there is or not. Higher up are the traditional Telegraph Hill dwellings—stucco, shingled and woodframe homes with bellied windows, and rents that rise proportionally with the elevation. Topping it all is Coit Tower, a phallic-shaped concrete column bequeathed to the city by Lillie Hitchcock Coit. As a child, Lillie was rescued from a blaze by a fireman, thereby beginning her lifelong fascination with men in uniform. Upon her death, in 1929, she willed $118,000 to the City of San Francisco for a monument to firefighters. The result is Coit Tower, a 210-foot (64 meter) landmark tower allegedly designed to resemble the nozzle of a fire hose. You can elevator to the top for terrific views over North Beach, San Francisco Bay and beyond. But before making the ascent, take some time to study the famous murals on the ground floor. A group of 25 artists were assembled in 1934 as part of the Works Progress Administration's attempt to lift America out of the Great Depression. Depicting the politics and culture of the era, as seen from the artists' eyes, the murals contain many allusions—both subtle and blatant—to Marxism and socialism. Soon after their unveiling the public outcry became so intense that the tower was closed for several months to allow certain parts of the murals, including a hammer and sickle, to be painted over. Check out the mural entitled "California Industrial Scenes," which depicts a multitude of unemployed workers, one of whom is holding a leaflet calling for a May Day protest for workers' rights. Make your way down Telegraph Hill via the Filbert Street or Greenwich Street steps. A long trek comprised of several flights of stairs, it's is one of the most lushly romantic walks in the city, winding its way through tall trees and hillside gardens, and offering some of the best views in the city.

SAN FRANCISCO'S STEEPEST TOP 10

Taxi company maintenance foremen maintain that hard-driving San Francisco cabbies burn out their brakes every 1,500 to 2,500 miles. But if you're in a rental car, who cares? Catching air down Filbert Street's 31.5 grade (it's one-way) and up intersecting Jones' 29-percent pitch (*Bullitt* style) is one of life's great experiences. Perhaps surprisingly, some of San Francisco's most celebrated slopes don't even make the grade: Lombard's 1000 block, known for its switchbacks as "The World's Crookedest Street," is only an 18 percent incline. Hyde Street, where the cable cars schuss down to Aquatic Park, is a mere 21.3-degree slope. And the point at which Mason Street plunges down Nob Hill's south face, next to the Mark Hopkins Hotel, is only 22.2 percent grade. Like the old maxim says, "When you get tired of walking around San Francisco, you can always lean against it."

10. Fillmore between Vallejo and Broadway (24 %)

09. Jones between Pine and California (24.8 %)

08. Duboce between Divisadero and Alpine (25 %)

07. Duboce between Castro and Divisadero (25 %)

06. Jones between Green and Union (26 %)

05. Webster between Vallejo and Broadway (26 %)

04. Duboce between Buena Vista and Alpine (27.9 %)

03. Jones between Union and Filbert (29 %)

02. 22nd Street between Church and Vicksburg (31.5 %)

01. Filbert between Leavenworth and Hyde (31.5 %)

Source: San Francisco City Bureau of Engineering

Fisherman's Wharf

Jefferson St (btw Kearny/Hyde). Technically "Fisherman's Wharf" refers to the "Fish Alley" on pier 45, but the term has come to encompass the entire Jefferson Street waterfront between Kearny and Hyde streets. A shared culture unites the entire area; namely an endless string of touristy schlock shops that extend across four malls: The Anchorage, The Cannery, Ghirardelli Square and Pier 39. At its worst, Fisherman's Wharf incorporates every insult known to tourism. A chaotic carnival of crass commercialism, the area is jam-packed with shops selling the worst kind of tourist-oriented junk (T-shirts, plush toys, refrigerator magnets), along with several classic tourist-traps masquerading as museums (Ripley's Believe it or Not, Guinness Book of World Records). In-between are dozens of mediocre-to-offensive restaurants, few of which care if they ever see a repeat customer. Worst of all, almost nothing is authentic about the Wharf anymore. There are few fishermen, and the sidewalk stands offering steamed shrimp and Dungeness crab sandwiches fly their catches in from Canada, and further. And yet, that's what the people want: Fisherman's Wharf has perfected its appeal to the lowest common denominator to become the most visited attraction in the city.

Fisherman's Wharf reached its peak in the late 1800s, selling more fish than all other West Coast ports combined. The mainly Italian fishermen sailed feluccas, 16-foot boats pointed at both the bow and stern. But signs of overfishing surfaced as early as 1900, and the situation was made worse by pollution and river damming. Today, commercial fishers rarely work inside the bay.

Pier 39 (at Stockton St) is the most dynamic of the waterfront shopping malls. Primarily an outdoor affair, the two-story, wooden planked wharf feels very much like a Rouse development, *a la* Boston's Fanuil Hall, Miami's Bayside Marketplace and New York City's South Street Seaport. Developed in the 1970s, the mall is home to important places like Puppets on the Pier, Turbo Ride Simulation Theatre, and Mel Fisher's Sunken Treasure Museum Store. After the 1989 Loma Prieta earthquake hundreds of sea lions that had hung-out around the Cliff House inexplicably moved down to Pier 39's K-Dock where they make their homes to this day. To the delight of store owners (and dismay of boaters who once operated out of this marina), the sea lions have become one of the waterfront's star attractions. Their numbers peak in January, with over 500 on the newly-reinforced docks. Pier 39 is also home to UnderWater World, a giant aquarium with a 300-foot-long tunnel through which you can walk while surrounded by sharks and hundreds of other marine animals.

Ghirardelli Square (900 North Point St), anchoring the other end of Fisherman's Wharf, is the other major mall on the block. Packed with shops like Little Cable Car Souvenirs, and the pet-gift shop Beastro by the Bay, few of the 60-plus "specialty" shops are really special. However, the elegant 19th-century factory and mill buildings that make up the Square are indeed extraordinary and worth exploring. After going belly-up selling gold prospecting supplies, Domingo Ghirardelli changed tack and began importing cocoa beans. In 1893 he took-over this former woolen mill where he made chocolate until the 1960s, after which production moved to the East Bay. The Square is known for staging lots of live entertainment in its West Plaza. Look for jugglers, magicians, mimes and live bands every Friday, Saturday and Sunday throughout the year.

The Cannery (2801 Leavenworth St), situated between Pier 39 and Ghirardelli Square, is yet another mall capitalizing on the daily onslaught of tourists to Fisherman's Wharf. At the turn of the last century, Marco J. Fontana, a former worker at the nearby Colombo Produce Market, devised a new method of canning fruits and vegetables. In 1907 Fontana built the world's largest cannery at Jefferson and Leavenworth streets, where tons of California fruits and vegetables were canned under the famous Del Monte label. Canning operations continued here until 1937; and in 1967 the Cannery was renovated. Today it is a lackluster maze of shops, galleries and restaurants, and home to the Museum of the City of San Francisco (*see* Other Collections, below).

The Anchorage, next door, is the worst mall of the lot. Its best attraction is the ATM, located in the courtyard opposite the Steelhead Brewery.

OK, so now that you know Fisherman's Wharf exists solely for tourists, go with your tongue firmly in cheek and have a good time. It's worth seeing at least once, just so you know what you're not missing. If you don't mind waiting in a long line, you can get to Fisherman's Wharf from Union Square by cable car. Both the Powell-Hyde and the Powell-Mason lines make the trip, which takes about 20-25 minutes.

Golden Gate Bridge

One of the world's most incredible pieces of outdoor sculpture, the majestic Golden Gate Bridge links San Francisco to Marin County. The world-renowned, Rust-Resistant Orange colored 1.7-mile span was built in four years, opening in 1937, at a cost of $33 million. The single-suspension span is anchored off the shores of the bay by twin towers that reach skyward 750 feet. The roadway, designed to sway 27.7 feet, is supported by two cables that contain 70,000 miles of wire which are stretched over the top of the towers and rooted in concrete piers on the shore. The bodies of ten workers, killed during a construction accident, are said to remain buried in one of the bridge's concrete piers. Since the bridge's opening, more than 1,000 people have taken deadly leaps from the span—a four-second drop onto concrete-hard waves; yet, several jumpers have survived the 80-mile-per-hour plunge.

If you've got the time and energy, the best way to get to the bridge is by foot, along the nearly four-mile-long Golden Gate Promenade that runs along the water past Fort Mason, Marina Green and the Presidio. You can safely walk or bicycle across the bridge, and there are parking lots at each end of the span.

Map labels (left side):

Fell · Oak · Page · Haight · Wall · Fred · Car · Parn

Stanyan

Arguello · 3rd Ave · Balboa · 5th · Cabrillo · 7th · 9th · 11th · Park Presidio · Funston · 15th · 17th · 19th · 21st · 23rd A · 25th · 27th · 29th · Cabrillo · 31st · 33rd · 35 · 3 · E

Conservatory of Flowers · Tennis Courts · AIDS Memorial Grove · Kezar Stadium · Mr King Jr Dr · Kezar Dr · Lincoln · Hugo · Irving

Kennedy Dr · Middle Dr E · California Academy of Sciences

DeYoung Museum · Japanese Tea Garden · Strybing Arboretum

Stow Lake

Boat House

Golden Gate Park · Lincoln

Marx Meadow · Speedway Meadow · Lindley Meadow · Spreckels Lake · Stadium

Fulton

Buffalo Paddock · Kennedy Dr · Riding Stables

Golf Course · John F. Kennedy Dr · Martin Luther King Jr Dr

Dutch Windmill · Soccer Fields · Murphy Windmill · Great Highway · La P · Ocean Beach

N

Golden Gate Park

Btw Fulton/Stanyan/Lincoln Way/Great Hwy. Tel. 415/753-7024.

It's hard to imagine San Francisco without Golden Gate Park. Its spacious and level greenery is an important counterpoint to the hilly concrete jungle. This huge green rectangle ingeniously blends rolling meadows, lakes, woods, formal dress grounds and rocky outcroppings, making it a wonderful place to explore (even when it's shrouded in fog). Designed in 1868 by Scotsman John McLaren, the park is one of the city's primary pressure valves; the place where urbanites come to run, blade, catch some sun or shade, and just release some pent-up urban steam. Unlike New York City's Central Park (America's other great urban green), where roads were sunk so as not to disturb the uniformity of the park, Golden Gate is traversed by a myriad of drives that effectively turn the land into a series of adjacent little parks. Sadly, for many, Golden Gate is a drive-thru park; you can practically see the whole thing without emerging from your car (this is California, after all). Of course, walking is the best way to go; especially on Sundays, when JFK Drive is closed to automobile traffic. A thousand acres of sand dunes have been tamed into a recreational and relaxation haven. The park offers gardens, lakes, playing fields, an archery range, baseball diamonds, 12 miles of bridle paths (see Chapter 6/Recreation & Exercise), the California Academy of Sciences, and a whole lot more. Free guided walking tours are conducted by **Friends of Recreation and Parks** (tel. 415/263-0991). Phone for tour times and reservations. Here's the round-up:

National AIDS Memorial Grove – The nation's only memorial to the victims of AIDS and those living with HIV is a bucolic dell built with meditative paths and flanked by a wall of redwoods. At the center is a concrete sculpture engraved with the names of thousands of victims.

California Academy of Sciences – The city's museum of natural history encompasses an aquarium and planetarium. See "The Top Museums," below, for complete information.

De Young Museum – The first art museum in the West is still one of the best. See "The Top Museums," below, for complete information.

Strybing Arboretum and Botanical Gardens – You don't have to be a plant lover to appreciate the unrivaled beauty of these gardens. In its attempt to cover the plant kingdom with encyclopedic completeness, the Arboretum is something of a "living library" for over 6,000 plant species, including an amazing stand of enormous California redwoods.

Conservatory of Flowers – When the Victorian-style glass Conservatory opens in 2001, it will be one of the finest greenhouses in the world. A floral utopia, the building is stunning, both inside and out. Surrounded by a rainbow of tulips, lilies and other flora, the glass kingdom houses an enormous collection of tropical plants and specialty flowers. There are some extraordinary plants from Madagascar, along with a "primitive garden" section which includes plants that were known to the dinosaurs.

Dutch Windmill – One of two windmills originally built to help irrigate the park, this traditional beauty is surrounded by more than 14,000 tulips and other flowers.

Japanese Tea Garden – A five-acre legacy from the 1894 Midwinter International Exposition, this is the oldest Japanese-style garden in the country. It is replete with bonsai and cherry trees, and contains an open-air pavilion where green tea and Japanese-style cookies are served.

Stow Lake – Golden Gate Park's Stow Lake has long been a popular spot with visitors and locals alike. It's a relatively quiet place for bird-watching, book reading and picnicking. It's also perfect for taking out a row- or pedal-boat and watching the world glide by (*See* Chapter 6/Recreation & Exercise for rental information.).

Buffalo Paddock – The park's small herd of bison can almost always be seen grazing near the fence along John F. Kennedy Drive.

Beach Chalet – This reconstructed 1929 building houses a fun brew-pub (*see* Chapter 9/Brew-Pubs/Micro-Breweries), as well as a comprehensive Visitor's Center for the park. Check-out the refurbished murals, too.

San Francisco's collection of museums is what one would expect from one of the world's great cities. Within the boundaries of Golden Gate Park are two of sterling reputation: the California Academy of Sciences, and MH de Young Memorial Museum. If you're a serious museum-goer, look into the San Francisco City Pass, which allows entrance to the city's top five museums (all the "Top Museums" below, with the exception of the Asian Art Museum), plus the Zoo and a one-hour Bay cruise, at a savings of 50% off the regular admission price. The pass is for sale at participating attractions and at the Visitor Information Center at the corner of Powell and Market streets.

Asian Art Museum

Golden Gate Park (near Fulton/8th). Tel. 415/379-8801. Open Tues-Sun 930am-5pm (first Wed of each month until 845pm). Admission $7; free first Wed of each month.

Until 2001, when the Asian Art Museum moves to the Civic Center, the city's pan-Asian collection of fine and decorative arts is housed in the middle of Golden Gate Park, adjacent to the De Young Museum (see below). Exhibits span the continent, from the Urals to India, usually culling pieces from the museum's own extensive collection of Chinese sculpture, Indian painting, Japanese prints, and weavings from newly independent Soviet republics. Almost everything the museum owns is old. Newer works are exhibited in temporary shows that are borrowed from other institutions. Recent presentations included a survey of jade objects, Hokusai prints, and Chinese Art since the death of Mao Zedong. Call for departure times of the excellent docent-led tours.

California Academy of Sciences

Golden Gate Park. Tel. 415/750-7145; Morrison Planetarium Tel. 415/750-7141. Open daily 10am-5pm (until 845pm the first Wed of each month). Admission $8.50; Planetarium $2.50; free the first Wed of each month.

The California Academy of Sciences, San Francisco's warehouse of history, is one of the world's largest institutions dedicated to the natural sciences. The Academy houses the Natural History Museum, Steinhart Aquarium, and Morrison Planetarium under one roof in the middle of Golden Gate Park. With over 14 million specimens and artifacts, the museum's scope is enormous. Begin with a detailed 3.5-billion-year journey of life on Earth, and continue with dinosaur fossils, an earthquake room that simulates several major shakers, moon rocks, an Insect Room with a bird-eating spider, the Gary Larson Hall (with original Far Side artwork), and a sparkling gem and mineral collection that includes a 1,350-pound quartz crystal.

Free docent-led tours are scheduled daily; phone for times.

The **Aquarium** is the Academy's highlight. In addition to enormous tanks of salt- and fresh-water fishes, it includes black-footed penguins in a temperature controlled enclosure, a "Swamp" that's home to alligators and turtles, a touch tidepool, and a Fish Roundabout; a 100,000-gallon doughnut-shaped tank that surrounds you while ocean fish circle. Of course, feeding times are best: the Penguins are fed at 1130am and 4pm, dolphins and seals are fed every two hours beginning at 1030am, and fish in the Roundabout eat at 2pm.

The **Planetarium** exhibits the usual sky shows, plus a regular schedule of "Laserium" special effects performances set to contemporary music. Phone for showtimes.

The museum is ridiculously crowded on weekends. It's best during the week after 3pm, when school groups are not clogging the building's arteries. The Academy Cafe serves made-to-order sandwiches, hamburgers and pizza, and is recommended only if you're starving.

California Palace of the Legion of Honor

Lincoln Park (34th/Clement). Tel. 415/863-3330. Open Thurs-Sun & Tues 10am-5pm, Wed 10am-845pm. Admission $7; free second Wed of each month. Additional charge for some special exhibitions.

The Legion's neoclassical exterior and dramatic Lands End setting contrasts with the traditional, homey exhibitions inside. Constructed in the 19th Century by sugar baron Adolph Spreckels, this Lincoln Park museum is home to San Francisco's best sculpture collection, as well as European tapestries, furniture, and model room interiors from the Middle Ages to the present day. Recent exhibitions have included decorative art from London's Victoria and Albert Museum, and a show focusing on Picasso during the War Years. One of Rodin's "Thinkers" is situated at the museum's entrance, below which are rugged cliffs, sandy beaches and the entrance to the Golden Gate. During museum hours the Legion Cafe serves decent lunches and snacks. The Museum Store offers a wide selection of art books, jewelry, posters, cards and gifts.

Exploratorium

in the Palace of Fine Arts, 3601 Lyon St (btw Jefferson/Bay). Tel. 415/563-7337. Open Tues-Sun 10am-6pm, Wed until 9pm. Admission $9; free first Wed of each month.

The Exploratorium is the funky and eccentric granddaddy of all children's science museums. Long before the word "interactive" ever preceded "museum," the Exploratorium invited people, especially young people, to experience and discover science on a very personal level. A pioneer in 1969, when it was conceived by physicist Frank Oppenheimer, the Exploratorium dramatically changed the way people experience museums, and the way laypeople understand natural phenomena. Begun with only a handful of items, some borrowed from NASA, it has grown to over 650 hands-on exhibits designed by artists and scientists. A characteristic recent exhibit, "Frogs," explained the idiosyncrasies of the creatures via sights, sounds and science. A great museum that's definitely not just for kids.

MH de Young Memorial Museum

Golden Gate Park (near Fulton/10th). Tel. 415/863-3330. Open Tues-Sun 930am-5pm (until 845pm first Wed of each month). Admission $7; free first Wed of each month.

Opened in 1895 by San Francisco Chronicle publisher MH de Young, his eponymous museum is a jumble of decorative and fine art from around the world. Some of the best pieces—including paintings by James Whistler and Georgia O'Keeffe, and architectural renderings by Frank Lloyd Wright—were donated by John D. Rockefeller III. The collection is particularly strong on tapestries from Asia Minor, and crafts and costumes from Africa, Oceania and pre-Columbian America. Eclectic temporary shows run the gamut from 1960s American fashions and Contemporary Art from Cuba, to photographs of San Francisco's old Chinatown and microminiatures from Armenia (tiny sculptures smaller than the eye of a needle). The museum's palatial architecture and glorious setting, in the heart of Golden Gate Park, are particularly special.

TOURIST TRAPS: THE WORST OFFENDERS

There are things in almost every city that no self-respecting local would ever dream of doing: expensive and gimmicky offerings that, first and foremost, are designed to separate tourists from their money. Like any good trap, most of the following are either nonverbal or dubbed into French, German, Spanish, Japanese and Italian.

Ripley's Believe it or Not!

175 Jefferson St (btw Mason/Taylor). Tel 415/771-6188. Open Sun-Thurs 10am-10pm, Fri-Sat 10am-midnight. Admission $8.50.

See a photo of a man with his lower lip over his nose! A model of a man with two sets of pupils in each eye! See a dinosaur made of chrome bumpers! A mock-up of a calf with two heads! A cable car made from 275,000 match sticks! See lots of stupid tourists! Believe it or not, this ridiculous "museum" is still open.

Wax Museum

145 Jefferson St (btw Mason/Taylor). Tel. 415/885-4975. Open daily 10am-10pm.

Can somebody explain to us the attraction of wax museums? Is it that people are so enamored with celebrity that even the unreal likeness of one can be as thrilling as meeting the actual thing? Is it that this is the closest to a "museum" that most people actually get? From the stupid (Frankenstein) to the inane (a Haunted Gold Mine and Medieval Dungeon), San Francisco's Wax Museum is a huge place offering dozens of tableaux on four floors. When we peeked in, all we could think of was... candles.

The Great San Francisco Adventure

Pier 39, 2nd Fl (at Beach/Embarcadero). Tel. 415/956-3456. Screenings daily, every 45 minutes from 10am-10pm. Admission $7.50.

Filmed in 70mm and projected onto a huge screen, the Great San Francisco Adventure is hosted by the ghost of an old San Francisco sea captain and his pelican friend who take viewers on a flight over the Golden Gate Bridge, a high-speed schuss down Lombard Street, and a stroll through Fisherman's Wharf and Chinatown. It's a decent, short destination film, but we'd rather spend 25¢ per minute at a peep show.

Turbo Ride

Pier 39. Tel. 415/392-8872. Open daily 1030am-830pm. Admission $8. Combine high-res film with mobile hydraulic seating, and you can barf from motion sickness without really going anywhere. In short, Turbo Ride is a rollercoaster simulator that takes passengers on virtual "adventures." Take your pick of four "perilous" journeys: Secrets of the Lost Temple, Dino Island, Smash Factory, and Alien Encounter. If there were lines to get in, you'd swear you were in a theme park.

San Francisco Museum of Modern Art

151 Third St (btw Mission/Howard). Tel. 415/357-4000. Open Mon-Tues and Fri-Sun 11am-6pm, Thurs 11am-9pm. Closed Wed. Admission $8; free first Tues of each month; half-price every Thurs 6-9pm.

Few American institutions have made as serious a commitment to building an impressive permanent collection in a relatively short time as the San Francisco Museum of Modern Art. The city's newest major museum is a stunner, both inside and out. The $63 million SoMa building, designed by Swiss architect Mario Botta, is itself a work of art. The museum has acquired many important works, including the only known preparatory drawing for "The Large Glass" (1915-23) by Marcel Duchamp; Andy Warhol's "Red Liz" (1962), one of the artist's famous images of Elizabeth Taylor set against a brilliant red background; and Magritte's "Personal Values" (1952), for which it paid $7.1 million, a record price for the artist. Of course, not everything here is of such high standard, but what is impressive is the sheer quantity and breadth of the work displayed. Recent exhibitions included a salute to Alexander Calder, a Paul Klee retrospective, an installation on supersurveillance, a show on experimental architecture from the 1960s, and a survey of ergonomical chairs. The museum is extraordinarily popular; Thursday nights have become something of a twentysomething singles scene, and weekends are packed with tourists. We can heartily recommend the casual ground level Caffe Museo, which serves respectable pizza and sandwiches; and the museum shop, which has quickly become one of the city's best gift stores. Free docent tours are conducted daily; phone for schedule information.

Ansel Adams Center for Photography

250 Fourth St (btw Howard/Folsom). Tel. 415/495-7000. Open Tues-Sun 11am-5pm (until 8pm the first Thurs of each month). Admission $2-$5; free first Thurs of each month.

One of the country's great photography museums exhibits a wide range of work by artists, journalists, scientists and entrepreneurs, and features many examples by Alfred Stieglitz, Man Ray, Edward Weston, Lee Friedlander, Cindy Sherman and Nicholas Nixon. As you'd expect, Ansel Adams' photos are always on display, in rotating exhibits from the permanent collection. Recent shows included contemporary photographers inspired by science, 50 Years of Polaroid Photography, and an Irving Penn retrospective.

Cable Car Barn Museum

1201 Mason St (at Washington). Tel. 415/474-1887. Open summer daily 10am-6pm, winter daily 10am-5pm. Admission free.

This noisy little Cable Car Barn is a unique and memorable place that houses the elaborate winding machinery—gears, pulleys and steel cables—that pull the city's cable cars through the streets. An underground viewing area offers a first-hand look at the giant wheels that pull eleven miles of cable at a steady 9.5 miles per hour. In the adjacent machine shop you can see the craftspeople who must make continuous repairs on the rolling landmarks. The "museum" side is also interesting, containing the world's first cable car, and detailed explanations of how it all works.

Cartoon Art Museum

814 Mission St (at Third). Tel. 415/227-8666 (recording) or 415/546-3922. Open Wed-Fri 11am-5pm, Sat 10am-5pm, Sun 1-5pm. Admission $4; pay what you wish first Wed of each month.

Bequests by "Peanuts" creator Charles Schultz and other top cartoonists have made this small museum the largest of its kind in the world. The permanent collection includes original art from comic books, magazines, animated film cels, advertisements and newspapers, some of which date from the early 18th century. Rotating exhibits and temporary shows augment the collection. The museum is located South of Market, in the historical Print Center building.

Chinese Historical Society Museum

965 Clay St (at Grant). Tel. 415/391-1188. Open Tues-Fri 10am-4pm. Admission free.

Operated by the Chinese Historical Society, this cultural museum endeavors to describe and preserve the immigrant Chinese experience in America. As with any good museum, a large part of this one is devoted to research, and tons of historical documents are catalogued here. For the casual visitor, the Society offers a window into the past via terrifically illustrated panels, intelligent narrative, and some colorful exhibits, including a full-size redwood sampan, an old Buddhist altar, and the best collection of opium pipes we've ever seen. Check-out the museum before exploring Chinatown and you will appreciate the neighborhood with a new perspective.

Musée Mécanique

Cliff House, 1090 Point Lobos Ave (at Great Highway). Tel. 415/386-1170. Open summer daily 10am-8pm, winter daily 11am-7pm. Admission free.

Musée Mécanique is a fancy name for a penny arcade; something of a living necropolis for arcade games of yore. The museum's got about a hundred fascinating mechanical contraptions from the beginning of the last century, all modified to account for inflation (bring plenty of quarters). Amongst the usual fortune-telling gypsy and dancing chicken machines you'll find lots of early kinescopes, a cast-iron wizard that rates your sexual prowess, and moving miniature scenes of "The Drunkard's Dream," "In the Sultan's Harem," and "The Opium Den." The Museum is located under the dining rooms of the Cliff House.

Museum of the City of San Francisco

The Cannery, 2801 Leavenworth St, 3rd Fl. (btw Beach/ Jefferson). Tel. 415/ 928-0289. Open Wed-Sun 10am– 4pm. Admission free. Most of this small museum's collection of historical everyday objects dates from before the 1906 earthquake. The best items are those that directly relate to the Big One, including the 3.5-foot high head of the *Goddess of Liberty,* a statue that once topped the quake-rattled dome of the old City Hall; and amazing photographs of completely devastated post-quake San Francisco. An adjacent wing of the museum houses dozens of vintage movie projectors, harking back to the days when the Bay Area was the center of California's motion picture industry. The museum is too small to warrant a special trip, but its convenient Fisherman's Wharf location (and free admission) make it a worthy stop on your exploration of the waterfront.

National Maritime Museum

Jefferson St (at Polk). Tel. 415/556-2904. Open daily 10am–5pm. Admission free.

The National Maritime Museum, situated in a fantastic art deco streamline moderne building that looks very much like an ocean liner, sits beside Aquatic Park, where kayakers, kite fliers, impromptu drummers, and even the occasional swimmer can often be found. The museum contains an impressive collection of large-scale model ships, and the larger-than-life figureheads that once adorned the bows of Gold Rush-era clippers. There is an exhibit tracing the history of steam navigation on the West Coast, and WPA-era murals depicting the lost city of Atlantis. Panoramic photographs of early San Francisco, juxtaposed with recent views, will challenge you to recognize the once-sleepy little 19th-century village in the busy skyline of today.

San Francisco Maritime National Historic Park

Hyde Street Pier (at Jefferson). Tel. 415/556-3002. Open daily 10am–5pm. Admission $4.

San Francisco was a major staging ground for American forces in the Pacific during World War II. The Bay Area was home to two huge naval shipyards, Treasure Island was an intelligence post and naval installation, and piers 35 and 45 were disembarkation points for troops headed towards Asia. The city's maritime heritage is celebrated at Hyde Street Pier with the largest collection of historic ships in the US. The most impressive is the triple-masted, square-rigged *Balclutha,* a beautiful steel-hulled ship that rounded the Horn many times loaded with British coal and California grain. The adjacent *Eureka,* an enormous sidewheel passenger ferry that once shuttled commuters between Sausalito and The City, is the world's largest floating wooden vessel. It's worth climbing onto the upper deck to see the beautifully restored and polished interior. Other boats on the pier include the 1895 schooner *CA Thayer,* the tugboat *Hercules,* the scow schooner *Alma,* and a restored Italian felucca. With the same ticket, you can also tour the *USS Pampanito,* a WWII fleet submarine docked at Pier 45.

San Francisco Zoo

Sloat Blvd (at 45th). Tel. 415/753-7080. Open daily 10am-5pm. Admission $9; free first Wed of each month.

The San Francisco Zoological Gardens opens new habitats all the time, but Gorilla World, Koala Crossing and the Primate Discovery Center (which is home to rare and endangered monkeys) are still the top draws here. Other hits include a walk-through aviary and an Insect Zoo. Docent tours are offered on Saturdays and Sundays at 1pm. The Zoo is located near the ocean, two miles south of Golden Gate Park. If you go, dress warmly as it's on the foggy end of the city.

Tattoo Museum

841 Columbus Ave (btw Greenwich/Lombard). Tel. 415/775-4991. Open daily noon-6pm. Admission free.

Part of a North Beach tattoo studio, this small gallery is something of a work in progress, displaying a myriad of historical photos, contemporary drawings and instruments related to the ink-slingers' art. It's definitely worth the price of admission (free).

UFO, Bigfoot, and the Loch Ness Monster Museum

709 Union St (at Powell). Tel. 415/974-4339. Open Tues-Sun noon-9pm.

As if more proof were needed that California is full of wackos, along comes a "museum" devoted to conspiracy theories, right in the center of the state's most "cosmopolitan" city. Curator and paranormal investigator Erik Beckjord is dead serious when it comes to aliens, whether they reside on our planet or just visiting. Exhibits include assorted photographs and documents relating to Area 51, faces on Mars, Nessie, Bessie (the Bay Area's own sea monster), and more. There is also a strange collection of ghostly photographs from Nicole Brown Simpson's former residence.

Wells Fargo History Museum

420 Montgomery St (at California). Tel. 415/396-2619. Open Mon-Fri 9am-5pm. Admission free.

Situated inside the Wells Fargo Bank, this small Museum houses the best collection of Gold Rush memorabilia and artifacts, most of which demonstrate the relationship between Wells Fargo and the development of the American West. Amongst lots of century-old photographs and papers, you'll find an original Concord stagecoach, several strong boxes, mining tools, and the gold nuggets that first attracted the 49ers (and the bank) here in the first place (sorry, no samples).

SPEC!AL-iNTEREST MUSEUMS

◆ African-American Museum,
Fort Mason, Bldg C, Tel. 415/441-0640.

◆ Ansel Adams Center,
250 Fourth St. Tel. 415/495-7000.

◆ California Historical Society,
678 Mission. Tel. 415/357-1848.

◆ Cartoon Art Museum,
814 Mission St. Tel. 415/227-8666.

◆ Chinese Culture Center,
750 Kearny St., 3rd floor. Tel. 415/986-1822.

◆ International Children's Art Museum,
The Ferry Bldg., Embarcadero. Tel. 415/772-9977.

◆ Jewish Museum of San Francisco,
Jessie Street Substation Building. Tel. 415/543-8880.

◆ Levi Strauss Museum,
250 Valencia St. Tel. 415/565-9159.

◆ Mexican Museum,
Third and Mission streets. Tel. 415/441-0404.

◆ Museo Italo-Americano,
Fort Mason, Bldg C. Tel. 415/673-2200.

◆ Museum of Money of the American West,
Bank of California, 400 California St. Tel. 415/765-0400.

◆ Museum of Russian Culture,
2450 Sutter St. Tel. 415/921-4082.

◆ National Maritime Museum,
Jefferson St. Tel. 415/556-2904.

◆ North Beach Museum,
Eureka Bank, 1435 Stockton St. Tel 415/626-7070.

◆ Pacific Heritage Museum,
608 Commercial Ave. Tel. 415/399-1124.

◆ San Francisco Center for the Book,
300 De Haro St. Tel. 415/565-0545.

◆ San Francisco Craft & Folk Art Museum,
Fort Mason, Bldg A. Tel. 415/775-0990.

◆ San Francisco Performing Arts Library & Museum,
399 Grove St. Tel. 415/255-4800.

◆ San Francisco Fire Department Museum,
655 Presidio Ave. Tel. 415/558-3210.

◆ Tattoo Museum,
841 Columbus Ave. Tel. 415/775-4991.

◆ UFO, Bigfoot, and the Loch Ness Monster Museum,
709 Union St. Tel. 415/974-4339.

◆ Wells Fargo History Museum,
420 Montgomery St. Tel. 415/396-2619.

05

EXPLORING
DiGGiNG dEEPER

THe fiNANCiAL diSTRiCt

Bordered by Washington, Market and Montgomery streets, and the Bay.

True to its name, the Financial District is San Francisco's business zone; home to banks, oil companies, insurance firms and, of course, plenty of major information technology players. Because it's built almost entirely on landfill, it's also one of the least safest places to be should a major quake hit. Few buildings in the hood survived the last Big One (1906), after which the area developed into the corporate canyon it is today. Zoning laws in most other parts of the city limit new buildings to just three stories, which makes this skyscrapered section of town even more desirable to developers.

During working hours these sidewalks are awash with suits darting to the district's many newspaper stands, cappuccino shops, shoe shine booths and flower stalls. None of it, though, would be unfamiliar to a native New Yorker, except that the faces are overwhelmingly white and people actually wait at corners for the lights to change.

The Financial District sprung up with the 49ers; **Wells Fargo Bank** (420 Montgomery St; tel. 415/396-2619) runs a history museum in its lobby (*see* Chapter 4/Other Collections).

The **Bank of America World Headquarters** (555 California St; btw Kearny/Montgomery), is San Francisco's tallest building. Covered with black Carnelian marble, it features a bar on the 52nd floor that's blessed with some of the best views of the city.

Nearby, the Embarcadero Center's four buildings offer dozens of shops geared to both local workers and visitors alike.

Skydeck, atop One Embarcadero Center (btw Front/Battery/Clay/Sacramento; tel. 888/ 737-5933), is the city's only indoor/outdoor observation area, and another destination for panoramic views of San Francisco.

Once derided as the "dunce cap," the quartz-aggregate coated **Transamerica Pyramid** (600 Montgomery St; btw Clay/Washington) is easily the city's most recognizable structure. There is no public access to the roof, but there's usually a decent art exhibit in the lobby.

Montgomery Street, which follows the original shoreline, is the Financial District's primary thoroughfare. Stroll along this stretch and you will see a wonderful row of historic red-brick buildings.

The area is also known for its **Jackson Square Historical District**, bounded by Washington, Kearny and Sansome streets, and Pacific Avenue. The region around Jackson Street's 400 block oozes with charm and is filled with a wonderful lineup of antique shops, as well as many offices of attorneys, architects, ad agencies and land developers. Though Jackson Square's re-awakening was relatively recent, the area and buildings it embraces date back to San Francisco's boozy, brawling Gold Rush days. The "entrance" to the Square, at the Jackson/Montgomery corner, was the site, in 1844, of the city's first bridge, built over a backwater, Laguna Salada, as a shortcut to the nearby bayfront. There were perhaps 30 white settlers in the outpost at the time; five years later there were 30,000. The area became the heart of the boom town's commercial life as miners dumped their nuggets and gold dust on the counters of Gold and Balance Streets to be weighed and assayed.

Landmarks of special interest on Jackson, between Sansome and Montgomery, are: 400 Jackson, dating in part from 1859; 415-31 Jackson, built in 1853 and used by Domingo Ghirardelli as his chocolate works prior to moving it in 1894 to the present Ghirardelli Square site; 441 Jackson, erected in 1861 on the hulls of two ships abandoned during the Gold Rush; 458-60 Jackson, first occupied in 1854; 470 Jackson, built in 1852, housed the consulates of Spain and Chile (1856-57) and France (1861-65); and 472 Jackson, constructed in 1850-52 using ship masts as interior supporting columns, served as the French Consulate from 1865-76. Also of historical import is 451 Jackson, built in 1866 to house the A.P. Hotaling & Company whiskey distillery. **Hotaling Place**, with its hitching posts and Dickensian air, is one of the quarter's most charming alleys. This quiet footway provides rear access to 722 Montgomery Street which sheltered California's first Masonic Lodge in 1849 and later, in the late 1850's, the Melodeon, where frock-coated toffs flocked to musical revues. Today, 722-28 Montgomery Street is sumptuously redecorated in red-and-plush-and-gaslight "Gold Rush Victorian." This look is emulated elsewhere in the neighborhood by a number of restaurants flaunting rich period decor.

Bordered by Geary, Powell, Stockton and Post streets.
Once the site of brutal Unionist rallies during the Civil War, Union Square has become an eclectic mix of business lunchers, fire-and-brimstone preachers, foreign shoppers, conventioneers and the homeless. Most of the city's hotels and theaters are located close by, as are the majority of the city's high-end shops. The Square is full of firsts: The turn-of-the century St. Francis Hotel, on the western side, was the first deluxe hotel in the city. The 1940s underground parking garage, below the Square, was the first of its kind in the western United States. And the self-cleaning toilet, shaped like a four-pack of toilet paper, situated on the square, was the first free-standing pay-as-you-go lavatory in the Bay Area. Some liberal city supervisors were opposed to the placement of a toilet here because they worried it would inspire police to arrest homeless people who preferred to urinate outdoors.

The 1,200-room **St. Francis Hotel**, named after the Patron Saint of San Francisco, should be your first stop. More specifically, make a b-line to one of the hotel's five outside Otis glass elevators; push "32" and watch the city emerge and unfold before you. The fastest glass elevator in the city, catapulting at a speed of 1000 feet per minute, offers a stereoscopic view of Union Square, downtown, Coit Tower and the Bay.

Back on solid ground, circle the Square and visit the high-end shops of the world. Tucked amongst the Neiman-Marcus, Macy's and Saks Fifth Avenue department stores, you'll find Bulgari, Cartier, Coach, Versace, Armani, Gucci, Hermes and all the other Euros. The world-famous Gump's nearby had its humble beginnings selling mirrors to bars and whorehouses. There's plenty for plebeians too, including Virgin Megastore, the Disney Store and Borders Books and Music.

Union Square is also the center of the theater district; home to the Golden Gate, Curran and Marines Memorial theaters, all of which are pop-houses featuring Broadway musicals.

Dip down **Maiden Lane**, between Grant and Stockton off the east side of the Square. The charm of this bucolic alley belies its exceedingly dangerous and bawdy past. Prior to becoming a genteel mall for restaurants and shops, Maiden Lane was one of the Barbary Coast's most lurid red light districts, and the site of regular homicides. **Circle Gallery** (140 Maiden Lane) is said to be Frank Lloyd Wright's 1949 model for the Guggenheim Museum.

On nearby Ellis Street is **John's Grill,** a historic 1906 restaurant that's best known as the regular haunt of Dashiell Hammett's fictitious sleuth, Sam Spade, hero of "The Maltese Falcon." Hammett, who lived across the street with playwright Lillian Hellman, was also known to frequent this pricey eatery. His favorite meal? Chops with baked potatoes and sliced tomatoes. If you're not up for dinner, stop in for a whiskey and some deep-fried oysters.

Around the corner, on Market Street, is the fabulous **Sheraton Palace Hotel**. You've got to check out the stunning Garden Court, an elegant tea room/restaurant with a magnificent massive skylight, marble columns, crystal chandeliers and tall palm trees. It's probably the most awesome room in California. Really. Before leaving, dip into the wood-paneled Pied Piper Bar and Maxfield's Restaurant, named for its original Maxfield Parrish mural (*see* Chapter 9/Cultivated Classics).

ThE tENdERLOiN

Bordered by Sutter and Mason streets, and Van Ness and Golden Gate avenues.

The Tenderloin is a neighborhood with such a seedy reputation that even the grungiest barflies and most decadent libertines are scared of it. There's no real reason to be, though. Sure, the junkies will beg for change, crack dealers will glare and hustlers might proposition you, but the encroachment of good Southeast Asian restaurants and trendy nightspots that are slowly converting the neighborhood into the "trendyloin" make it worth visiting. Of course, always keep your head up so that your heart is left in San Francisco and not a piece of your ass. Squeezed between tourist-filled Union Square, upscale Nob Hill, and the political Civic Center, the Tenderloin is also home to the majority of the city's tourist-class hotels. Things tend to get scarier the closer you get towards Van Ness Avenue and Market Street. Arguably, the two most famous neighborhood landmarks are the **Mitchell Brothers O'Farrell Theater,** known for quality sex shows for decades (*see* Chapter 9/Sex); and the **Glide Memorial United Methodist Church** (330 Ellis St, at Taylor; tel. 415/771-6300), with its wildly famous pastor, Cecil Williams, whose inspirational sermons and rockin' choir have attracted nationwide fame. Services are held Sundays at 9 and 11am.

Bordered by Market, Leavenworth, Post and Franklin streets.
True to its name, the Civic Center is the neighborhood that encircles City Hall. The mayor and city supervisors legislate from here, surrounded by a new main library, the opera, and symphony. Curiously, the center of municipal authority and seat of high society is also one of the poorest neighborhoods in San Francisco. The area's parks and pedestrian boulevards are more frequently filled with cardboard homeless shelters and shopping carts than culture lovers and high powered city officials. It's an ironic situation that lead one former Supervisor to petition the board to invite Fidel Castro to visit and offer advice on the homeless problem.

The recently remodeled **City Hall** (200 Polk St, at Van Ness; tel. 415/554-4000), with its gleaming gold-leafed dome, is a stunning beaux-arts-style building that originally opened in 1915. Following the 1989 Loma Prieta earthquake, this National Historic Landmark underwent a multi-year seismic upgrading that necessitated the removal and replacement of more than 75,000 pieces of stone and hardware, after which nearly every space in the building was returned to its 1915 configuration. Free docent-lead tours are offered Monday through Friday at 10am, noon, 2pm and 4pm from the South Light Court.

The new **Main Library** (at Grove/McAllister), fronted by a revolving chrome "L" sculpture across Civic Center Plaza, contains over one million books and 400 electronic work stations surrounding a five-story atrium. True to the community it serves, the library contains a well-stocked Gay and Lesbian room.

The old library, across the street, is slated to be the new home of the **Asian Art Museum**, which is currently in Golden Gate Park.

The **War Memorial Opera House**, next door, is another local renovated landmark that has reopened to rave reviews. Named in honor of the post WWII peace treaty between the US and Japan, which was signed on this site, the lavish house is now home to one of the world's foremost opera companies (*see* Chapter 9/Classical Music).

On the corner of Van Ness and Gough is the **Louise M. Davies Symphony Hall**; and flanking the other side of City Hall is the **Veteran's Building**, a 1930s structure housing the Herbst Theater and a thousand-seat lecture hall.

ChiNAtOWN

Bordered by Broadway, Taylor, Bush, and Montgomery streets.

Chinatown is a wondrous place: a tangle of narrow streets crammed with exotic-produce markets, street vendors hawking stir-fried noodles, drugstores with dried seahorses and deer antlers; cheerful pagoda-topped phone booths and, everywhere you look, an impossible clutter of signs, most of which are in Chinese. Restaurants are packed shoulder to shoulder along Chinatown's tiny alleyways (the best are listed in Chapter 8); and Grant Street is awash with vendors hawking knock-off designer watches, sunglasses and handbags, as well as cheap toys and electronics.

As is the case with Chinatowns throughout North America, this one is thriving and expanding into adjacent neighborhoods. Unlike the Italian community in North Beach, which is gasping its last breath, Chinatown is growing in all directions. At the same time, it's transforming into a kind of Southeast Asiatown, as Vietnamese, Thai, Malay, and Cambodian immigrants pour-in to toil in the neighborhood's over-crowded sweatshops and hygienically-challenged restaurants.

CHiNAtOWN

San Francisco's Chinatown was the first Cantonese settlement in America. There was barely a Chinese presence in San Francisco until the 1850s, when some 15,000 laborers came to work the gold mines, or support the Gold Rush industry. The community settled around **Portsmouth Square** (btw Grant, Kearny, Washington and Clay streets), which today is the distressingly ugly heart of an otherwise fun-to-look-at neighborhood.

It was an uneasy relationship from the beginning. The European-American settlers were spooked by the Chinese culture, and generally avoided the Asian immigrants unless they were looking for labor, sex, opium or a fight. Throughout the 19th Century European-Americans showed bitter hostility towards the Chinese, often culminating in organized violence against the entire community. Gangs regularly beat and robbed them, burned shops at random, and cut-off Chinamen's queues, or pigtails, just for a laugh. Much worse, Chinese were hung by their queues, and even brutally tortured and murdered in racist attacks. The racism came from the top. Successive California governors vociferously attempted to halt the "Yellow Tide," including Leland Stanford (founder of Stanford University), who argued in the state legislature that any more of those "degraded and distinct people would exercise a deleterious effect upon the superior race." On April 5, 1874, almost twenty thousand people turned out for a rally in support of Chinese deportation.

The Chinese in turn became ever more inward and pulled together to protect the community, enforce laws and even mete out punishments. This was done in the form of the Six Companies, a circle of elders that included the community's richest and best-educated members.

The **Chinatown Gateway**, a dragon-topped portal at Grant Avenue and Bush Street, is the natural starting point to explore the neighborhood. From here, Grant Avenue runs the eight-block length of Chinatown with an overdone orientalism that bears little resemblance to anything in China. Stroll through the crowded streets, past dragon-entwined lamp posts and pagoda-topped buildings with arched eaves, carved cornices and filigreed balconies. Peek into shops crammed with wares that are rare, fine and facsimile: art objects from old China; porcelain and fabric from Hong Kong; and T-shirts and tourist kitsch from the good old US of A.

However, beyond all the tacky gift shops and tourist traps, there exists an authentic Chinatown well worth exploring. A couple of blocks up Grant, at the corner of California Street, is San Francisco's first Catholic cathedral, **Old Saint Mary's Church** (660 California St, at Grant; tel. 415/288-3800), which was built largely by Chinese laborers, with brick brought around Cape Horn, and granite cut in China. When it was completed in 1854, the structure towered above the surrounding city. Today, due to the flamboyance of the surrounding Chinese architecture, you could almost walk by without noticing it.

St. Mary's Square, a tranquil, tree-shaded retreat diagonally across the street, is presided over by an imposing 12-foot **statue of Sun Yat-Sen,** founder of the Chinese Republic (1911-1913).

If, as they say, dragons are benevolent, the **Bank of America's** branch at 701 Grant Street fairly glows with goodwill. Gold dragons ornament the front columns and doors, and 60 dragon medallions line its facade.

Just around the corner, at 743 Washington Street, is the oldest existing oriental-style edifice in the quarter, which was built after the 1906 earthquake. Now the **Bank of Canton,** this three-tiered "temple" formerly housed the Chinatown Telephone Exchange. "China-5," as it was known until 1949, when the dial system took over, was staffed by 20 operators whose fluency in five dialects, and phenomenal memories enabled them to accommodate the hundreds of Chinese subscribers who disregarded phone numbers and demanded to reach their party by name.

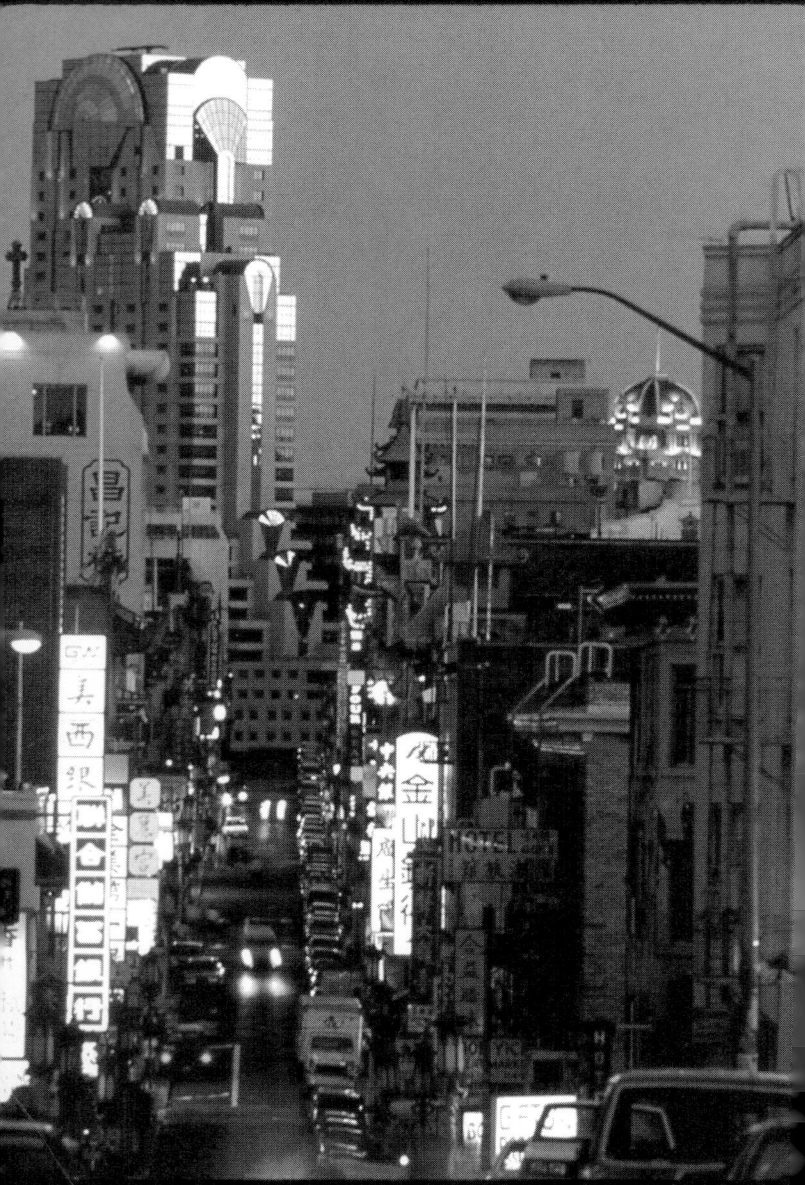
GW
HOTEL

In recent years, the main Chinese market
ct has shifted a block west, stretching along
ton Street's 1000-1200 blocks. Here you can
bowed by old ladies jostling for bargain
of bok choy, along with golden glazed ducks
ole drawn pigs, lichee nuts, sharks' fins,
full of fish, and crates of cackling
.

Some of the most interesting parts of
wn are the many narrow streets and
s that riddle the district. From afar, most
the back entrances to restaurants and shops,
re worlds are buzzing within each one. In
h century, many were home to sex slaves
um dens. For almost 90 years, until 1939,
e girls were brought here by Chinese
ssmen who imprisoned them in small cells,
"cribs," in which they spent the majority of
brief lives. Required to remain naked, the
s would call out to passersby, "Chinese girl
! Your father just go out!" (In some parts of
ina it was considered a good thing to bang
e same girl your father did—assuming it
asn't your mother). Disease festered in the
ribs, and few of the girls lived much past the
age of twenty. A far classier bordello was located
at the corner of Waverly Place and Ross Alley.
Today you can dip into **Waverly Place** for a peek
at some fine Buddhist temples, including the **T'ien
Hou Temple**, the oldest Asian prayer hall in the
country, where you can do like the locals and burn
some incense at the feet of the giant Buddha.

Ross Alley, between Jackson and Washington
streets, is infamous for its sweatshops, many of
which can be glimpsed through an open window
or door. While you're at it, step into the tiny
Golden Gate Fortune Cookie Factory (56 Ross
Alley) to see how these thoroughly Chinese-
American specialties are made.

For an excellent overview of the neighborhood
and its residents, check out the **Chinese Historical
Society Museum**, 965 Clay St, at Grant;
tel. 415/391-1188. (see Chapter 4/Other Collections
or complete information).

NORth bEACh

Bordered by Columbus Avenue, Washington and Beach streets, and the Embarcadero.

What's amazing about North Beach is that, while it's become one of the priciest neighborhoods in town, it has never lost sight of its humble past. Begun as part of the rough-and-tumble Barbary Coast, the neighborhood still reeks with old-school strip shows that were once considered risqué (*see* Chapter 9/Sex); despite the fact that the area's once dominant Italian population has dwindled to under 10%, the neighborhood remains home to the city's best pasta restaurants, pastry shops and cappuccino bars. And, although its intimate connection with the Beats in the 1950s is long gone, there is still something of a Bohemian edge in North Beach's cafes and dive rock bars.

The beach that was once here disappeared under landfill a century ago, when gold struck and San Francisco rocked with pubs, whorehouses, and gambling parlors (not unlike Prague today! -ed).

North Beach blossomed into the city's Italian quarter after the Great Earthquake of 1906, when tens of thousands of immigrants from The Boot trotted over here to work as fishermen, toil in Ghirardelli's Chocolate Factory, and pack produce in the California Fruit Growers Association's nearby canneries. Once known as "Little Italy," vestiges of the quarter's Roman Age are dwindling, so that only a handful of garlic-laden pasta restaurants remain. For the time being, though, the best Italian sandwiches can still be found at **Molinari's Delicatessen** on Columbus Avenue, which continues to make its own prosciutto and mozzarella; and great espresso is still steamed at Cafe Trieste, Steps of Rome, and Cafe Roma.

With the encroachment of rich Midwesterners to the northeast and Chinese to the southwest, San Francisco's Little Italy is shrinking like a dried salami. Rising rents are partly to blame, but the disappearance of Italians from North Beach largely coincided with the white-flight that affected many American cities in the decades following World War II. Back in the 1950s, this Italian neighborhood provided an expatriate haven for the icons of the Beat Generation and other dissatisfied white populists who wrote poetry, danced and drank in the cafes of what was then considered a low-end neighborhood. Cheap rent and casual cafes attracted the likes of Allen Ginsberg, Jack Kerouac, Neal Cassady and Lawrence Ferlinghetti (the latter poet still lives close by). Favorite Beat hangs included the now-defunct Co-Existence Bagel Shop, the egalitarian City Lights Bookstore, and Vesuvio Café, which was immortalized in Kerouac's *Dharma Bums*.

Poet and publisher Lawrence Ferlinghetti opened **City Lights** in 1953, and immediately began publishing the works of his friends. His issuance of Ginsberg's revolutionary poem, "Howl," two years later caused a public scandal that climaxed with the winning of a landmark obscenity case. Occupying a prominent corner on Columbus Avenue, City Lights is said to be the first store in America to feature paper-back books and continues to be a dynamic neighborhood institution, not just a touristic monument to another age.

It seems almost ridiculous now, but when aspiring actress Carol Doda bared her breasts at the **Condor** nightclub on June 19, 1964, she became the first regular "exotic" dancer in America, and single-handedly began the topless era. Tourists from around the country came to San Francisco just to get a peek at the hedonistic, liberal Mecca. Sadly, the Condor is now just a run-of-the-mill sports bar; but plenty of topless clubs remain in North Beach, in the part closest to the Financial District.

A proper tour of North Beach should begin at Kearny Street and Columbus Avenue, where Chinatown is pushing hard against the former Italian neighborhood. With the Transamerica Pyramid at your back, cruise the length of Columbus, dipping into the historic side streets at will. The local street names alone—including Saroyan Place, Jack Kerouac Alley and Via Ferlinghetti—prove that this has long been something of a literary stomping ground. Only in the last generation have the European-style mom-and-pop shops been replaced by tony shops and trendy restaurants. While plenty of people still celebrate the neighborhood's past, very few actually pine for the old days. Ourselves included. We dig the new diversity that mixes the traditional old with the vibrant new. North Beach's gentrification has attracted tons of terrific restaurants, upscale clothing boutiques and loads of people who come to eat, drink and be very. Not coincidentally, the neighborhood is also the epicenter of the city's current swing craze (*see* Chapter 9/Swing Dancing).

Washington Square Park (bordered by Union, Filbert, Powell and Stockton streets), a small green popular with sunbathers and early-morning tai chi practitioners, is dominated on the north side by the distinctive twin spires of **Saint Peter and Paul Church**. Built in 1924, the Italian Catholic church is still known as the "Fisherman's Church," so-called for the vocation of many of its original parishioners.

Fior d'Italia, directly across the green, on Union Street, was established in 1886 and claims to be the oldest Italian restaurant in the United States.

To the east is **Telegraph Hill**, one of San Francisco's very best places to live (if you're lucky enough to have a garage). Named for a Morse Code signal station that once stood here, the Hill is dotted with beautiful beshrubbed cottages commanding top views, and top dollars. Telegraph Hill is topped by **Coit Tower**, a slender monument to the city's firefighters, and there's no better way to reach it than via the Filbert Steps (*see* Chapter 4/Top Sights). The 377 step climb from Sansome and Filbert streets wends its way through verdant flower gardens and charming 19th-century cottages. Napier Lane, a narrow plank walkway, leads to Montgomery Street; turn right and follow the path to the end of the cul-de-sac where another stairway continues to Telegraph's panoramic summit.

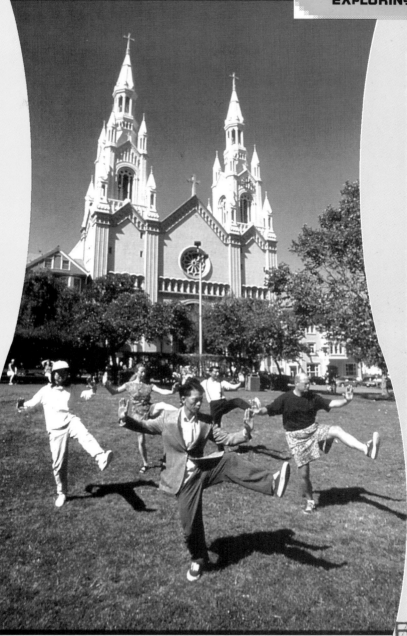

To the west is that famously corkscrewed block of **Lombard Street** (between Hyde and Leavenworth streets) that's mistakenly known as the world's "crookedest" street. Vermont Street, between 20th and 22nd streets, is actually crookeder. Two blocks south, Filbert Street offers the city's steepest vertical descent (*see* Chapter 4/San Francisco's Steepest Top 10).

RUSSIAN hiLL

Bordered by Van Ness and Columbus avenues, Broadway and Fisherman's Wharf. Named for the Russian explorers and trappers who came to San Francisco to trade with the Spanish, Russian Hill devolved into an artists and writers quarter before becoming the tony neighborhood it is today. Jack London, Frank Norris, Mark Twain, and Ambrose Bierce, all did a spell on the Hill, as did Jack Kerouac, who wrote in Neal Cassady's little attic on Russell Place.

Affluence came relatively late to this perfectly situated knoll above North Beach and Fisherman's Wharf. In addition to unobscured views of Alcatraz and the Golden Gate Bridge, Russian Hill is blessed with lots of quirky side streets, wonderful staircases, plenty of sun, and an abundance of flora that appealed to San Francisco transplants of the early 1970s. Rising rents have since pushed bohemians elsewhere, but Russian Hill still boasts its share of characterful bookstores, and creative sushi spots, not to mention the ever-present jingle of cable car bells.

The neighborhood's best houses are simple, arty affairs, designed in the early 1900s, that feel much cozier than the elaborate Victorians that populate the majority of the city.

Russian Hill's steep inclines deter most tourists; and that's a good thing as far as locals are concerned. Walking along on the neighborhood's flower-filled stairways is an experience you won't soon forget. There are lots of great views, and more than a few places where you'll feel as though you've made a fantastic personal discovery. Make your way to **Vallejo Summit**, said to be the nucleus of Russian Hill, and absorb the majestic views. The stairs on Taylor Street, between Green and Vallejo, lead to the top of the Hill. Keep an eye out for the flock of red-headed, chartreuse parrots that live in the surrounding trees. Finally, you may want to descend via the famously crooked **Lombard Street,** a worthy walk even for those without cameras around their necks.

NOb hiLL

Bordered by Bush, Larkin and Stockton streets, and Pacific Avenue.

Tradition-bound Nob Hill is synonymous with posh hotels and old money. Many people think that Nob Hill affords the best views in the city, a point that wasn't lost on the turn-of-the-century tycoons Charles Crocker, Mark Hopkins, Collis Huntington and Leland Stanford, who combined their vast resources to build the Central Pacific Railroad. The "Big Four," as they were known, built unbelievably ornate mansions atop Nob Hill, all of which, with the exception of the brownstone Flood Mansion (which is now the private Pacific-Union Club), were demolished after the 1906 earthquake and fire.

The hill's summit is now capped by a trio of hotels: The Fairmont, The Huntington and the Mark Hopkins, along with Grace Cathedral, the Pacific-Union Club, the Masonic Temple Auditorium, and Huntington Park.

The Fairmont, opened in April 1907, is perhaps the most famous hotel in San Francisco. Because it looks so much like a fancy hotel should, the Fairmont has provided the backdrop for many films including "The Towering Inferno," "The Rock," "Sudden Impact," and Hitchcock's "Vertigo." For a terrific view, take the glass elevator that rises 24-stories above street level where, on a clear day, you can see forever, or at least as far as Oakland and Berkeley.

The **Top of the Mark** restaurant and bar, at the top of the Mark Hopkins Hotel, offers a similar view from a posh interior (see Chapter 9/Rooms With a View).

For a glimpse of Nob Hill's heydays, step into the Huntington Hotel's Big Four Restaurant, which is decorated with lots of memorabilia and photographs from that era.

Grace Cathedral (1100 California St, at Taylor; tel. 415/749-6300) is San Francisco's little bit of Europe, designed after Notre Dame in Paris, and fitted with bronze replicas of the Doors of Paradise that grace the Campanile in Florence. In addition to holding regular masses, the Episcopal church also maintains a full schedule of concerts that run the gamut from choirs singing Handel's coronation anthems to members of the Drepung Loseling Monastery performing sacred songs from Tibet.

Nearby **Huntington Park** is worth a visit for its formal gardens, Dancing Sprites sculpture, and replica of a 16th-century Tortoise Fountain.

Bordered by Market, Eleventh, Berry streets and the Bay.
San Francisco's machine shop and warehouse district has turned post-industrial hip as museums, nightclubs, and a plethora of start-up internet firms have replaced light industry and flophouses. SoMa's revitalization was intensified by the destruction of the Embarcadero Freeway, a horrible shadow-casting offramp of the Bay Bridge that was destroyed in the 1989 Loma Prieta Earthquake.

In the 1970s, Folsom Street, between Eighth and Eleventh Streets, became something of a center for the city's hardest-core gay bars and clubs. Mega dance clubs soon crept into adjacent streets, where there were no neighbors to be disturbed by booming sound systems and partying crowds. To this day, SoMa remains the king of clubs.

The blocks surrounding Second and Third streets have come to be known as **Multimedia Gulch,** and are home to software designers, post-production companies, audio producers, and the city's film and video industry.

SoMa has also been the site of the city's most intensive urban renewal projects. The heart of this billion-dollar infusion of public capital is the 22-acre **Yerba Buena Center,** a very contemporary convention center and cultural complex. The **Yerba Buena Center for the Arts** (701 Mission St; tel. 978-ARTS) is devoted to showcasing multiculti art and artists, and features diverse programming in dance, theater, music, visual arts, films, installations and festivals.

The center adjoins **Moscone Convention Center,** the city's premier convention and exhibition facility.

Zeum (221 Fourth St; tel. 415/777-2800), a children's center atop Yerba Buena Gardens, is a high-tech arts center combined with a full-size ice rink, bowling center, and the original carousel from "Playland-At-The-Beach."

Another anchor in the development of Yerba Buena Gardens is the **San Francisco Museum of Modern Art,** designed by Swiss architect Mario Botta. The nearby **Ansel Adams Museum for Photography** and **Cartoon Art Museum** have turned the hood into a full-fledged museum district.

The centerpiece of Yerba Buena is the **Esplanade,** a one-block area of green that includes terrace cafes, an outdoor performance area (with a lawn seating 5,000), and a walk-through waterfall incorporating an etched glass memorial to Dr. Martin Luther King, Jr.

For a taste of old SoMa, head to the **Pacific Bell Telephone Building** (140 New Montgomery St), a 1920s-era skyscraper which now houses a small Communications Museum.

Built in 1874, the **Old US Mint building,** at Fifth and Mission streets, is another old schooler that's worth visiting. A legacy of the city's silver age, the mint produced over 750 million dollars in coins, and at one time housed a third of all American gold reserves.

Nearby **Rincon Center** is also worth a visit. This thoroughly modern mall on Spear Street contains 27 historical WPA murals.

MiSSiON dIStRiCT

Bordered by Cesar Chavez (Army), Market, Dolores and Potrero streets.

It's hard to believe when you look at it now, but the area surrounding Mission Dolores, the oldest extant building in San Francisco, was once the chi-chiest neighborhood in the city. Things pretty much went downhill during the next century, so that by the 1970s the Mission District had become a run-down, crime-ridden Hispanic ghetto. A turn-around began in the 1980s, as rising rents pushed the poorest families out in favor of recent college graduates, mid-level administrative workers and hard-peddling bike messengers. Today rundown tenements, with paint peeling down to their ankles, rub shoulders with once-magnificent movie palaces, and beautifully remodeled Victorians that get nicer and nicer the closer one gets to the Castro. The result is an excellent mix of budget bodegas, high-style coffee bars, low-life check-cashing places, quirky used furniture shops, 99-cent stores and excellent taquerias that, taken together, create the perfect environment for lowriding Latinos and dejobbed urban sophisticates. Suits don't work too well here. Most San Franciscans only come to the Mission at night, when the dozens of bars on Mission and Valencia streets (between 16th and 24th streets) become the epicenter of the city's straight nightlife.

Founded June 29, 1776, a date considered to be San Francisco's birthday, **Mission Dolores** (Dolores/16th sts; tel. 415/621-8203) is one of 21 missions that were constructed by early Catholic missionaries along the California coast, each a single day's walk from the next. Built with adobe, redwood and Native American sweat, the mission is the oldest extant structure in the city. Highlights of the Moorish-style church include a highly-adorned altar, and a small garden cemetery that's a permanent home for some of the city's most significant early residents, including Belle Cora, the Gold Rush-era's most celebrated madam. The red and gold umbrella and papal insignia to the right of the altar signifies that the church is a Basilica, an honorary designation bestowed by Pope Pius XII. Check out the stained-glass windows depicting the entire string of California missions, and the small museum that provides an instant historical crash-course. Mass is held each Sunday at 8 and 10 am, plus a noontime mass in Spanish.

The other reason to visit the Mission District during daylight hours is to tour the neighborhood's many **outdoor murals**. There are dozens of giant urban-ethnic wall paintings depicting political struggles and cultural icons, from feminist trailblazers to musician Carlos Santana. The biggest concentration of murals can be found in and around **Balmy Alley**, off 24th Street, between Treat and Harrison streets.

hAIGHt-ASHbURY

Bordered by Franklin, Grove, Webster, and Page streets.
Synonymous with the Summer of Love and the heydays of hallucinagenics, it's hard to resist comparing contemporary Haight-Ashbury to a hangover. Each day, Haight Street is awash with tattooed and pierced skateboarders, vaguely employed twentysomethings, homeless can-collectors, and suburban style-hounds shopping for the latest retro fashions. Nobody around here, it seems, is interested in letting go of the hippie legend that's

so enticing to teen angst rebels, and profitable for store owners. Back in the day, Janis Joplin, The Grateful Dead, Jefferson Airplane and disparate bands of lesser known youth roamed these streets with anarchists and runaways. Today, upscale boutiques are beginning to replace vintage clothes stores, and the historic corner of Haight and Ashbury is now flagged on either side with The Gap and Ben & Jerry's. But the Haight remains far from Disneyfied. This is still the place to find psychedelic poster stores and head shops, the air still wafts with the smell of cheap reefer, and dropouts still beg for change (though today they're often looking to buy lattes).

The main drag of Haight Street, between Divisadero and Stanyan streets, still guarantees a great afternoon out. In addition to colorful shops and lots of sidewalk eye-candy, you can gawk at the former **home of the Grateful Dead** (710 Ashbury Street) and the **house where Janis Joplin lived** (112 Lyon Street). Check-out the intersection of Haight and Ashbury streets (sometimes referred to as "Hashbury") and take a little trip in your mind.

ThE LOWER hAiGHt

Haight Street between Buchanan and Divisadero streets. The hardscrabble reality of the Lower Haight makes nearby Haight-Ashbury seem like Disneyland by comparison. Here, at the bottom of Haight Street, one is confronted with punks, clubbers, dealers (crack, anyone?), low-lifes, and all manner of the vaguely employed, hanging out, getting high, and comparing tattoos. No trendy boutiques here. But the Lower Haight is the neighborhood to visit when looking for cheap grub (the Squat and Gobble), serious scarification (Body Manipulations), or a decent piss bar (Noc Noc). On sunny days, nearby Duboce Park (called "Dogshit Park" by petless locals) is over-run by leather-collared canines and their latte-sucking owners.

COLE VALLEY

This sleepy neighborhood above the Haight gets mention here because of **Tank Hill**, a craggy outcropping high above the city that offers some of the best views anywhere. Unlike nearby Twin Peaks, this bucolic spot is something of a secret with tourists, and locals are more than happy to keep it that way. Get there via a footpath and wooden staircase at the end of Belgrave Avenue, off Stanyan Street.

ThE CAStRO

Bordered by Market, Church, and 24th streets.

San Francisco's unequal male-to-female ratio began with the Gold Rush and increased during World War II, when the city was the jumping-off point for soldiers heading to the Pacific. Many men, who were dishonorably discharged due to their sexual orientation, were attracted by this city's relative permissiveness and San Francisco became Second Chance City, a place to start over. Once a blue-collar, Catholic neighborhood, the Castro was transformed in the 1970s, and is now so inextricably related to sexual dissidents it's practically a synonym for "gay." True to stereotype, the Victorians were painted, the neighborhood

cleaned up, and real estate values went through the proverbial roof.

Today, the Castro District is as much a gay theme park as it is a residential haven. A proper tour of the neighborhood begins at the corner of Castro and Market streets, where a huge rainbow flag waves above the entrance to Gay Zion. **Castro Street** is jam-packed with restaurants, bars , T-shirt shops, clothing stores, and home-and-garden retailers, all squarely aimed at local SINK SCUM (Single, Independent, No Kids, Self-Centered Urban Males). And heavy demand means there's never any shortage of tight tank tops and leather

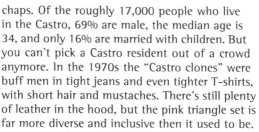

chaps. Of the roughly 17,000 people who live in the Castro, 69% are male, the median age is 34, and only 16% are married with children. But you can't pick a Castro resident out of a crowd anymore. In the 1970s the "Castro clones" were buff men in tight jeans and even tighter T-shirts, with short hair and mustaches. There's still plenty of leather in the hood, but the pink triangle set is far more diverse and inclusive then it used to be.

Nothing brings people together more than a crisis, and AIDS has left an indelible mark on the neighborhood. A tour of the Castro should include a stop at the **Names Project Visitors' Center** (2362 Market St, at Castro; tel. 415/863-1966), which is a growing memorial for people who have died from AIDS. The Names Project oversees the creation of the AIDS Memorial Quilt, an enormous community art project that is made of tens of thousands of three-by-six-foot panels, each dedicated to an AIDS victim. Here visitors can see quilt panels, learn about the Project, and even create their own memorials (sewing machines and materials provided). It's open Mon noon-630pm, Tues-Wed, and Fri noon-7pm, Sat-Sun noon-5pm.

Back on Castro Street, there is never any shortage of people to ogle, cruise, stare at or engage in conversation. Check-out the 1923 landmark **Castro Theater**, San Francisco's best-loved movie palace specializing in international art films and American classics (*see* Chapter 9/Film). You'll also notice that many small businesses have been replaced by chain stores. This has caused the Castro to impose a moratorium on coffee bars (read: Starbucks) in fear that the influx of chains will damage the character of the neighborhood. Make your way to the commercial heart, at 18th and Castro streets, then trek around the surrounding residential neighborhood to check-out all those stunning Victorian houses so perfectly painted in that distinct San Francisco look.

Bordered by 22nd, Dolores and Market streets, and Glen Canyon Park. Named for San Francisco's last Mexican mayor, Jose de Jesus Noe, whose ranch used to occupy this land, the Valley has evolved into something of an extension of the adjacent Castro district. A sunny oasis in this terminally overcast city, Noe Valley has long attracted new immigrants, from the Irish, who created something of an Emerald Enclave, followed by Germans, Mexicans and, lately, gay men who have painstakingly restored the neighborhood's elegant Victorians. The main commercial thoroughfare, 24th Street, is lined with shops, pubs and restaurants catering to the new local bohemians, and nearby Church Street contains several cafes and upscale shops.

ThE EMbARCAdERO

On the Bay, between Pier 41 and China Basin.
With the post-quake removal of the Embarcadero Freeway, the downtown waterfront district has been transformed into a sunny bayside promenade, perfect for walking, blading and exploring. Cast off from King Street to explore the waterfront renaissance, which includes outdoor cafes, wide palm-studded sidewalks, and tidal stairs that descend to the water's edge. Herb Caen Way, along the southern Embarcadero, is punctuated with historic plaques and pylons recalling people and events of the Barbary past.

Ever since the clipper ships transported hordes of 49ers to these shores, San Francisco's historic coming-of-age has been most eloquently retold in the history of its waterfront. In 1849, when the Gold Rush struck, over 700 ships sailed to the little trading post of Yerba Buena (today's San

Francisco), swelling the local population from 400 to 25,000 in a single year. Landfill was dumped on the carcasses of hundreds of abandoned ships, and the Embarcadero was born. Eventually San Francisco's border was extended a full six blocks east from the natural shoreline. Resourceful entrepreneurs then put some old ships to use, converting them into saloons, warehouses, lodgings, a jail and even a church. Meanwhile, the sailor-saturated area around the port became the notorious Barbary Coast.

To accommodate the ever-increasing flow of shipping, engineers planned a great seawall that would neatly round out the city's northeast waterfront. It took 46 years (1878 to 1924) to create the Embarcadero, a 12,000-foot long bulkhead that added 800 acres to the city and eighteen miles of usable docking space.

The Ferry Building, at the center of the Embarcadero, with its conspicuous 19th-century clock tower modeled after the Cathedral Tower in Seville, Spain, became a landmark, and the symbol of San Francisco. During the last half of the 19th century as many as 50 ferries simultaneously shuttled citizens in and out of the city in a constant stream. The building now houses the World Trade Center and the San Francisco Port Authority.

After World War II, shipping gradually shifted across the Bay to Oakland, where the port offers better access to inland cities. This trend accelerated in the 1960s when the Port of Oakland built container shipping facilities. The once great Embarcadero piers, partially overshadowed by a double-decker freeway, were relegated to storage areas, or abandoned to rot in the Bay.

tWiN PEAkS

Originally named by the Spanish "Indian maiden's breasts," Twin Peaks has always captivated and lured admirers. The spectacular view is the main draw, encompassing everything from Bay to breakers, including all five Bay Area bridges. Typically, the Peaks are a lopsided pair, separated by a small valley that serves as the anchor for **Sutro Tower**, the city's biggest (and ugliest) telecommunications tower. Tourists come in droves to stand atop the south peak which, at 922 feet, is the second highest summit in the city. The area is also a haven for hikers and nature lovers; several steep stairway walks will reward you with some of the city's last remaining bit of wilderness.

tHE PRESidiO

Main entrances at Lombard St (at Lyon), Presidio Blvd (at Broadway), Arguello Blvd (at Jackson), and Lincoln Blvd (at 25th Ave). Tel. 415/561-4323.
In the 1990s, after 200 years as a government-owned military post, the Presidio was officially decommissioned and transferred from the Sixth US Army to the Golden Gate National Recreation Area, creating the nation's newest National Park. It's an enormous windfall for the city—1,400-acres of prime, waterfront property right on the tip of the Peninsula.

Much of the Presidio is untamed parkland, encompassing 11 miles of hiking trails and 14 miles of bike routes. There is also a golf course, a private water system and more than 800 buildings, over half of which have historic significance. Plans call for developing more recreational space throughout the Presidio, including the rehabilitation of historic buildings for new park purposes; conversion of some buildings into an international center for research and education on environmental and cultural issues; restoring the historic forest; and replanting 285 acres of native flora.

Hiking and biking are the best ways to enjoy the Presidio. There are spectacular views of the Golden Gate Bridge and San Francisco Bay, and a very unusual pet cemetery, the final resting place of dogs, cats, and even Peep the pigeon.

ThE MARiNA

Bordered by Van Ness Ave, Greenwich and Lyon streets, and the Bay.
Filled-in and developed for the 1915 Panama-Pacific International Exposition, this former marshland has become prime real estate for San Francisco's straightest and most conservative yupsters. At least that's the stereotype. The Marina's stucco houses are inhabited by former middle-Americans who work in the Financial District by day, and vie for parking spaces with other Beemer and SUV owners each night. Chestnut Street,

between Fillmore and Divisadero streets, is the commercial center of the enclave filled with stores aimed at admirers of Pottery Barn, Starbucks and Martha Stewart.

True to its name, the best part of the Marina is its proximity to the water. It's easy to have an athletic outdoor lifestyle when you can easily rollerblade or jog on the flatlands along Marina Green while enjoying spectacular views of the Golden Gate Bridge, San Francisco Bay and the Marin Headlands. At its western end, the Marina abuts **Presidio Park** and the **Palace of Fine Arts** (3601 Lyon St, btw Jefferson/Bay; tel. 415/563-6504).

Home to the **Exploratorium** science museum (*see* Chapter 4/The Top Museums), the Palace was a focal point for the Panama Pacific Exposition, a self-congratulatory pat on the back that celebrated the city's rise from the ashes of the 1906 earthquake. Built with imposing Corinthian colonnades, and surrounded by lush gardens and cherry trees, it's a wonderfully romantic place to stroll.

Fort Mason Center, holding down a park in the east, is a former military installation turned thriving cultural center, filled with theaters (including the Magic), museums (Museo Italo-Americano, African-American Museum, and the San Francisco Craft & Folk Art Museum), and **Greens**, the city's top vegetarian restaurant. It's located at Marina Blvd (entrance at Buchanan). Tel. 415/441-5706.

Who cares if the Marina district is built on landfill that turns to jelly in an earthquake? All other times it's one of the most comfort-addicting spots in the world.

Bordered by Broadway, Lyon, and Lombard streets and Van Ness Avenue.

Cow Hollow is old-time vernacular for the valley lying west of Van Ness Avenue between Russian Hill and the Presidio. Nowadays it is mainly applied to the area around Union Street's 1600 to 2200 blocks, a patch of former grazing ground that's now best known for high-density shopping. The cows were banished by the Board of Health in 1891, after which the Hollow developed into a sedate residential and commercial district. **Union Street's** regeneration began in the late 1950s with a few stylish antique shops and home furnishing showrooms. The movement quickly gathered momentum and by 1964, Cow Hollow had developed a into flourishing shopping sector. It's beautiful, in a Martha Stewart kind of way; passages between buildings lead to flower-filled courtyards wrapped with boutiques. In good weather, business overflows through Dutch doors into doll-size patios. This seven-block stretch of Union Street abounds with home furnishings showrooms; antiques and handicraft galleries; and shops purveying custom clothes, art objects, imports, books, gifts, linens, specialty foods, fabrics, and feminine fripperies. Some of the most important structures in the neighborhood include:

1980 Union Street, one of the district's most striking Victorian compounds fashioned from three circa 1870 residences, including a pair of "wedding houses" (identical bungalows joined by a common center wall). It is now home to several shops and restaurants.

2040 Union Street, a three-story mansion built around 1870 by James Cudworth, one of Cow Hollow's first dairy men, is now filled with boutiques.

2963 Webster Street, a Vedanta Society Temple, was built in 1905-1908 as a reflection of Hindu religious philosophy. Its amazing amalgam of Moorish columns, cusped arches, crenellated towers and onion domes are visible from Union Street.

3011 Steiner Street, located three doors north of Union Street, is a two-story vintage clapboard house. It's carriage entrance (which now houses Pane E Vino restaurant) was a Wells Fargo stagecoach stop in the 1880s.

If you happen to be in the neighborhood on the second or fourth Thursday of the month (between noon and 3pm), check-out the **Octagon House** (2645 Gough St, at Union; tel. 415/441-7512). It's a perfectly eight-sided home from 1861, restored inside and out by the National Society of Colonial Dames in America. In addition to period furnishings, you'll find a collection of documents and signatures from 54 of the 56 men who signed the Declaration of Independence, and a deck of Revolutionary War-era playing cards that have no Kings, Queens or Jacks. Admission is free.

PACifIC hEIGHtS

Bordered by Van Ness Avenue, Broadway, Divisadero, and Pine streets.

Known for gorgeous mansions untouched by the post-quake firestorms of 1906, "Pac Heights" (most easily pronounced with a bourbon in one hand and a stiff upper lip) is a quiet residential neighborhood with lots of old money and Mexican gardeners, and stunning bay views. In short, it's the most prestigious place to live for the city's wealthiest families (i.e. the Getty's and the Gund's). A local mansion tour should include Jackson and Washington streets near Alta Plaza Park, and the Broadway bluff between Lyon and Webster streets (the views!). Of particular note are the **Whittier Mansion** (2090 Jackson St), the Willis Polk-designed **Bourn Mansion** (2550 Webster St); and the **Spreckels Mansion** (2080 Washington St), which is now home to romance novelist Danielle Steele.

The **Haas-Lilienthal House** (2007 Franklin St), a 19th-century 28-room stunner on Franklin Street, has been made into an Architectural Heritage museum.

Fillmore Street, between Sutter and Washington streets, is the Heights' main shopping strip, bursting with quaint furniture shops, high-end hair salons, boutique organic groceries, and almost as many thrift shops as Manhattan's Upper East Side. Sunday morning strolls on Upper Fillmore have become an addicting habit for countless dog-walkers, cappuccino-sippers, and independent-bookstore-browsers. If possible, leave the neighborhood at Broadway and Lyon streets by descending the stairs towards the Palace of Fine Arts. The walk down a dozen flights of majestic stone steps is one of the very best, with trees from the Presidio rising up on one side, and rows of ornate mansions aligned on the other.

Bordered by Van Ness Avenue, and Eddy, Steiner, and Pine streets.

J-Town, or Nihon Machi, as it is known to the city's ethnic Japanese, was erected soon after World War II with the release of interned Japanese-Americans. Less than five percent of the city's 12,000 Japanese-Americans actually live in the neighborhood, but most seem to identify with this collection of homes amidst sterile malls, stark plazas and understated community centers. The district is dominated by the three-block-long **Japan Center,** a late-60s cultural ideal, anchored by a bowling alley and a multiplex cinema. The mall bustles with shops dealing in all manner of Nipponiana, and innumerable that restaurants roll out such similarly mediocre udon and sushi you'd swear they share a single kitchen. **Peace Plaza**, at the center of the mall, is dominated by a five-tiered pagoda donated by the Japanese government. Nearby is an arched bridge over Webster Street that's said to be modeled after the Ponte Vecchio in Florence.

It's worth checking-out J-Town to spy the homes along **Cottage Row** (bound by Webster, Fillmore, Bush, and Sutter streets). These former servants' quarters, set on a narrow park, are some of the city's coolest homes.

hAYES VALLEY

Bordered by Franklin, Grove, Webster, and Page streets.

One of San Francisco's fastest gentrifying neighborhoods, Hayes Valley has the feeling of being the district *de jour.* Lodged between the Lower Haight and the Civic Center, it's just as easy to buy crack as it is to get opera tickets, depending on which direction you walk. Within the last half-decade, Hayes Valley has undergone a massive transformation ushering in young money and a small strip of youthful boutiques catering to the arrivistes. The arrival of a few adventuresome merchants (and the 1996 demolition of a nearby housing project) has meant that great restaurants and cafes have replaced liquor stores and check-cashing booths, and boarded-up storefronts have transformed into antique shops, clothing stores and wine bars. All the while, the neighborhood remains culturally and economically mixed, as well as decisively metrosexual and fiercely independent. A great place to explore.

tHE WEStERN AdDiTiON

Bordered by Masonic Ave, and Fell, O'Farrell, and Franklin streets.

Because it encompasses so many diverse neighborhoods, the Western Addition can't be pigeonholed in a single, pithy sentence. If there's a single unifying thread in this section of hyphenated-Americans (Japanese-, African-, Chinese-), its the Victorian architecture, best exemplified by the famous painted ladies around Alamo Square—you know, that picture-postcard row of houses with the downtown skyscrapers in the background.

The Addition is "western" in relation to the Civic Center, and was built to accommodate the middle-class men and women of the city, a position that it still fulfills to this day. The heavily African-American Fillmore neighborhood is something of a "Harlem West," while nearby Francisco Heights and eastern Jordan Park are both wealthier and whiter.

HONNEUR ET PATRIE

ThE RIChMONd

Bordered by The Presidio, and Arguello Ave, Fulton St and the Pacific Ocean.

Known as "The Avenues" by locals, the Richmond is a huge swath of land between Golden Gate Park and the Presidio that is something of a stucco suburbia within the city. The Avenues—numbered two to Forty-eight—are quiet residential neighborhoods known for perpetual fog and multiple immigrant communities, including, Russian, Irish, Jewish, and enough Chinese to make this something of a Chinatown Lite.

Commercially The Richmond centers on Clement Street and Geary Boulevard, both of which are getting more Asian by the minute.

Meanwhile, a five-block stretch of Sacramento Street near Presidio Avenue is coming into its own as something of a local low-cal Union Street.

For visitors, the best part of the neighborhood is by the ocean. On a Pacific bluff, overlooking Ocean Beach and Seal Rocks, stands **Cliff House** and the remains of **Sutro Baths,** a once-spectacular indoor sea-water swimming pool. Erected in 1909, the current Cliff House restaurant complex replaced an earlier landmark building that had burned to the ground. On the ocean side of the House is the **Musée Mécanique** arcade (*see* Chapter 4/Other Collections), and **Camera Obscura,** a walk-in camera, invented by Leonardo di Vinci, that projects an extraordinary view onto a back wall.

Just offshore are the abrupt outlines of **Seal Rocks,** usually inhabited by shore birds and a colony of sea lions. You'll need binoculars for a close-up. On a clear day you can see to the Farallon Islands, some 30 miles away.

Lincoln Park, out by the rugged cliffs of Land's End, is home to an incredible 18-hole golf course and the **California Palace of the Legion of Honor** art museum (*see* Chapter 4/The Top Museums).

EXERCiSiNg: fiTNESS ANd SPORtS

BEACHES

Ocean Beach
The Great Highway (at the western edge of Golden Gate Park). Tel. 415/556-8371.

Contrary to middle-American belief, San Francisco is not a beach town. Even in the height of summer the water is colder than a lawyer's heart, and only pre-pubescent boys seem able to take the plunge sans wetsuit. The air temperature is rarely beach-worthy and when it is, cold winds and gray fog often cut a day at the beach into a half-day, or less. That said, when it's time to hit the sands, Ocean Beach is where most locals head. For starters, this is the largest beach in the Bay Area, reaching four miles from Cliff House in the north to Fort Funston in the south. Our favorite stretch runs right past Golden Gate Park but, unfortunately, rip tides and monster waves make swimming here dangerous. Surfers love Ocean Beach for its raw waves and open ocean that offers unobstructed views to the horizon.

Baker Beach
Lincoln Boulevard (at Pershing).

Baker is the city's other great beach. Descend the stairs, just off Lincoln Boulevard, and walk south along the sand where you can see the great Golden Gate Bridge reaching across to the Marin Headlands directly across the Bay. This part of the beach is popular with nudists; gay men mostly. As you continue along the half-mile strip of beach the sands become more egalitarian, catering to all manner of SF society: Whites, Blacks, Asians, Surfers... everyone's here.

BICYCLING

San Francisco street cycling is not for amateurs; the massive hills keep most cyclists at bay, literally. Peddling along the water—around the perimeter of the peninsula—and into Golden Gate Park, is a great way to see the city. The ride into Marin across the Golden Gate Bridge is another great day out (see Chapter 10/Day Trips).

Almost a half-dozen bike-rental companies offer high-end mountain bikes for about $25 to $35 per day. The best are **Adventure Bicycle Company**, 968 Columbus Ave (tel. 415/771-8735); **Holiday Adventures**, 1937 Lombard St (tel. 415/567-1192); **Blazing Saddles**, Pier 41-Fisherman's Wharf (tel. 415/202-8888); and **American Rentals**, 2715 Hyde St (tel. 415/931-0234). All the companies include maps and directions for itineraries that range from an easy trek to Sausalito (and back by ferry) to the strenuous, legendary 38-mile loop across the trails of Mt. Tam, where the mountain bike was invented.

Captain Case Powerboat & Waterbike Rental

W10 Schoonemaker Point Marina, 885 Liberty Ship Way, Sausalito. Tel. 415/331-0444. Open daily 10am-6pm. Boston Whaler rentals $50-$90 per hour. AE, MC, V.

Captain Case is the best place to rent a power-boat. Boston Whalers to be exact. There's nothing fancy about these basic metal motorboats, but they can move quickly and are reputed to be virtually unsinkable. Once mobile, you can fly past the San Francisco skyline, check out the Golden Gate from below, visit the Sausalito Houseboats and, if you're lucky, even catch a tan.

Cass' Marina

1702 Bridgeway (at Litho), Sausalito. Tel. 415/332-6789. Open daily 9am-4pm. MC, V.

Experienced sailors can rent a sloop from Cass', one of the oldest charter marinas in the Bay Area. They've got nice boats, ranging in size from 22-foot day runners to 65-foot cruisers that sleep six. Novices can hire a skipper with their boat, and even a crew to serve a gourmet sunset dinner on board.

Stow Lake Boat Rentals

50 Stow Lake Dr (near 19th Ave), Golden Gate Park. Tel. 415/752-0347. Open summer, daily 9am-5pm; winter daily 9am-4pm. Hourly rentals: $10 rowboats; $11 pedal boats; $14 electric motor boat. No cards.

Golden Gate Park's Stow Lake has long been a popular spot with visitors and locals alike. It's a relatively quiet place for bird-watching, reading and picnicking. It's also perfect for taking out a row- or pedal-boat and watching the world glide by.

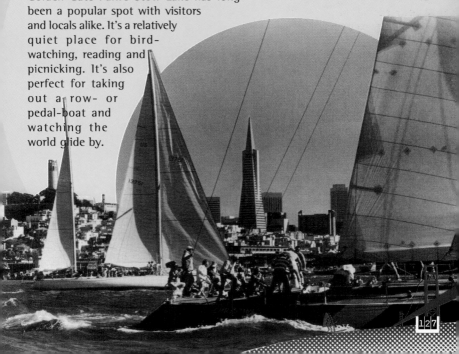

SPORES

BOWLING

Japantown Bowl
1790 Post St (at Webster). Tel. 415/921-6200. Open Mon-Thurs and Sun 9am-1am, Fri-Sat nonstop. Prices: $3-$3.50 per game; $1.50 shoe rental. MC, V. Packed with college graduates intent on recreational slumming, this 40-laner attracts kitsch-hunting low rollers with disco bowling and other special events. You can almost always get a lane when the urge hits—even at 3am, if it's a weekend. Unfortunately, the bar has to close at two.

CLIMBING

Mission Cliffs Rock Climbing
2295 Harrison St (at 19th). Tel. 415/550-0515. Open Mon, Wed and Fri 630am-10pm; Tues-Thurs 11am-10pm; Sat-Sun 10am-6pm. Prices: $15 per day. Urban climbing reaches its zenith at this top-of-the-line indoor climbing center. A former warehouse, the facility incorporates lead-climbs and top-roping routes for all levels of rockers. There's even a large bouldering area. Basic belay classes are offered daily and all equipment can be rented on the premises.

GOLF COURSES

Harding Park Golf Course
Harding Rd at Skyline Blvd. Tel. 415/664-4690. Open daily dawn-dusk. Fees: $28 Mon-Fri, $33 Sat-Sun.
Located across from the city zoo, Harding is a relatively flat, 6,743 yards, Par 72 course named for the former US president Warren G. Tons of trees provide the challenge, along with a large lake that duffers must play around. The adjacent 9-hole Fleming Course is a 2,300-yard, Par 32 green that's perfect for a quick round.

Golden Gate Park Municipal Golf Course
47th Avenue (at Fulton). Tel. 415/751-8987. Open daily 9am-6pm. Fees: $9 Mon-Fri, $10 Sat-Sun.
The price is certainly right at this city center municipal course. It's a relatively simple 9-hole affair (1,370 yards, Par 37) that's popular with hackers and the more than occasional first-timer.

Lincoln Park Golf Course
34th Avenue (at Clement). Tel. 415/221-9911. Open daily dawn-dusk. Fees: $23 Mon-Fri; $27 Sat-Sun.
One of the very best public courses anywhere, Lincoln Park is well-known for its awesome beauty, quality design and extremely reasonable greens fees. The 5,158-yard, Par 68 links is located on a steep bluff overlooking Golden Gate Bridge and the Bay, and there's a 1/3 discount for twilight play.

HORSE RIDING

Golden Gate Park Riding Stables

John F. Kennedy Drive (at 36th Ave). Tel. 415/668-7360. Open daily 8am-6pm. Prices: $40 private lesson, $25 trial ride. No cards.

These stables rent horses for trotting in Golden Gate Park. Jockeys don't need any training; just a wad of cash and a signature on a liability waver gets you on the mount. The trail ride follows 12 miles of bridle paths in the park.

ICE SKATING

Kristi Yamaguchi Holiday Ice Rink

Justin Herman Plaza (at Market/Embarcadero). Tel. 415/956-2688. Open Nov-Feb, Sun-Thurs 10am-10pm, Fri-Sat 10am-1130pm. Admission: $7; Skate rental: $3.50-$4.50.

A terrific outdoor rink for figure skaters and hockey speedsters, the Yamaguchi rink is a decent-sized oval, with a dramatic location at the foot of Market Street. Ninety-minute sessions run throughout the day.

POOL & BILLIARDS

Chalkers

1 Rincon Center (btw Spear/Mission). Tel. 415/512-0450. Open Mon-Wed 1130am-1am, Thurs-Fri 1130am-2am, Sat 2pm-2am, Sun 3-11pm. Tables: $6-$15 per hour. AE, MC, V.

After a brief stint as an upscale fad in the 1980s, pool has thankfully returned to its scummy roots. Not so in San Francisco, where Chalkers continues to attract cab-sav swillers by the Range Rover load. Its faux-swank decor includes high ceilings, plush carpeting and imitation oils by great European masters. There's a full bar with several specialty beers on tap, and an interesting grazing menu. And, oh yes, there are also thirty antique and custom pool tables.

Hollywood Billiards

61 Golden Gate Avenue (btw Taylor/Jones). Tel. 415/252-9643. Open nonstop. Tables: $8-$14 per hour.

For our money, the best pool halls are divvy places with tons of tables, good lighting and late closing times, if any at all. That's why Hollywood Billiards is one of the best pool halls in the city. The place hops throughout the week, but insiders rave about Wednesday's "ladies night," which is hugely popular with cruising lesbians.

IN-LINE SKATING

Because of the hills, most street bladers are confined to low-lying neighborhoods along the Embarcadero and around Golden Gate Park. But that covers an awful lot of ground. A fantastic paved path runs around the perimeter of the peninsula, from SoMa to the Golden Gate Bridge. On Sundays, Golden Gate Park is closed to cars, and bladers have the run of the streets. Near the east end of the park there's a popular skate pad where regular skating events are held.

Friday Night Skate (2549 Irving St; tel. 415/752-1967), held each Friday at 8pm, is becoming one of the largest weekly sporting events in California. Begun in 1993, the event now attracts hundreds of rollers who skate through a broad swath of city from Fisherman's Wharf and the Marina, to SoMa and the Embarcadero. Everyone is welcome. The Skate begins at Bryant Street & The Embarcadero.

In-line and conventional skates can be rented from several places in the city. Marina Skate & Snowboard (2271 Chestnut St; tel. 415/567-8400) is the best place for those skating around Fisherman's Wharf. Skates on Haight (1818 Haight St; tel. 415/752-8375) is perfectly situated for those planning a day in Golden Gate Park. Both places charge about $6/hour; $20/day.

TENNIS

Golden Gate Park Tennis Complex
Golden Gate Park. Tel. 415/753-7100.
Twenty-one hard courts in the park are well-maintained and available free to the public on a first-come, first served basis. Some reservations are also accepted (see phone number above), but courts are often available for walk-ons.

SPECTATOR SPORTS

BASEBALL

Oakland Athletics

Oakland-Alameda County Stadium. Tel. 510/638-0500 or Tel. 510/568-5600. Box office open Mon-Fri 9am-6pm, Sat 10am-4pm. Admission $5-$25.

Despite a roster of top young players, the A's pitching is still thin and their manager seems perpetually in danger of being fired. Happily, O-A Stadium is a great ballpark with a booming sound-system, terrific seating, and easy access, via BART.

San Francisco Giants

Pac Bell Park. Tel. 415/467-8000 or 800/SF-GIANT. Box office open Mon-Fri 830am-530pm. Admission $7-$35.

On Opening Day, in April, 2000, the baseball Giants will have christened their new stadium in San Francisco's China Basin neighborhood. After 42 seasons at Candlestick Point, the team takes their show to Pacific Bell Park, a high-tech ballground just seven blocks from the Moscone Convention Center. The Giants are always exciting to watch, and their new home should make them one of the league's hottest tickets.

BASKETBALL

Golden State Warriors

Oakland-Alameda County Arena. Tel. 510/762-BASS or 888/GSW-HOOP. Box office open Mon-Sat 10am-5pm. Admission $15-$250.

There might be better basketball teams, but few have more loyal fans. Oakland is a basketball city and this recently refurbished arena is a wonderful place to watch professional hoops.

131

FOOTBALL

Oakland Raiders

Oakland-Alameda County Stadium. Tel. 510/639-7700. Box office open Mon-Sat 9am-5pm. Admission from $55.

The bottom-of-the-league Raiders do absolutely nothing to help their city's already flagging image. Yet, their die-hard fans are some of the game's most loyal, even forgiving the team for its dismal 13-year stint in Los Angeles.

One nice thing for visitors is that it's always easy to find a last-minute seat at the terrific Oakland-Alameda County Stadium, which boasts a great sound system and perfect sightlines, even from the cheapest seats in the house. Take BART from San Francisco directly to the Coliseum.

San Francisco 49ers

3Com Park. Tel. 415/468-2249. Box office open Mon-Fri 9am-5pm. Admission $50; parking $20.

San Francisco 49ers' regular season games are some of the hardest sports tickets to get. Even in a rebuilding year, the Niners bring a fiercely loyal crowd to every game they play. As of this writing the team still calls Candlestick, er, make that 3Com Park, home, though they are agitating for a new stadium to be built next door. The old wind tunnel is known for the best stadium food in the league (read: steak burritos, garlic fries, Ben & Jerry's ice cream, Gordon Biersch beer).

ICE HOCKEY

San Jose Sharks

San Jose Arena. Tel. 408/287-9200 or 800/888-2736. Box office open Mon-Fri 930am-530pm. Admission $17-$80.

The Sharks are a God-awful team with one of the best arenas in the land. The team performs its ice-capades at a predictably high-tech Silicon Valley facility, fronted by a landmark ten-story glass pyramid. Get there by CalTrain, from the 4th and Townsend Street Station in San Francisco to the Tamien Station in San Jose.

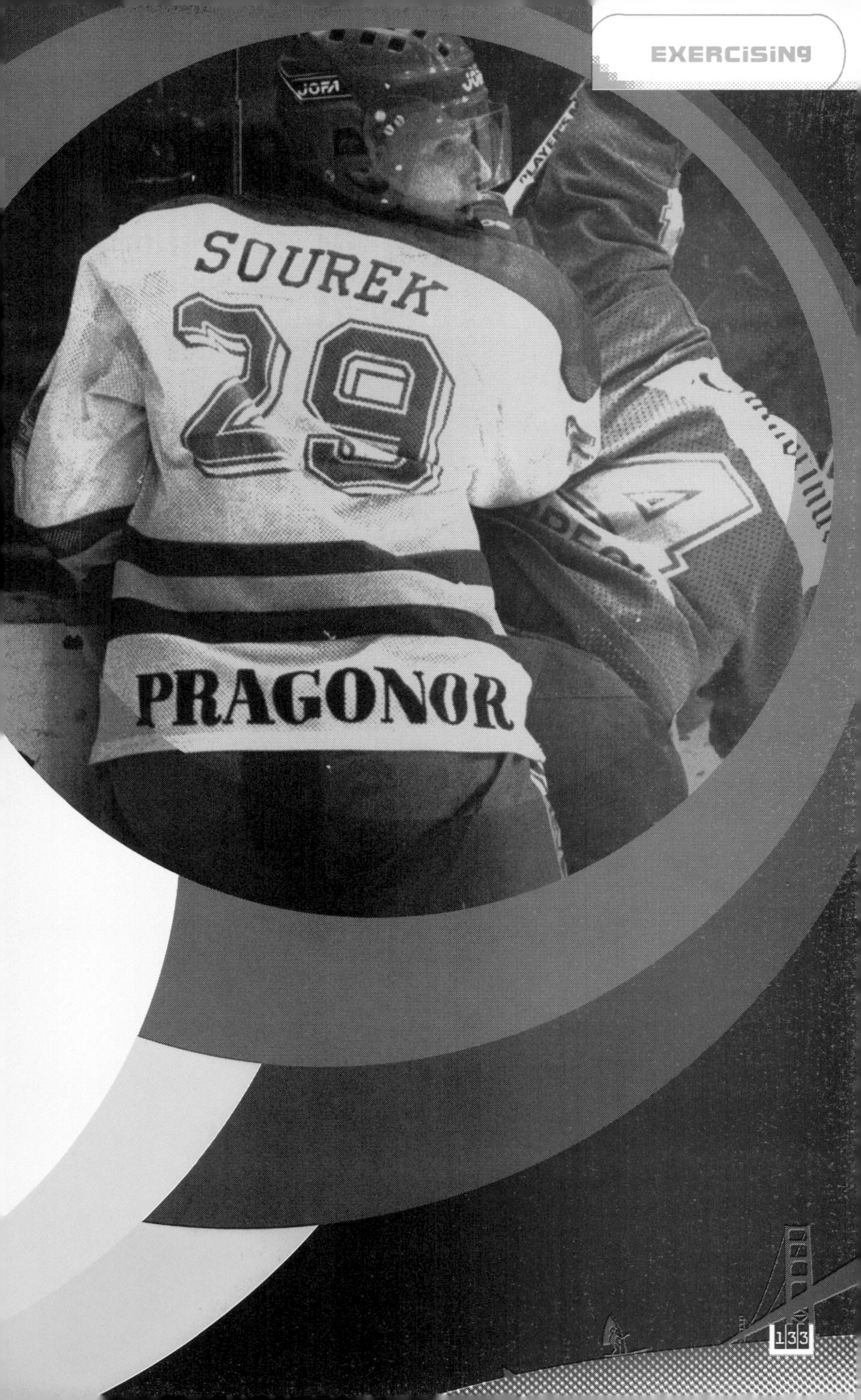
JOFA
SOUREK
29
PRAGONOR

¶
¶
#07

STROH⊂

Zuckerman

When it comes to variety, San Francisco is not the best shopping city in the world, but its relatively small size makes shopping manageable; you can confidently cover an entire neighborhood in a single afternoon. Shops of a feather flock together on strictly-defined, walkable strips (*see* The Neighborhoods, below). Strangely, fashions tend to be either very conservative or intensely avant, with precious little inbetween. The best strategy: pick the neighborhood that interests you and make a day of it.

ThE NEiGHbORhOODS

- **Union Square** is retail ground-zero for luxury shopping and department stores. Post Street, on the north side of the square, is particularly rich with high-end stores from Brooks Brothers to Versace (*see* High-End Hotlist).
- **Fillmore Street**, in Pacific Heights, is younger and trendier; well worth a stroll for it's mid-range international boutiques and plethora of thrift stores.
- **Haight-Ashbury** continues to groove off its 1960s seductiveness, offering a long strip of hip-meets-hippiewear for both locals and visitors.
- **Hayes Valley**, by the corner of Hayes and Gough streets, has become one of the city's most forward-thinking fashion districts. It's a great place to shop for Avant clothes, deco furnishings and all manner of eclectic goodies.
- **Noe Valley** shops cater primarily to gays and families who live in the neighborhood. Twenty-Fourth Street between Castro and Dolores is the district's epicenter.
- **Sacramento Street**, between Presidio and Locust streets, is particularly loaded with antiques shops, crafts galleries and clothing boutiques serving one of the city's most upscale neighborhoods.
- **Union Street**, in Cow Hollow, is great at promoting itself as one of the city's premier shopping strips. In truth, the street is brimming with conservative old-ladies' fashions and kitschy gift shops that are united by their inability to impress us.

Alfred Dunhill
250 Post St (btw Grant/Stockton). Tel. 415/781-3368.
Bally
238 Stockton St (at Union Square). Tel. 398-7463.
Brooks Brothers
201 Post St (at Grant Ave). Tel. 415/397-4500.
Bulgari
237 Post St (btw Grant/Stockton). Tel. 415/399-9141.
Burberrys
225 Post St (btw Grant/Stockton). Tel. 415/392-2200.
Cartier
231 Post St (btw Grant/Stockton). Tel. 415/397-3180.
Chanel Boutique
155 Maiden Lane (btw Grant/Kearny). Tel. 415/981-1550.
Coach
190 Post St (btw Grant/Kearny). Tel. 415/392-1772.
Gianni Versace
60 Post St (at Kearny). Tel. 415/393-1505.
Giorgio Armani
278 Post St (btw Grant/Stockton). Tel. 415/434-2500.
Gucci
200 Stockton St (at Geary). Tel. 415/392-2808.
Hermes
212 Stockton St (btw Geary/Post). Tel. 415/391-7200.
Kenneth Cole
166 Grant Ave (btw Post/Geary). Tel. 415/981-2653.
Louis Vuitton
230 Post St (btw Grant/Stockton). Tel. 415/391-6200.
MaxMara
175 Post St (btw Grant/Kearny). Tel. 415/981-0900.
Montblanc
120 Grant Ave (at Post). Tel. 415/403-4000.
Nicole Miller
50 Post St (at Kearny). Tel. 415/393-1505.
Polo/Ralph Lauren
in Crocker Galleria, 50 Post St (at Kearny). Tel. 415/788-7656.
Sulka
255 Post St (btw Grant/Stockton). Tel. 415/989-0600.
Tiffany & Co.
350 Post St (btw Stockton/Powell). Tel. 415/781-7000.
Wilkes-Bashford
375 Sutter St (btw Grant/Stockton). Tel. 415/986-4380.

bOOkS

Aardvark's Books

227 Church St (btw Market/15th). Tel. 415/552-6733. Open Mon-Sat 1030am-1030pm, Sun 930am-1030pm.

This independent bookseller stands out from the chains with a huge selection of new and used books, and leftist, egg-headed shop assistants. Something of a cash cow for college students who need to sell old feminist theory books in order to pay rent, Aardvark's is a great place for both serious books and inexpensive day reads in Golden Gate Park.

Barnes & Noble

2550 Taylor St (at North Point). Tel 415/292-6762. Open daily 9am-11pm.

B&Ns Fisherman's Wharf superstore is a particularly wonderful place to browse. In addition to books, you'll find music, software, a news-stand, a cafe and lots of comfortable chairs for lounging.

Borders

400 Post St (at Powell). Tel. 415/399-1633. Open Mon-Thurs 9am-11pm, Fri-Sat 9am-midnight, Sun 9am-9pm.

Borders dominates the north-west corner of Union Square with its four-story megastore that includes a music/video department, espresso bar and one of the largest selections of mainstream magazines in the city. There's an excellent travel section too.

City Lights

261 Columbus Ave (btw Pacific/Broadway). Tel. 415/362-8193. Open daily 10am-midnight.

A vestige of 1950s North Beach, this Lawrence Ferlingetti-backed bookshop is a testament to the endurance of literature, poetry and bohemian sensibilities. Ginsberg's Howl is a perennial best-seller. The store focuses upon the outrageous and classic, so you're just as likely to find a Dennis Cooper novel as you are a book of Baudelaire's poetry.

A Clean Well-Lighted Place for Books

601 Van Ness Ave (at Golden Gate). Tel. 415/441-6670. Open Sun-Thurs 10am-11pm, Fri-Sat 10am-midnight.

This independent bookseller stands out from the chains with its huge selection, professional staff and dense calendar of events featuring some of the world's top authors. It is particularly strong on art books, fiction, cookbooks and travel.

A Different Light

489 Castro St (btw Market/18th). Tel. 415/431-0891. Open daily 10am-midnight.

Specializing in gay and lesbian oriented books, A Different Light carries Joan Crawford biographies, lesbian erotica, light porn and queer theory compilations. Although you may have to suffer through the soundtrack from Hair while shopping for Chastity Bono's memoir, its also a good place to find information on local gay and lesbian interests.

McDonald's Book Shop

48 Turk St (at Market). Tel. 415/673-2235. Open daily 10am-6pm.

Hunkered down in one of the seedier streets of the Tenderloin, McDonald's is something of an anomaly in a part of town where it seems few people even know how to read. The enormous shop takes a page from the old school of bookselling, with dusty, disorganized stacks in a claustrophobic environment. But patience is often rewarded with that obscure out-of-print novel or volume of poetry you've been looking for.

Rizzoli

117 Post St (btw Grant/Kearny). Tel. 415/984-0225. Open Mon-Sat 10am-7pm, Sun 1030am-6pm.

Easily among the most beautiful bookshops in the city, Rizzoli's interiors could be the subject of a coffee table book of its own. This upscale and arty retailer is not the place to look for the latest Danielle Steele novel.

Stacey's

581 Market St (at 2nd). Tel. 415/421-4687. Open Mon-Fri 830am-7pm, Sat 10am-7pm, Sun 10am-6pm.

This large generalist shop also specializes in computer oriented texts. The cellar and first floors carry the standard bookstore fare, while the upstairs is a virtual wet dream for silicon heads.

Rand McNally Map & Travel Store

595 Market St. Tel. 415/777-3131. Open Mon-Fri 9am-630pm, Sat 10am-6pm, Sun 11am-5pm.

Packed with travel guides, maps, language tapes, videos, globes and atlases, Rand McNally stocks everything for the global traveler.

Thomas Bros. Maps and Books

550 Jackson St (at Montgomery). Tel 415/981-7520. Open Mon-Fri 930am-530pm.

One of the oldest shops on Jackson Square, Thomas Bros. carries an extensive selection of domestic and international travel books, and maps ranging from pocket- to wall-size.

CAMERAS & PhOtOGRAPhY

Adolf Gasser

181 2nd St (btw Mission/Howard). Tel. 415/982-4946. Open Mon-Sat 9am-6pm.

Professionals and film students know Adolf Gasser for refrigerated films, replacement camera parts and accessories, and top-quality used equipment.

Camera Boutique

342 Kearny St (btw Bush/Pine). Tel. 415/982-4946. Open Mon-Fri 9am-6pm, Sat 10am-5pm.

Not only does this all-purpose camera shop have the latest in analogue and digital equipment, they also stock used cameras and rentals, and have a sizable collection of antiques. Quality developing, too.

Body Manipulations

3234 16th St (btw Dolores/Guerrero). Tel. 415/621-0408. Open daily noon–7pm.
Ask any local where they got their family crest branded onto their back and the answer will probably be Body Manipulations. What better way to say "I love you" than to have your sweetie's initials permanently scarred on your biceps?

Gauntlet

2377 Market St (at Castro). Tel. 415/431-3133. Open Mon–Wed and Fri–Sat noon–7pm, Thurs noon–9pm, Sun 1–6pm.
Something of a Castro Street institution, Gauntlet was one of the first clean, well lighted places in the city to do nipple piercing. Such renown translates into prices that are on the high end of the spectrum, but for neophytes to piercing, there's no substitute for experience.

Sephora

1 Stockton St (at Market). Tel. 415/392-1545. Open Mon–Sat 10am–8pm, Sun 11am–7pm.
Packaged with the clean lines and high style of designer perfume, Sephora is an immaculately clean, twin-story shop specializing in high-quality beauty supplies. The ground floor of this one-stop emporium is devoted to fragrances and bath products for both men and women, while the upper level is exclusively for cosmetics. Throughout the store are self-serve stations containing Q-tips, make-up sponges and removers, so you can try all you want without any hard sell. Can't find the perfect shade? Visit the custom-blending area where assistants will even mix lipsticks to match your shoes.

Bebe

2133 Fillmore St (btw Sacramento/California). Tel. 415/771-2323. Open Mon-Fri 10am-8pm, Sat 10am-7pm, Sun 11am-6pm.

Up-to-the-moment derivatives mean moderately-priced knockoffs of the top designer styles. Look for well-tailored dresses, suits, tops and other feminine wearables that will get you past the velvet ropes.

Betsey Johnson

160 Geary St (btw Grant/Stockton). Tel. 415/398-2516. Open Mon-Sat 11am-8pm, Sun noon-8pm.

In addition to Johnson's trademark skintight flesh-wrappers, you'll find plenty of feminine urban trashwear made with leather, lace and fishnet. Check-out her new line of peek-a-boo lingerie.

Emporio Armani

1 Grant Ave (btw O'Farrell/Geary). Tel. 415/677-9400. Open Mon-Sat 11am-8pm, Sun noon-8pm.

Armani's Union Square shop features the designer's less-pricey collections that include those trademark crisp suits.

Jil Sander

135 Maiden Lane (btw Grant Ave/Kearny). Tel. 415/273-7070. Open Mon-Sat 10am-6pm.

San Francisco's schmashion mavens have embraced this epitome of basic German style as their own. This boutique carries Sander's complete lines for both men and women.

Citizen

536 Castro St (btw 18th/19th). Tel. 415/575-3560. Open Mon-Sat 10am-8pm, Sun 10am-7pm.

Tight lycra T-shirts, tank tops and other uniforms of gay streetwear are the specialties of this house. Always trendy, Citizen stocks anything from glittery western wear to simple white shirts with creative crests, along with the ever-popular sleeveless undershirts.

Diesel USA

101 Post St (at Kearny). Tel. 415/982-7077. Open Mon-Fri 10am-8pm, Sat 10am-7pm, Sun noon-6pm.

Dance club meets clothing store at this awesome showplace for the Italian clothes horse. House DJs work the turntables while shoppers browse through four floors of pricey, must-have Italian fashions.

143

House of Blue Jeans
979 Market St. Tel. 415/252-2929.
Open Mon-Sat 11am-7pm, Sun 1130am-530pm.
One of the largest Levi's selections in the birthplace of the bluejean, they also stock casual shirts, sweats and shorts.

Nomads
556 Hayes St (btw Octavia/Laguna). Tel. 415/864-5692. Open daily 11am-7pm.
Nomads clothes successfully straddle the fence between street and clubwear (which in San Francisco is a very narrow fence). From ravvy soccer jerseys to loose hemmed sweaters, this is one forward thinking shop that refuses to be typecast.

Rolo
25 Stockton St (at Market) Tel. 415/989-7656. Open Mon-Sat 10am-8pm, Sunday 11am-7pm.
Freshjive skate/club gear and shimmery Reflexite jackets in neon colors jam the racks, while shelves bulge with imported British marshmallow-shaped sneakers. The Kangol caps of yesterdecade have been replaced with the ubiquitous NY Yankees baseball cap, and old (looking) shirts bearing the names of '30s sports clubs from Chicago to Havana.
  Branch: 450 Castro St (btw Market/18th). Tel. 415/626-7171. Open Mon-Sat 10am-8pm, Sunday 11am-7pm.

Settemezzo
419 Columbus St (btw Vallejo/Green). Tel. 415/398-4664. Open Tues-Sun 11am-7pm.
This small North Beach outpost sells Diesel, Gene Meyer, Paul Smith and other streetwise casual creations. Turnover is so quick that the pants you're thinking about buying can practically disappear while you're mulling it over.

CLOthiNG--DiSCOUNt

Goodwill As Is
86 11th St (at Market). Tel. 415/575-2197. Open Mon-Sat 9am-6pm.
No one, from tweaked-out speed freaks and local homeless, to second-hand clothes dealers and fashion hounds, can pass up bargains like these: Everything costs $1. Versace gowns with the tags still on them, vintage Pucci shirts—you never know what you'll find in this filthy South of Market warehouse, providing you have the patience to sift through hundreds of bins of leg warmers and acid-washed denim.

Rolo Outlet

1301 Howard St (at 9th). Tel. 415/861-1999. Open
Mon-Sat 11am-7pm, Sun noon-6pm.

Depending on what the trendsetters snubbed last season, the racks can be
full of great designer outfits or pink sequined tank tops. Bargains prices
are the only certainty.

Ross Dress for Less

1645 Van Ness Ave (btw California/Sacramento). Tel. 415/775-0192.
Open Mon-Sat 930am-9pm, Sun 11am-7pm.

Drag queens, temp workers, and everyone else looking for 80%
markdowns on oversized or overstocked Calvin Klein ensembles, flock
to Ross hoping for a lucky break. Unfortunately most of the offerings
aren't high-end, and one is more likely to find last season's Contempo
Casuals than mint Dolce & Gabbanas. But there's always hope.

CLOthING--fOOtWEAR

Bulo Women/Bulo Men

418/437A Hayes St (btw Gough/Octavia). Tel. 415/864 3244. Open
Mon-Sat 1130am-630pm, Sun noon-6pm.

Bulo's neighboring shops specialize in mid-priced knockoffs of the hottest
international styles. Offering terrific shoes and boots, all priced under $200,
Bulo is something of a 9-West for the sartorially savvy but budget limited.
The women's store is both more sparse and more flamboyant (read: more
sparkle, more sling back, more platform) than the men's store across the street.

Dal-Jeets

1744 Haight (btw Cole/Shrader). Tel. 415/752-5610. Open
daily 11am-7pm.

Taken together, the Haight and Valencia street stores offer what is
probably the largest selection of Doc Martens in the Bay Area. A long
way from their clunky steel-toe roots, DMs now run the gamut from
suede boots to sandals.

Branch: 541 Valencia St (btw 16th/17th). Tel. 415/626-9000.
Open Mon-Fri noon-7pm, Sat noon-8pm, Sun noon-6pm.

Gimme Shoes

2358 Fillmore St (btw Clay/Washington). Tel. 415/441-3040. Open
Mon-Sat 11am-7pm, Sun noon-6pm.

While sandals, mules and the occasional loafer do appear on these shelves,
Gimme can't seem to get enough of square-toed shoes and boots. High-
end Italians share floor space with the likes of Britain's Patrick Cox and Dirk
Bekembergs. The Fillmore Street store caters to women, while the Grant
Avenue shop is mainly for men.

Branch: 50 Grant Ave (btw O'Farrell/Geary). Tel. 415/434-9242.
Open Mon- Sat 11am-7pm, Sun noon-5pm.

Gucci

200 Stockton St (at Geary). Tel. 415/392-2808. Open Mon-Sat 10am-6pm, Sun noon-5pm.

The only real way to enter this attitude-laden boutique is with a manner that's so disarmingly casual that it'll throw the black-clad model/salespeople off-guard; an especially tough act when you're eyeing a pair of thousand-dollar loafers. What the hell, try on a few different pairs (then ask if they have a wallet to match).

John Fluevog

1697 Haight St (at Cole). Tel. 415/436-9784. Open Mon-Sat 11am-7pm, Sun noon-6pm.

Essential for any hipster worthy of the title, Fluevog's quality, comfortable footwear can at times be over-the-top; but you'll always feel fabulous bouncing down the street in a pair of Angels with the trademark Gibson Swirl.

Kenneth Cole

in the SF Shopping Centre, 865 Market St (at 5th). Tel. 415/227-4536.

Great styling and chic aesthetic keeps Kenneth Cole at the head of foot fashions for both men and women. Most designs are created in-house. Unfortunately the staff isn't particularly helpful, but it's hard to have it all.

Luichiny

1529 Haight St (btw Cole/Clayton). Tel. 415/252-7065. Open Mon-Sat 11am-7pm, Sat 11am-8pm, Sun 11am-7pm.

Fashion-forward seems like a drowsy understatement about this edgy shop, where boots and shoes often border on the absurd. You wouldn't want to show up for a job interview in a pair of their thigh-high platforms, but you wouldn't want to go bar hopping in the Mission without them. Blue plastic floors and wrought iron shoe racks help make shopping here an otherworldly experience.

NaNa

2276 Market St (btw Noe/16th). Tel. 415/861-6262. Open Mon-Thurs 11am-9pm, Fri-Sat 11am-930pm, Sun 11am-7pm. NaNa's exciting melange of club gear, retro-print shirts, kitchy lighters and fabulously extreme shoes can transform even the most rigorous Banana Republican to an instant hep-cat, guaranteeing swift entrance into bars like the Orbit Room and The End Up. Like passionate love, nothing here lasts forever, but that's the (low) price one pays for style.

Niketown

278 Post St (at Stockton). Tel. 415/392-6453. Open Mon-Fri 10am-8pm, Sat 10am-7pm, Sun 11am-6pm.

A multilevel paean to the ubiquitous swish sneaker, Niketown assaults the senses with loud music, high-decibel sports sounds and flashing video walls screaming at shoppers to "Just..." well you know. It's an intense multimedia shopping experience, occasionally heightened by picketers out front decrying the company's Third World labor practices.

Macy's
170 O'Farrell St (btw Stockton/Powell). Tel. 415/397-3333. Open Mon-Sat 10am-8pm, Sun 11am-8pm.

Occupying a good chunk of Union Square, Macy's is one of the biggest department stores in the city. Actually, it's two stores. The larger West Building is five mammoth floors of women's fashion and home furnishings. Menswear and accessories are across Stockton Street, in the East Building. Macy's seems to be a bit less expensive than rival department stores, but a salesperson can be as absent as a cop when you need one.

Nieman Marcus
150 Stockton St (btw Geary/Market). Tel. 415/362-3900. Open Mon-Wed & Fri 10am-7pm, Thurs 10am-8pm, Sun noon-6pm.

Known locally as "Needless Mark-Ups," this temple to high-end, high priced fashion is popular with platinum-carded socialites and office workers who've just received their year-end bonuses. Armani, Donna Karan, Calvin Klein and Versace are all well represented, along with caviar and fine wines on the top floor.

Nordstrom
865 Market St (btw 5th/6th). Tel. 415/243-8500. Open Mon-Sat 930am-9pm, Sun 11am-7pm.

Famous for great service and an amazing no-questions-asked shoe return policy, Nordstrom has become San Francisco's footwear king. The department store branched out long ago to include bridge-line designer clothing for working women and social butterflies, but it's the shoes that keep customers returning.

Saks Fifth Avenue
384 Post St (btw Stockton/Powell). Tel. 415/986-4300. Open Mon-Wed & Fri 10am-7pm, Thurs 10am-8pm, Sun noon-7pm.

Saks is a great store. They have terrific selections of women's designerwear and excellent, if conservative, Men's Store offerings on the next block (see below). The window displays are legendary, and prices are not too far out of this world.

Saks Men's Store
220 Post St (btw Stockton/Grant). Tel. 415/743-5184. Open Mon-Wed & Fri 10am-7pm, Thurs 10am-8pm, Sun noon-7pm.

One of Union Square's most recent additions, Saks Men's store outfits gents from head to toe with everything from suits and ties to shoes and clubby designer wear. We usually bypass the store's first four floors, which are stuffy and expensive, and head straight to the discounted Gucci, Dolce & Gabbana and Helmut Lang clothes up top.

Cliff's Variety

497 Castro St (btw 18th/Market). Tel. 415/431-5365. Open Mon-Sat 930am-8pm.

Part housewares shop, part pick-up joint, Cliff's is a Castro institution where you can find everything from Great Neck hammers and Alessi cookware to a date for Saturday night. Check it out.

Don't Panic!

541 Castro St (btw 18th/19th). Tel. 415/553-8989. Open Mon-Thurs 10am-10pm, Fri-Sat 10am-11pm, Sun 11am-9pm.

Packed with yay-gay clothing and accessories, Don't Panic gives new meaning to "outerwear" with T-shirts proclaiming "I'm Not Gay But My Boyfriend Is," "Nobody Knows I'm A Lesbian" and the like.

Does Your Father Know?

548 Castro St (btw 18th/19th). Tel. 415/241-9865. Open Mon-Thurs 930am-10pm, Fri-Sat 930am-11pm, Sun 10am-9pm.

Sure, they've got penis-shaped pasta and lots of adult videos, playing cards and magnets. But the best items in this shop are the anatomically super-endowed Billy Dolls (as well as his Latin friend, Carlos), which come dressed in a variety of guises (sailor, leatherman, club kid). It's all very tasteful, of course.

FAO Schwarz

48 Stockton St (btw Market/Geary). Tel. 415/394-8700. Open Mon-Sat 11am-6pm, Sun 11am-5pm.

This play palace is so awesome that most kids believe it when their parents tell them they're actually in a toy museum. The frivolity includes house-sized stuffed animals, mini-Porche automobiles that actually work, a wall of M&M chocolate candies sorted by color, and an excellent selection of plush Gund animals and high-end theme Barbies.

Gump's

135 Post St (btw Grant/Kearny). Tel. 415/982-1616. Open
Mon-Sat 10am-6pm.

Luxe china, jade figurines, high-end soaps and beautifully blown glasswork
make this two-story extravaganza akin to a fine Asian art gallery. Gump's
great craftsmanship doesn't come cheap, and only the brashest socialites dare
list their wedding registries here. The two-story golden Buddha, in the
center of the store, is reason enough to visit.

PlaNet Weavers Treasure Store

1573 Haight St (at Clayton). Tel. 415/864-4415. Open Sun-Thurs 10am-8pm,
Fri-Sat 10am-9pm.

If you're not frightened by wind chimes and clouds of incense, PlaNet Weavers
will entice with their only-in-San Francisco brand of Zen/Hippie clutter. A virtual
one-stop shop for all your astral needs, you could fill a New Age monastery with
their great selection of candles, incense, funky musical instruments and gift cards.

Sanrio

39 Stockton St (btw Market/Geary). Tel. 415/981-5568. Open Mon-Sat
10am-8pm, Sun 10am-6pm.

You'd have to go to Japan to top this colorful collection of Asian kitsch
—stuffed animals, stationary, cosmetics, stickers, candy and clothes—most
of which is emblazoned with the various Sanrio franchises: Hello Kitty,
Keroppi, Twin Stars, ad nauseum. We go for their cool photo booths
where your face is printed onto stickers and stamp pads.

SF MoMA Museum Store

151 3rd St (btw Mission/Howard). Tel. 415/357-4035. Open Fri-Wed 1030am-630pm, Thurs 1030am-930pm.

The shop on the ground floor of the Museum of Modern Art is the best place in the city for glossy art books, post-modern postcards, trippy posters and über-designy home furnishings (think Williams-Sonoma meets IM Pei).

TT Globetrotter USA

418 Sutter St (btw Stockton/Powell). Tel. 415/434-1120. Open Mon-Sat 10am-6pm, Sun 11am-5pm.

The entire line of Tintin adventure books is sold here alongside umbrellas, T-shirts, watches, home furnishings and other souvenirs emblazoned with images of the young Belgian detective and his faithful dog. Keeping Tintin company are other "Euro-peon" characters, including Asterix, Barbar and The Little Prince.

Uncle Mame

2241 Market St (btw Noe/Sanchez). Tel. 415/626-1953. Open Mon-Thurs noon-7pm, Fri-Sat noon-11pm, Sun noon-5pm.

A nostalgia buff's dream come true, Uncle Mame carries such offbeat rarities as the earring-wearing Magic Ken Doll, Mr. T Coloring Book, ET the Extra-Terrestrial Hand Soap and various other icons of American Pop culture. Prices can be steep ($100-plus for a talking Pee-Wee Herman doll), but as a museum of Americana this place is tops.

hOUSEWARES & fURNISHiNGS

Design for Living

1612 Market St (btw Gough/Franklin). Tel. 415/864-7477. Open Tues-Sun noon-6pm.

A vintage store specializing in the Modernist era, DfL offers furnishings from designers that reads like a Who's Who of the greats: Eames, Sarineen, Mies van Diro—they're all here.

Limn Company

290 Townsend St (btw 3rd/4th). Tel. 415/543-5466. Open Mon-Fri 930am-530pm, Sat-Sun 11am-530pm.

While technically a furniture store, the homewares sold here are so edgy and artistic you'd be hard pressed not to imagine you're in a museum. The place is packed with cool furnishings and knickknacks from big name designers that are worth taking out a second mortgage for.

MAGAZINES

Cafe de la Presse

352 Grant Ave (at Bush). Tel. 415/398-2680. Open daily 7am-11pm.

As the name implies, Cafe de la Presse stocks a wide selection of international newspapers and magazines and serves them up with croissants and cafe au lait. You can browse through anything you want, but if you spill on it, you buy.

International Magazine Store

225 Bush St (at Montgomery). Tel. 415/439-8858. Open daily 7am-11pm.

IMS boasts the largest selection of domestic and international magazines in the city. You can find most anything here from Vogue Babini to Bang Me Blue Boy.

MALLS

The Fisherman's Wharf area is basically a single string of shopping malls, selling the worst crap known to tourism. It's hard to say which is worse but here's our attempt, in ascending order: **Ghirardelli Square** (900 North Point), a former chocolate factory; **Pier 39** (at the Embarcadero and Beach), a wooden "festival marketplace"; **The Cannery** (2801 Leavenworth), a former Del Monte peach packing plant; and **The Anchorage** (2800 Leavenworth), a block-square open-air complex. *See* Chapter 4/Crucial San Francisco for complete information.

Crocker Galleria

50 Post St (at Kearny). Tel. 415/393-1505. Open Mon-Fri 10am-6pm, Sat 10am-5pm.

Billing itself as an upscale shopping experience, Crocker puts its two-story roof over heads you don't normally associate with a mall (Polo/Ralph Lauren and Versace to name two). The concept works for two reasons: Its user-friendly layout makes it easy to compare the styles and prices of high-end designers, and price tags tend to be lower here than in other high-rent boutiques around Union Square. Best of all, there are no mallrats, Ricky Lake Girls or other teen angst rebels.

San Francisco Shopping Centre

865 Market St (at 5th). Tel. 415/495-5656. Open
Mon-Sat 930am-8pm, Sun 11am-6pm.

Anchored by Nordstrom's department store, this seven-story city
center mall is far better than most. Good mid-range shops include
Benetton, J. Crew and Club Monaco, though you'll also have to put
up with non-events like Gymboree, Hold Everything and Sam Goody.

Stonestown Galleria

3251 20th Ave (at Winston). Tel. 415/759-2626. Open
Mon-Sat 10am-9pm, Sun 11am-6pm.

Dotted with lowbrow shops like Contempo Casuals, Lady
Foot Locker and Sunglasses Hut, the Galleria is a
thoroughly horrible place filled with boring suburban
shops that appeal to Lord knows who. Still, some
candyassed tourists insist on making the long trek to
the edge of the Sunset District to dine at the Food
Court. Perhaps they're homesick.

MUSiC

Amoeba

1855 Haight
St (at Stanyan).
Tel. 415/
831-1200.
Open Mon-Sat
10am-10pm,
Sun 11am-9pm.
Perfectly suited
for eclectic
Haight Street,
Amoeba offers
a tremendous
selection of used
and vintage
vinyl, movies and
compact discs, as
well as tons of
new stuff.
B-bands like Jon
Spencer Blues
E x p l o s i o n
occasionally drop by
for free in-store
performances.

Reckless Records
1401 Haight St (at Masonic). Tel. 415/431-3434. Open
Mon-Sat 10am-10pm, Sun 10am-9pm.
Because it's not as massive as its competitors, this neighborhood shop is often overlooked by Haight's tourist
legions and so is left with a better selection of used LPs and
CDs than its neighbors.

Tower Outlet
660 3rd St (btw Brannan/Townsend). Tel. 415/957-9660.
Open Mon-Fri 10am-530pm, Sat noon-5pm.
We love this place because they carry tons of overstock from
Tower megastores which they sell for about one-third off.
Used videos are also available for not much more than the
price of a rental. Perhaps best of all, you can find back
issues of import magazines like The Face for under a buck.

Tower Records
2525 Jones St (at Fisherman's Wharf). Tel. 415/885-
0500. Open daily 9am-midnight.
The best of the chain stores. Tower stocks plenty of indie
stuff along with major labels. Opened in 1968, it's a huge
space, with a separate area for classical music where
overstocked items are priced under a buck.
Branch: 2280 Market St. Tel. 415/621-0588.

Tweekin'
593 Haight St (at Clayton). Tel. 415/626-6995. Open Mon-
Thurs 11am-7pm, Fri-Sat 11am-8pm.
All house all the time, Tweekin' is the vinyl-only headquarters
for an unmatched selection of club music. Famous with
local DJs, the shop stocks all the obscure 12" remixes that
you just can't find in the chains.

Virgin Megastore
2 Stockton St (at Market). Tel. 415/397-4525. Open
Mon-Thurs 9am-11pm, Fri-Sat 9am-midnight, Sun
10am-10pm.
You could easily spend hours combing through CDs, books,
videos and CD-ROMs in this expansive three-story complex
near Union Square. There are lots of listening stations in which
to hear new music, but beware the greasy headphones.

Good Vibrations

1210 Valencia St (at 23rd). Tel. 415/974-8980. Open daily 11am-7pm. Women-owned Good Vibes brings sodomy and deviation into the mainstream with its clean, bright store and "sex positive" attitude. Helpful assistants are all too happy to illustrate the features of their dildos and butt-plugs, and have even amassed a small historical museum of pleasure tools. Ask to see The Mule.

SPORtS

Copeland Sports

901 Market St (at 5th). Tel. 415/495-0928. Open Mon-Fri 10am-8pm, Sat 10am-7pm, Sun 10am-6pm.

From Adidas bath sandals and baseball bats to wind breakers and yogi mats, Copeland carries clothing and equipment for almost every imaginable activity. They've got a great collection of name-brand gear from Patagonia and The North Face, and a huge selection of sneakers. In short, it's the best sporting goods shop in the city.

DLX Skateboards & Clothing

1831 Market St (btw Guerrero/Pearl). Tel. 415/626-5588. Open Mon-Sat 11am-7pm, Sun 11am-6pm.

One of the few stores in the city catering exclusively to skaterats, DLX is where serious borders get their decks and gear, including clothing that's way too cool for skool.

Valencia Cyclery

1065 Valencia St (btw 21st/22nd). Tel. 415/550-6600. Open Mon-Sat 10am-6pm, Sun 10am-4pm.

The mountain bike is a local invention, created for riding the trails of Marin's Mount Tam. Stocking the biggest selection, and offering the best deal, on all sorts of bikes and accessories, Valencia Cyclery has become the Mother of all San Francisco Bike Shops.

StAtiONARY & PENS

Montblanc

120 Grant Ave (at Post). Tel. 415/403-4000. Open Mon-Sat 10am-6pm, Sun noon-5pm.

The snow-capped Montblanc pen has long been one of the world's finest writing instruments, as well as a sign of financial success. No Bic Rollerballs here: pens range from $175 to more than $16,000, but they'll throw in a case free. The Meisterstuck collection includes matching desk accessories, leather goods, watches, jewelry and eyewear.

Papyrus

2109 Fillmore St (btw California/Sacramento). Tel. 415/474-1171. Open Mon-Fri 10am-7pm, Sat 10am-6pm, Sun 11am-6pm.

Ever since Martha Stewart extolled the virtues of this San Francisco-based chain on her TV show, "Living," Papyrus has been doing brisk business with its high quality stationary and note cards. In addition to the standard Ann Geddes baby cards, the well-stocked shop also trades in sealing-wax kits, calligraphy pens and other accessories.

Branch: 2 Embarcadero Center (btw Clay/Front). Tel. 415/781-8777. Open Mon-Fri 830am-7pm, Sat 10am-6pm, Sun noon-5pm.

VidEO

Leather Tongue

714 Valencia St (at 18th). Tel. 415/552-2900. Open Sun-Thurs noon-11pm, Fri-Sat noon-midnight.

Student films, semi-new releases and classics like *The Poseidon Adventure* lurk in the depths of this two-floor store where breath takes a back seat to depth.

Le Video
1231 9th Ave (btw Lincoln/Irving). Tel. 415/566-3606.
Open daily 10am-11pm.
With over 65,000 titles, Le Video stocks an impressive selection of European, Indian and Japanese films, along with traditional fare. They've got memorabilia, DVD and LaserDiscs too.

Naked Eye News and Video
533 Haight St (btw Fillmore/Steiner). Tel. 415/864-2985.
Open Mon-Thurs 10am-10pm, Fri-Sat 10am-11pm, Sun 11am-10pm.
Despite a notoriously rude Dr. Jekyl/Mr. Hyde staff and humorously disorganized shelving, this is a great place to find offbeat and obscure indie classics. There's lots of unique zines, too.

Video Control
2095 Market St (btw 14th/Church). Tel. 415/621-1426.
Open Sun-Thurs 11am-11pm, Fri-Sat 11am-midnight.
Located just steps from that McVideo behemoth, Blockbuster, Video Control stocks independents that corporate guys won't touch, including a particularly comprehensive selection of gay classics like Boys In the Band and the somewhat steamier Hot Times in Havana.

fOOd & dRiNk

Ferry Plaza Farmers' Market
Green (at the Embarcadero). Tel. 415/981-3004. Open year-round, Saturday 8am-130pm; Easter-Thanksgiving, Tues 11am-3pm.
Each weekend the city's healthiest early-risers head to the Farmers' Market for terrific, locally-grown produce, specialty foods and some prepared dishes made by area restaurants. It's also a terrific social scene that offers visitors an authentic glimpse into city life.

Napa Valley Winery Exchange
415 Taylor St (btw Geary/O'Farrell). Tel. 415/771-2887.
Open daily 10am-7pm.
If you can't get to the Wine Country, this well-stocked shop will set you up with hard-to-find bottles from some of Northern California's best small-production wineries. They supply airplane-ready boxes and can ship worldwide.

EAtiNG
ThE RESTAURANt SCENE

Specialties of the House

Don't let those ubiquitous Rice-a-Roni commercials fool you; San Francisco is a food-lover's kind of town. The city has more restaurants per capita than any other in the US and, for quality and variety, even rivals New York City. Great cuisine from practically every corner of the globe is represented here and many of the best kitchens are on the forefront of America's fascination with all things multiculti. The Pacific Rim in particular has taken San Francisco by tsunami; the storm is so pervasive you can hardly escape it. Many, if not most, of the city's top chefs are enthusiastically scrambling East and West, and it seems as though every new restaurant includes menu items that ginger glazed or shiitake mushroomed.

A kind of post-ironic retroism is the second characteristic of contemporary San Francisco dining. Rich foods, strong drinks, designer ties and sexy dresses are on the ins. And the multi-year rally of tech stocks has facilitated a trend towards expensive meats and upscale preparations. Complex entrees, richly flavored with time-consuming stock-reductions, are remarkably common, though they routinely top $30 and more. And grape nuts are well catered to all over town; this is wine country, after all.

It's safe to say that some of the best dining in the world is in San Francisco; the result of a confluence of hyperlatives: some of America's best chefs, finest ingredients and prettiest people converge nightly in the peninsula's top restaurants.

Since 1849 when Tadich Grill, the city's first real restaurant, opened, San Francisco has been something of a culinary pioneer. The Bay Area is the birthplace of lots of food firsts including the first martini (1860), the first authentic Chinese food delivery service (1939), and the first fern bar, Henry Africa, which opened in 1970. Cioppino, the local version of an Italian fish stew, debuted here in 1900; the mai tai, that king of tropical cocktails arrived in 1944; and Irish coffee is said to have been created here in 1952. But not all home-grown inventions are ones to be proud of. Witness that white-trash staple, chicken tetrazzini (1908), and its cousin Green Goddess salad dressing, which was first made at the Palace Hotel in 1915.

The Reservations Game

As sure as death and taxes, there's always a restaurant of the moment; one in which every night is like a movie premiere, filled with film stars, models, musicians, the media elite, athletes, restaurateurs, garmentos and generic rich people. Within the first two weeks of opening everyone will trample through, before quickly heading off to the Next New Thing. If you want to be there too, it's time to use some muscle, work the phones and call-in favors. When white-hot slows to simmering, street-wise mortals can get reservations about a week in advance. Unless you have connections, or don't mind being seated at 6pm or 11pm, we advise you to reserve a table as far in advance as possible (the country code for the USA is 1; the city code for San Francisco is 415. From Great Britain dial 00-1-415 plus the local number).

COVETED TABLES: AVANT-GUIDE TO GETTING ONE

For a Tough Reservation:

Restaurant: Good afternoon, Haute Restaurant, may I help you?
Avant-Guide: Hello, who am I speaking to?
Restaurant: (caught slightly off-guard) This is Joanne.
Avant-Guide: (with feigned recognition) Oh, hi Joanne! This is (your name). I need a table for four tonight at nine-o'clock, can you do it? Say "yes."
Restaurant: (laughs) Well, we're booked solid, Ms. (your name), but I'll see what I can do. Can you hold-on a moment?
Avant-Guide: Thank you very much, it's *really* important.
(short pause)
Restaurant: Ms. (your name), we can fit you in at 8:30, is that OK?

For a Really Tough Reservation:

Restaurant: Good afternoon, Haute Restaurant, may I help you?
Avant-Guide: Hello, who am I speaking to?
Restaurant: (caught slightly off-guard) This is Joanne.
Avant-Guide: (with feigned recognition) Oh, hi Joanne! This is Randy Thomas at CKA Talent. I'm calling for my client (your name). She needs a table for four tonight at nine-o'clock, can you do it? Say "yes." (continue with above script).

Tipping

Listen-up Europeans! American waiters expect to be tipped about 15 percent of the total bill. In San Francisco that's an easy calculation–just double the sales tax (8.5%) that's tacked-on to the bottom of every check.

Kibbles & Bits

* Lunch is usually 25-50% cheaper than dinner.
* Although we may say some nasty things in the reviews below, we enthusiastically recommend all the restaurants we list.
* You can drink the water.

Cheaper Eats

You should know that most of the city's restaurants offer lunch menus that are 25-50 percent cheaper than the dinner prices quoted below. In addition, most top restaurants offer special set-priced early-dinner menus. These are usually three-course affairs, involving an appetizer, entree and dessert for $20-$30 per person. That's a real bargain, but you've got to eat early as the restaurant expects you to vacate your table by 8pm.

Our reviewers have no connection with any establishment listed in this guidebook or on the Avant-Guide Web site. All restaurant visits are anonymous, and expenses are paid by Avant-Guide.

WhERE tO dINE WhEn dINING ALONE

Of course you can eat solo in any restaurant: a good book or magazine can be far better companions than some human beings we've shared tables with. When dining alone we shy away from quiet places with stuffy service in favor of lively surroundings and bar chairs. Here's where to go when you're on your only...

REStAURANts bY AREA, PRiCE & CUSiNE

	PRICE	CUiSINE	PAGE
CASTRO/NOE			
Fuzio	$	American Avant	181
Hamano Sushi	$$$	Japanese	166
CHINATOWN			
Lichee Garden	$	Chinese	178
Yuet Lee	$	Chinese	183
DOWNTOWN			
Bix	$$$	American Avant	171
Cafe Akimbo	$$	Californian	176
Cafe Claude	$$	French/Bistro	176
Dottie's True Blue Cafe	$	American Classic	184
Farallon	$$$$	Californian	172
Fleur De Lys	$$$$	French Avant	165
Garden Court	$$$	Californian	185
Globe	$$$	American Avant	172
MC²	$$$$	Californian	174
Postrio	$$$$	Californian	167
Sam's Grill	$$$	American Classic	168
Sears Fine Foods	$	American Classic	185
Tadich Grill	$$	American Classic	169
Yank Sing	$$	Chinese	180
HAIGHT-ASHBURY			
Cha Cha Cha	$$	Caribbean	177
Indian Oven	$$	Indian	178
Sweet Heat	$	Mexican	182

The cost ($) reflects the average price of a dinner with one drink and tip

$ = Under $16
$$ = $16-$30
$$$ = $31-$50
$$$$ = Over $50

162

	PRiCE	CUiSiNE	PAGE
MARINA			
Fuzio	$	American Avant	181
Greens	$$$	Vegetarian Avant	173
Sweet Heat	$	Mexican	182
MISSION			
Blowfish Sushi	$$$	Japanese	176
Bruno's	$$$	Mediterranean	171
La Cumbre Taqueria	$	Mexican	181
Slanted Door	$$$	Vietnamese	167
Ti Couz	$	French/Crepes	182
NOB HILL			
Ritz-Carlton Terrace	$$$$	Mediterranean	185
NORTH BEACH			
Black Cat	$$$$	Eclectic	182
Caffe Greco	$	Italian/Cafe	181
Enrico's	$$$	Mediterranean	168
Fuzio	$	American Avant	181
Mario's Bohemian	$	Italian/Cafe	181
Rose Pistola	$$$	Italian	174
Tommaso's	$$	Italian	169
Washington Sq. B&G	$$$	American Classic	175
RICHMOND			
Mel's Drive-In	$	American Classic	183
Ton Kiang Restaurant	$$	Chinese	180
SOMA			
Boulevard	$$$$	American Avant	164
Fringale	$$$	French/Bistro	165
Hamburger Mary's	$$	American Classic	182
Hawthorne Lane	$$$$	Californian	166
Lulu	$$$	Mediterranean	173
Thirsty Bear Brewing	$$	Spanish	179
SUNSET			
Ebisu	$$$	Japanese	177
PJs Oyster Bed	$$	Cajun/Creole	178
UNION STREET			
Doidge's Kitchen	$	American Classic	184
Mel's Drive-In	$	American Classic	183
VAN NESS/POLK			
Harris'	$$$$	American/Steak	177
La Folie	$$$$	French Avant	166
Mario's Bohemian	$	Italian/Cafe	181
Mel's Drive-In	$	American Classic	183
Swan Oyster Depot	$$	Seafood	169
Sweet Heat	$	Mexican	182
WHARF/EMBARCADERO			
Scoma's	$$$	Seafood	180
The Waterfront	$$$	Californian	175

Boulevard

1 Mission St (at Steuart). Tel. 415/543-6084. Lunch Mon-Fri 1130am-2pm;
dinner daily 530-1030pm; bistro menu Mon-Fri 215-515pm. Main courses
$24-$32. AE, MC, V.

Boulevard is yet another baby of designer/restaurateur Pat Kuleto, who teamed
up this time with top local chef Nancy Oakes. Kuleto regularly knocks-out
competition with a signature one-two punch that combines funky, urban design
with top-notch New American cooking. Boulevard is a stylish, bustling bistro in
a gorgeous, historic building near the Embarcadero waterfront. The trio of
dining rooms are vaguely art-nouveau wonderlands, florabundantly dressed with
kaleidoscopic mosaic tiles, decorative ironwork, rich wood paneling, and a
domed brick ceiling that keeps noise levels intense. The restaurant is large and
busy, attracting a lively mix of visiting celebs, globobosses, local business
arrivistes, and plenty of in-the-know gastro-gnomes. Boulevard is one of those
rare places where the food is as good as the people-watching.

Typical starters on the innovative, frequently-changing menu might include
crab cakes, butternut squash soup, and ahi tuna sushi, followed by wild mushroom
risotto, roast duck or Oakes' signature maple-cured pork loin. Order garlic mashed
potatoes with everything, and save room for dessert, the selection of which is
always stellar. The restaurant's wine list is one of the city's best, and several good
buys are always on offer. Reserve a table in the back room where you'll be
treated to sweeping views of the Bay Bridge and Ferry Building.

Fleur de Lys

777 Sutter St (btw Jones/Taylor). Tel. 415/673-7779. Reservations required. Kitchen open Mon-Thurs 6-9pm, Fri-Sat 530-1030pm. Main courses $29-$37; tasting menu $65. AE, MC, V.

From the opulent midnight-at-the-oasis dining room to the foie gras and caviar menu, everything about Fleur de Lys screams Serious Restaurant! Dressed, with lots of greenery, mirrored walls, plush fabrics and elegantly laid tables, this is a very formal "destination place," meant to be the main part of an evening rather than a mere prelude to some other entertainment. Although the tented dining room feels rather buttoned-up (jackets and ties required), the sophisticated French/California cuisine couldn't be more *a la mode*. Chef Hubert Keller has a seemingly natural ability to invent cross-cultural dishes that dance in the mouth and are a beauty to behold. Exemplary meals might include roasted sea scallops with wild mushrooms, spinach-wrapped lamb with garlic and truffle oil, or venison with black chanterelle sauce. Regulars often come here for the tasting menu, which, for an additional $25, can be paired with a different wine for each of the four courses.

Each guest is treated like nobility by a fawning waitstaff that never lets a glass become empty nor an emptied plate lie. Depending on whom you're dining with, Fleur de Lys can feel either gentlemen-clubby or amorous. Reserve the main room when planning to celebrate, or a side room when you're making a proposition.

Fringale

570 Fourth St (btw Brannan/Bryant). Tel. 415/543-0573. Reservations recommended. Kitchen open Mon-Fri 1130am-3pm and 530-1030pm, Sat 530-1030pm. Main courses $13-$20. AE, MC, V.

Fringale is a great name for a restaurant, considering that it's the word Parisians have for the urge to eat. In San Francisco, Fringale is a really nice bistro/restaurant that's perfect for anything, be it a few appetizers and a good bottle of wine, or a multi-course banquet. The restaurant is the brain-child of Paris-trained chef/owner Gerald Hirigoyen, whose sophisticated, yet low-key dining room has been such a success that he's already opened another instant hit, **Pastis** (1015 Battery St; tel. 415/391-2555). This cozy, low-key South of Market dining room can only accommodate about 15 tables, all of which are occupied most nights. The bottom line here is great food, reasonable prices, and an all-around comfortable dining experience you wouldn't mind recreating night after night. This is an exceedingly capable kitchen that's completely comfortable turning out starters like prawns sautéed in Pastis with lemon & fresh herbs, and sea scallop-and-avocado napoleon with mango & pepper. These might be followed by salmon with braised leeks & fried onions, fricassee of sweetbreads with garlic, or chicken with caramelized parsnips & braising greens. Best of all, food this good is shockingly affordable.

Hamano Sushi

1332 Castro St (at 24th). Tel. 415/826-0825. Reservations not accepted. Kitchen open Mon 6pm-930pm, Tues-Sat 530-1030pm, Sun 530-930pm. Main courses $11-$17. AE, MC, V.

Hamano's deep bow to the trinity of great sushi—high quality, absolute freshness and thick cuts—make it one of the city's top-rated Japanese restaurants. But it's not just raw fish; the restaurant's full-on Nipponese cuisine includes award-winning chicken, beef, pork, and salmon teriyaki; seafood and vegetable tempura; and excellent sukiyaki (sliced beef and vegetables in savory broth). Hamano's dining room is nothing special, the Noe Valley location is a schlep, and the service can be insultingly horrible—even nasty. Taken together, it's proof that we will put up with a lot for the holy grail of fish.

Hawthorne Lane

22 Hawthorne St (btw Howard/Folsom). Tel. 415/777-9779. Reservations required. Kitchen open Mon-Thurs noon-130pm and 530-10pm, Fri noon-130pm and 530-1030pm, Sat 530-1030pm, Sun 530-10pm. Main courses $24-$32. AE, MC, V.

Five years running and Hawthorne Lane continues to be one of the city's most difficult reservations. They got everything right here. Chef/owners Anne and David Gingrass (formerly of Spago and Postrio fame) opened with their following firmly in tow, and then never failed to live up to the food press' considerable hype. Needless to say, the food's the thing here; homegrown American meals with Asian and Mediterranean influences translates into entrees like seared pepper-and-ginger-coated tuna, intensely flavored roast Sonoma lamb au jus with crispy eggplant spring rolls, and Chinese-style roast duck, a signature dish that's moist and meaty inside but has a magnificent skin that crackles like a potato chip. Homemade duck sausage and designer pizzas hark back to the owners' Postrio days. For dessert, the pair have enlisted Nicole Plue, one of the city's most esteemed pastry chefs, whose specialties are involved variations on creme brulee.

The restaurant's light, sophisticated dining room is a happy place that's always somewhat youth-infected due to its proximity to SoMa's nightclubs. Reserve the main dining room, rather than the cafe, or go alone and snag one of the seats at the long bar.

La Folie

2316 Polk St (btw Green/Union). Tel. 415/776-5577. Reservations recommended. Open Mon-Sat 530-1030pm. Main courses $27-$35. AE, MC, V.

La Folie is for dedicated foodies who crave a serious meal but don't feel like dressing up for dinner. Lyon-trained chef/owner Roland Passot, who runs the restaurant with his wife, Jamie, and brother Georges, has created a *vrai Français* menu that San Franciscans have taken to like ducks à l'orange. The passionate kitchen is regularly voted one of the best in the city, as it consistently turns out Artful dishes of meat, fish and fowl, most of which are doused with intensely-flavored stock reductions. The dining room, like the service, is charming, informal, intrusiveless, and thoroughly professional, making La Folie popular with wealthy couples and PODs (people on dates). There's a great wine selection, and a knowledgeable sommelier. Insiders know to splurge on the five-course tasting menu, which allows diners to chose from the regular carte for about $60.

Postrio

Prescott Hotel, 545 Post St (btw Mason/Taylor).
Tel. 415/776-7825. Reservations recommended. Kitchen open daily 7am-11pm.
Main courses $20-$30; breakfast $8-$15. AE, MC, V.

Soon after Wolfgang Puck earned his toque at Spago in LA, he brought his show to Northern California and immediately wowed local foodies who know chow. More than a decade later, Postrio remains one of the city's hottest mealtime tickets. Puck got famous for his pizzas, and Postrio's hard-working wood-burning oven turns out these designer pies at a furious pace. Even if it's not on the menu, insiders order Jewish Pizza, topped with smoked salmon and cream cheese. Typical appetizers include foie gras terrine with fig-onion compote, and smoked trout with baby greens and caper raisin sauce. Entrees run the gamut from herb-roasted veal with curried peaches and baby spinach, to chicken breasts with sauternes-mustard sauce sided with savoy cabbage and a potato knish. Desserts are extensive, and because the restaurant is located in a hotel it's one of the few top eateries where you can get breakfast. Look for cinnamon banana pancakes, homemade granola, and eggs scrambled with lobster, mascarpone and chives. Designer Pat Kuleto's fun interior makes every entrance feel like a gala event. A trio of dining areas is something of a three-ring circus: The main dining room is the center ring, designed for destination diners who've made reservations; level two is more intimate, with good views of the kitchen and dining room; and the less formal upper level, which contains a lively bar and pizza oven, is the last resort for walk-ins.

Slanted Door

584 Valencia St (btw 16th/17th). Tel. 415/861-8032. Reservations recommended. Kitchen open Tues-Sun 1130am-330pm and 530-10pm. Main courses $12-$18. AE, MC, V.

At Slanted Door that holy trinity of trendy, stylish and delicious come together to make a really great restaurant. Culinarily, the restaurant represents the epitome of haute Vietnamese cooking. Chef/owner Charles Pham regularly wows diners with amazing dishes like striped sea bass, which is stuffed with shrimp, scallops and chicken, then wrapped in phyllo dough and served in a cloying tomato sauce. This is not fusion food, it's a sophisticated take on Vietnamese cuisine, created with almost 100 percent organic ingredients. Preparations are traditional, often stir fried with fish sauce, garlic, and ginger, and rarely miss their intended marks. Other winning entrees include sautéed glass noodles with tree-ear and shiitake mushrooms, tofu and bamboo shoots; and clay-pot catfish with caramelized onion and garlic. There is an unusually varied wine list and wonderful tea menu. The restaurant's Mission location pulls in a youngish crowd that's attracted to attitude-free service and high noise levels. It's a fun spot that often devolves into one of the most rollicking parties in town. Eat dessert elsewhere.

Enrico's

504 Broadway (at Kearny). Tel. 415/982-6223. Reservations accepted. Kitchen open Mon-Thurs 1130am-1130pm, Fri-Sat 1130am-midnight, Sun 1130am-11pm. Main courses $15-$21. AE, MC, V.

Enrico's has one of the finest pedigrees in the city. Originally opened in 1958, it was San Francisco's first Parisian-style sidewalk cafe. The original owner, Enrico Banducci, was the impresario behind the Hungry I, one of America's great nightclubs of the Fifties and Sixties. Banducci was a legend in his time, helping launch the careers of Barbra Streisand, Lenny Bruce, the Smothers Brothers, and Bill Cosby, who later gave Enrico $100,000, no strings attached, to save the coffeehouse. But times change. Enrico went bankrupt, and the famous open-air deck of this legendary landmark was bordered up in 1988. Two years later the restaurant reopened with a new Spanish-California menu, and the hordes have returned en masse. The best part of Enrico's is its heated terrace overlooking Broadway, and the live jazz that often plays in the background. Food here is good, not great, and includes something for everyone, from crispy salmon rolls with red pepper dipping sauce, to house-cured pork chops. The best entrees come from the wood-burning grill and include Sonoma duck breast, flat iron steak, and a line of haute couture pizzas. There's pastas, soups and salads too. True to its roots, Enrico's is perhaps best for coffee and dessert. They're open later than most other restaurants in the neighborhood, and serve a healthy dose of nostalgia with every plate.

Sam's Grill

374 Bush St (btw Kearny/Montgomery). Tel. 415/421-0594. Reservations Recommended. Open Mon-Fri 11am-9pm. Main courses $12-$18. AE, MC, V.

Begun as an oyster bar on nearby California Street in 1867, Sam's is a masculine, Old World grill with private booths and a meaty menu of carteological no-nos that seems terminally locked in the '50s. At its present location since 1946, Sam's is packed with power-lunching suits by day, and a smattering of tourists and locals by night. It's a traditional place with a menu to match, featuring some of the best charcoal-broiled seafood, steaks, chicken and chops in the city. Sides, including creamed spinach and artichoke hearts, are particularly special and are ordered separately. In addition to a half-dozen types of fresh fish, the kitchen is particularly known for Olympia oysters in a milk stew, and the Hang Town Fry, a traditional San Francisco meal of scrambled eggs with bacon and oysters that originated during the Gold Rush, and is said to have been one of the most popular last meals requested by condemned men.

Swan Oyster Depot

1517 Polk St (btw California/ Sacramento). Tel. 415/673-1101. Reservations not accepted. Kitchen open Mon-Sat 8am-530pm. Main courses $10-$25. No cards.

Swan Oyster Depot serves the best bivalves in San Francisco. Or maybe it just seems that way due to its rich history, never-ending crowds and inimitable counter seating. Opened in 1912, Swan is old skool, hole-in-the-wall San Francisco—a pre-nouveau haven from the highfalutin dining that's now happening everywhere else. The best way to experience this place is solo or duo, at the long marble counter, where you can watch the famously accommodating chefs in action. The emphasis of course is on seafood, and clam chowder is the specialty of this house. Thin and creamy, and bursting with clams and potatoes, a bowl of soup and some crusty sourdough bread makes the perfect San Francisco lunch. The rest of the short menu includes oysters on the half-shell, as well as fresh crab, shrimp and Maine lobster served with either a zippy cocktail sauce or thousand island dressing. Fin fish is only available raw and to go.

Tadich Grill

240 California St (btw Battery/Front). Tel. 415/391-1849. Reservations not accepted. Kitchen open Mon-Fri 11am-930pm, Sat 1130am-930pm. Main courses $11-$40. MC, V.

One of the oldest restaurants in California, Tadich Grill is an American Regional classic specializing in all things fishy. But no one really comes here just for the food. The restaurant is a living landmark, founded in 1849 by a trio of Croatian immigrants. Moved to its current address in 1967, the restaurant remains a noisy and bright San Francisco institution. It's a grand, important space with a long bar, polished brass, white tablecloths, and very private wooden booths that are regularly warmed by the city's most important asses: titans of politics and industry who come here daily to jaw over comfort food like lobster thermidor, cioppino, and pan-fried petrale sole, a small native flounder. Reservations are not accepted and there's almost always a wait at what is sometimes a three-deep bar. Like many places of this vintage, Tadich is known for killer drinks and thoroughly professional waiters with a reputation for crustiness.

Tommaso's Restaurant

1042 Kearny St (btw Broadway/ Pacific). Tel. 415/398-9696. Reservations accepted. Kitchen open Tues-Sat 5-11pm, Sun 4-10pm. Main courses $11-$15. AE, MC, V.

There was a time, in the 1970s and '80s, when Tommaso's was the nouveau pizza pie against which all others were judged. This venerable restaurant is said to have inspired Wolfgang Puck's designer pizza craze, and once attracted a celebrity roster that was the toast of the town. Times may have changed, but Tommaso's, which first opened in 1935, has not budged an inch. The menu includes some rigorously unambitious Italian-American specialties like veal marsala, eggplant parmesan, and chicken cacciatore, but the main draw here is the wood-fired pizzas. Really good pizza is the kind that measures at least one foot across and has a crust so thin you could slide it into a record sleeve. These crisp pies don't disappoint. More than a dozen different toppings are available, but regulars swear by the basic Neapolitan with cheese and tomato sauce. Noisy and dimly lit, Tommaso's homey ambiance is pure North Beach. Some say the restaurant is better than ever, now that mere mortals can easily snag a table.

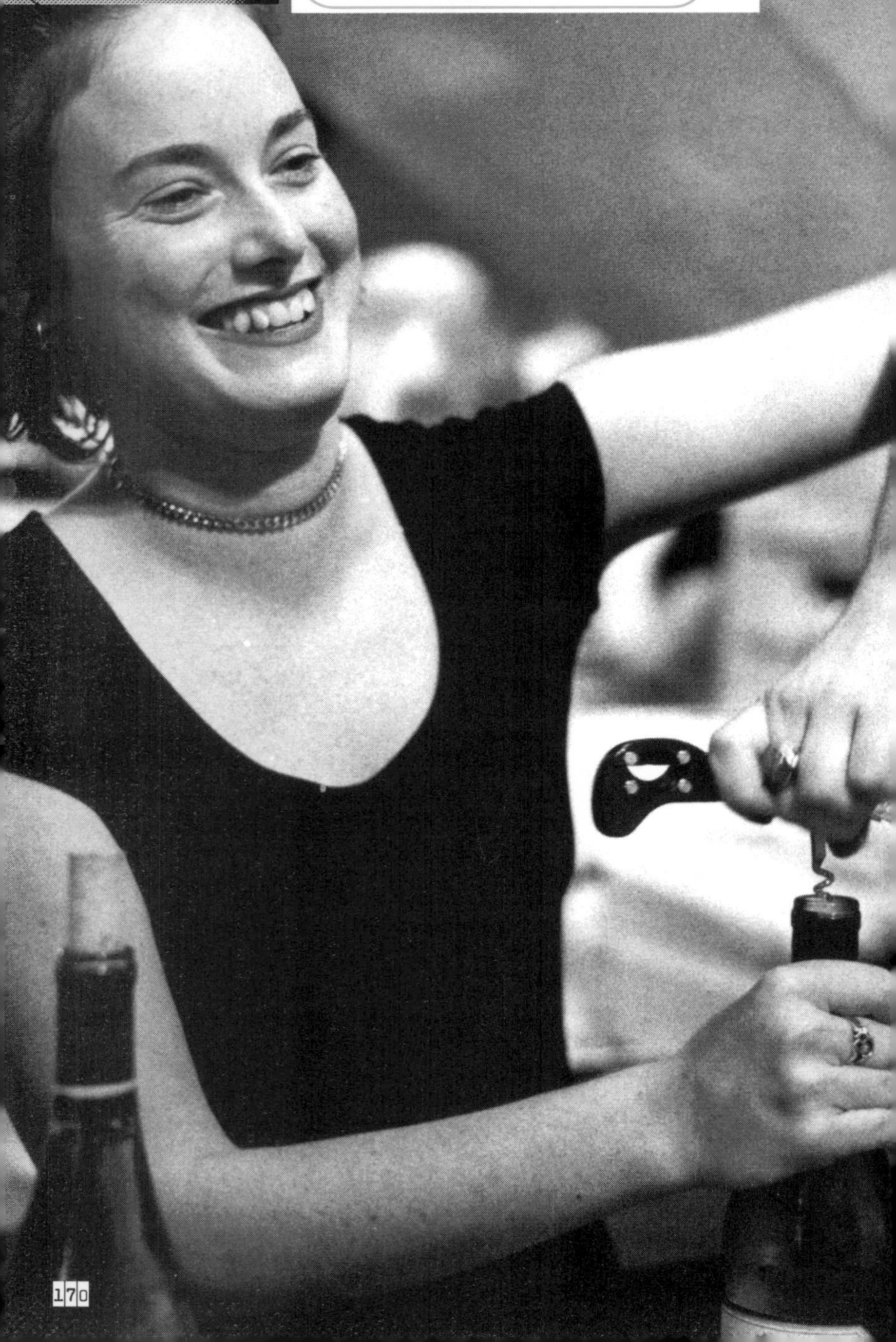

Bruno's

2389 Mission St (btw 19th/20th). Tel. 415/550-7455.
Reservations recommended. Kitchen open Tues-Thurs 630pm-11pm, Fri-Sat 630pm-midnight. Main courses $17-$22. AE, MC, V.

As if more proof were needed that retro is way in, Bruno's provides it with a groovy restaurant/lounge that remains one of the hottest places in the Mission. The restaurant's main dining room is pure Americana, decked out with original '60s furnishings and oversized red vinyl booths that are so comfortable most guests install themselves for the night. Featuring excellent cocktails and groovy jazz most nights (see Chapter 8/Live Jazz & Blues), Bruno's is all about the scene, baby. With two bars and an interestingly eclectic crowd, the place can get as loud as a Hawaiian shirt, creating something of a celebratory atmosphere that's best experienced with a bevy of friends.

Perhaps the only thing that's modern about this place is the menu, a well-executed selection of New American offerings that includes gnocchi with seared scallops, Sonoma quail with Moroccan spices, and grilled steak with morel sauce. Desserts are particularly outstanding, and the wine list includes lots of drinkables priced around $25.

The lounge is open until 2am most nights and serves appetizers throughout the week, including Mondays, when the restaurant is closed.

Bix

56 Gold St (btw Jackson/Pacific). Tel. 415/433-6300. Reservations recommended. Kitchen open Mon-Thurs 1130am-11pm, Fri 1130am-Midnight, Sat 530pm-Midnight, Sun 6-10pm. Main courses $16-$23. AE, MC, V.

Looking very much like an upscale 1930s speakeasy is supposed to look, Bix is the ultimate art deco supper club with swoony surroundings, live lounge music, and a good looking crowd enjoying colorful cocktails and fru-fru foods. Hidden in a film-set alleyway, the dramatic retro experience starts even before you walk in the door. Once inside, everything about Bix screams "swank," from the snooty maitre d's and the elaborate bar murals, to the dimly lit bi-level dining area and soothing late-night jazz. Although the food can't equal such perfect surroundings, the kitchen does manage to turn-out decent meals that reflect the opulent American theme. Winning starters include steak tartare with toasted olive bread, and crispy potatoes with smoked salmon, creme fraiche and caviar. Typical main courses on the seasonal menu include filet mignon with roasted potatoes, seared Chilean sea bass with shiitake mushroom risotto, and the restaurant's signature chicken hash—the choice of regular cognoscenti. There's an adventuresome wine list with lots of good choices under $30.

The best seats are on the wrap-around balcony with its unobstructed sightlines and reasonable sound levels. Typical of restaurants in the neighborhood, Bix is popular with business folk by day, and Prada-wearing beautiful people by night. It often stays open until one or two in the morning and has the reputation for being something of a singles scene. Dress for success.

SCENES

Farallon

450 Post St (btw Mason/Powell). Tel. 415/956-6969. Reservations recommended. Kitchen open Mon–Thurs 1130am–1030pm, Fri–Sat 1130am–11pm, Sun 530–1030pm. Main courses $20–$26. AE, MC, V.

Farallon, the latest offering from über restaurateur Pat Kuleto, is all about the sea and being seen. An architectural and gastronomic delight, the restaurant is revealing itself as San Francisco's king of all things fishy, attracting the city's top echelon of fish-lovers and shellfish-ionados. Built with fantastical furnishings that include playful pink and purple "jellyfish" light fixtures and sculpted kelp-like pillars, the trippy decor is a splashy theatrical delight designed with a flash that falls well short of trash. Amazingly, the wonderful dining room is bested by the kitchen, which is under the direction of Stars alumnus Mark Franz. Many insiders make meals based entirely on appetizers including house-made caviar, scallop ceviche, Spanish mackerel tartare, and another half-dozen taste treats. Entrees also combine the freshest seafood with complicated sauces. Witness roasted turbot with lobster, seared wild striped bass with lobster and morel mushrooms, and roast monkfish with grilled foie gras. Lamb, fowl, and beef also make appearances. Wines are well-selected with a large choice of half-bottles, and wines by the glass. Foodies in the know often speak of Farallon in superlatives: the best food, the most wonderful decor... in short, one of San Francisco's very best restaurants. Even with reservations you'll have to wait at the octopus theme bar. Dress elegantly and reserve a table in the Pool Room, as opposed to the more secluded mezzanine. A lighter-priced cafe menu is offered at lunch, and menu items are limited between 230 and 5pm.

Globe

290 Pacific Ave (btw Battery/Front). Tel. 415/391-4132. Reservations recommended. Kitchen open Mon–Fri 1130am–1am, Sat 6pm–1am. Main courses $13–$20. AE, MC, V.

Fashionable, fun and jammed at all hours, Globe is the San Francisco restaurant we'd most like to own. It's hard to imagine a more successful scene spot than this polished Financial District dining room. It's just an unpretentious rectangle storefront with tightly-spaced tables, exposed brick walls, and an exhibition kitchen. But the wonderful, eclectic menu and bustling atmosphere are like magnets for upscale downtowners. Globe is known as the place where chefs from other restaurants go after their own kitchens close. The menu caters to both grazers and gorgers with everything from potato soup and grilled sardines, to Atlantic salmon and calf's liver with onion marmalade. A well-stocked raw bar and decadent desserts round out the offerings. Between 3pm and 6pm the kitchen is open for appetizers only.

Restaurant Lulu

816 Folsom St (btw Fourth/Fifth). Tel. 415/495-5775. Reservations recommended. Kitchen open Sun-Thurs 530-1030pm, Fri-Sat 530-midnight. Main courses $12-$22. AE, MC, V.

Huge and bustling, Lulu is a continuously buzzing grill with excellent sightlines, good food and train station acoustics that force the kitchen staff to wear headsets and microphones in order to communicate with each other. Everything about this SoMa spot is big, from the colossal windows and warehouse-high ceilings to the lengthy wine list, robust flavors and generous portions of food. Roasted mussels, the restaurant's justifiably popular signature dish, arrive piled high on an iron skillet and are as simple and delicious as you can get. And while you might want to skip the lackluster pastas and pizzas, meats from the wood fired rotisserie are absolutely delicious. The best of these are leg of lamb, rosemary chicken, and pork loin. Make reservations, go with a group with whom you have nothing much to talk about, and think about packing some ear plugs.

Greens

Fort Mason Ctr, Bldg A (at Buchanan). Tel. 415/771-6222. Reservations recommended. Lunch Tues-Sat 1130am-2pm; dinner Mon-Sat 530-930pm; brunch Sun 10am-2pm; late-evening desserts Mon-Sat 930pm-11pm. Main courses $13-$18. AE, MC, V.

Greens is legendary for being the nation's first truly gourmet vegetarian restaurant. Executive chef Annie Sommerville, author of several best-selling Greens cookbooks, remains at the top of her genre, inventing adventurously creative meals that almost always hit their intended marks. Organic produce is sourced from the nearby Zen Center's Green Gulch Farm, and blended into dishes that are all over the culinary map—Asian, Mediterranean, European, Mexican... the results are so good that most patrons aren't even vegetarians. Like any top restaurant, meals are created with a balance of colors and contrast of textures. Recent selections have included Moroccan carrot soup with spiced yogurt and cilantro; pastry turnovers filled with corn, zucchini, red onions and asiago cheese; corn crepes with smoked cheese, marjoram and tomatillo sauce; and eggplant and roasted pepper pizza with gaeta olives, provolone and fontina cheeses. On Saturdays the restaurant serves a four-course, $40 fixed price dinner exclusively. The interesting wine list includes lots of pleasant surprises, and even a few good buys. Sunday brunches are particularly wonderful and might include buttermilk pecan pancakes with a mound of fresh berries. The dining room is a welcoming, woody place with tall ceilings and comfortable redwood furnishings. Book a table by the window for terrific views of the bay and Golden Gate Bridge.

MC²

470 Pacific Ave (at Montgomery).
Tel. 415/956-0666. Reservations
recommended. Kitchen open Mon-Fri
1130am-230pm and 530-10pm, Sat-
Sun 530-1030pm. Main courses $18-
$26. AE, MC, V.

Built with sleek, designer lines that feel
like architectural Prada, MC² is a self-
consciously stylized see-and-be scene
spot that, were it in L.A., would be
celebrated as the film-set restaurant of
the month. The no-expense-spared
industrial dining rooms feature exposed
seismic bracings, immense glass partitions
and raw brick walls, softened by leather
banquettes, Phillippe Starck-designed
chairs and stools, and moderate sound
levels. The minimalist art installation
decor attracts buttoned-up business
types at lunch, who opt to sit in the
sun-bright covered atrium. At night,
black-clad Ketel-One drinkers and slinky-
dressed waifs covet the banquettes in the
rear of the main dining room.

The fussy Franco-Japanese food
definitely takes a back seat to the scene.
But that's not to say there aren't some very
good dishes. Sardines with grilled
eggplant, and foie gras with apple sherry
sauce are both memorable starters, and the
meats and fish in red wine reductions are
consistently delicious. Skip the ho-hum
desserts in favor of a dessert wine from the
extensive and fair-priced list.

Rose Pistola

532 Columbus Ave (btw Green/Union).
Tel. 415/399-0499. Reservations
recommended. Kitchen open Sun-Thurs
1130am-midnight, Fri-Sat 1130am-
1am. Main courses $16-$20. AE, MC, V.
Easily one of the most popular
restaurants in North Beach, Rose Pistola
is a gold mine that continues chef Reed
Hearon's extraordinary run as one of San
Francisco's most prolific restaurateurs.
Although it only opened in the late 1990s,
the restaurant has the atmosphere of an
institution. It's filled with rich woods,
leather upholstery, Italian art-glass tiles
and an open kitchen; all of which

contributes to the din of success ("ka-ching!"). A jazz combo raises the volume most nights after 9pm. You've got a lot more clout than us if you walk in and find the table you've reserved is actually ready. And you have a lot more restraint if you can walk past the antipasti bar without ordering a large combo plate with your aperitif. Fried squash blossoms, warm octopus, roasted peppers, and prosciutto with figs and porcini oil are typical starters. Main course specialties include roast fish with fennel and tapenade, wood oven-roasted rabbit, and a wonderfully fishy cioppino. Late eaters should note that the kitchen often runs out of the best dishes early, and the menu is severely limited after 11pm.

Washington Square Bar & Grill

1707 Powell St (at Union). Tel. 415/982-8123. Reservations recommended. Kitchen open Mon-Thurs 1130am-4pm and 5-1030pm, Fri-Sat 1130am-4pm and 5-1130pm, Sun 1130am-4pm and 5-10pm. Main courses $8-$16. MC, V.

The "Washbag," as it is affectionately known, has long been a top destination for moneyed locals. It's an historic woody tavern with a long, polished bar, a dozen intimate tables, and a friendly '21' Club vibe. Catering to the comfort-addicted for decades, the oak-paneled restaurant remains essentially the same as it ever was. But the professional waitstaff, powerful cocktails and updated American menu are now pulling in a younger crowd. Uniformly excellent meals are equally divided amongst old and new classics. The former celebrates an age when blissfully unaware diners guiltlessly indulged in fist-sized medallions of beef, and includes oysters Rockefeller, steaks, pork chops, grilled fish, and a terrific burger. Newer, lighter meals include risotto with clams, mussels, and shrimp; and crisp, baked black seabass with roasted vegetables.

The Waterfront

Pier 7 (Embarcadero at Broadway). Tel. 415/391-2696. Reservations recommended. Kitchen open Mon-Fri 1130am-230pm and 530-10pm, Sat-Sun 530-10pm. Main courses $21-$27. AE, MC, V.

Proof positive that a great view and extraordinary food are not mutually exclusive, The Waterfront wows with the stunning combination of stellar bay views and inspirational cuisine that's as good as you can find anywhere. Maverick celebrity chef Bruce Hill, who trained in some of the city's best kitchens, turns out combinations so extravagantly inventive they're almost mystifying. Witness, for example, lotus-braised monkfish, a gigantic beggar's purse filled with baby vegetables and seared monkfish. It's brought to the table in a lotus leaf that's cut at the bottom so everything falls out in a dramatic puff of steam when the waiter lifts it up. The lion's share of the menu is given over to complex starters, and insiders regularly make a full meal of these. The best includes house-smoked sturgeon and warm roasted beet salad, roast-garlic flan, and sautéed foie gras with crispy fennel. The superb easy-to-negotiate wine list is packed with quality and value.

The restaurant's cement exterior belies its stunning multi-million-dollar interior that's perfectly understated so as not to detract from the scene—either out the window or in the trendy, high-decibel dining room.

Blowfish Sushi

2170 Bryant St (at 20th). Tel. 415/285-3848. Reservations recommended. Kitchen open Mon-Thurs 1130am-230pm and 5-1030pm, Fri 1130am-230pm and 5-1130pm, Sat 5-1130pm. Main courses $10-$15. AE, MC, V.

There's always something of a party atmosphere at this rollicking, album-oriented sushi spot that features Japanese-techno decor, a pulsating sound system, and Northern Puffer, a nonlethal cousin of Japan's notorious tiger fugu sashimi. The action-hero manga decor is a Japanese boy's wet dream, featuring nonstop video screens and original animation cels of masculine villains and large-breasted, round-eyed waifs. It's a slick, dance-clubby space whose real purpose is only given away by the pebble-topped sushi bar and excellent sake menu. All the fresh-fish hits are here, amply cut and served in pairs. Fished from North Carolina waters, the restaurant's namesake puffer is not as intense, either in taste or deed, as its illegal (in California) Japanese counterpart. It will set you back about $30 to discover the slightly shellfishy taste and experience the mild numbing sensation the meat imparts.

Cafe Akimbo

116 Maiden Lane (btw Grant/Stockton). Tel. 415/433-2288. Reservations recommended. Kitchen open Mon-Thurs 1130am-330pm and 530-9pm, Fri-Sat 1130am-330pm and 530-10pm. Main courses $10-$15. AE, MC, V.

Although Cafe Akimbo is one of the very best values around Union Square, there are few tourists here. They can't find the place. Secreted on the second floor of a discreet building on tiny Maiden Lane, the restaurant is the epitome of a find. The reward is a warm atmosphere, and very good cooking at about two-thirds the price of its comparable neighbors. The menu is brief and to the point, specializing in a few well-chosen dishes that the kitchen knows well. The cuisine is an East-West fusion (what else?), offering excellent starters like paté-packed spring rolls with mango sauce, and tandori prawns with kiwi and lime. Entrees encompass several choices from both turf and surf and, if you're lucky, will include the restaurant's signature braised beef short ribs in port wine. Chocolate-based desserts here are state of the tart.

Cafe Claude

7 Claude Lane (btw Grant/Kearny). Tel. 415/392-3515. Reservations recommended. Kitchen open Mon-Fri 1130am-330pm, Sat-Sun 1130am-330pm and 530-10pm. Main courses $8-$13. AE, MC, V.

Cramped and crazy, Cafe Claude is so French you expect a dog to be under the next table. Everything in these twin dining rooms seems imported from France—every table, spoon, salt shaker and waiter. And Piaf is on the turntables at all times. The menu also reads like a survey of bistro classics: cassoulet, seafood gratin, croque monsieur, and onion soup served bubbling in crocks. And with prices topping out at about $13, Cafe Claude is a terrific value. Plenty of regulars pop in for coffee and creme brulee, or stand at the zinc bar with a glass of wine. There's usually live jazz on weekends.

Cha Cha Cha

1801 Haight St (at Shrader). Tel. 415/386-5758. Reservations not accepted. Kitchen open Mon-Thurs and Sun 1130am-4pm and 5pm-11pm, Fri-Sat 1130am-4pm and 5pm-1130pm. Tapas $5-$7.50. AE, MC, V.

Count us amongst the hordes of Cha3 fans. An Upper Haight institution, this high-energy spot is a trippy tropical-exotica paradise with great food and neighborhood-appropriate artistic atmosphere. It's a rare night that Cha Cha Cha is not a rollicking party, fueled by powerful pitchers of sangria, and amazing tapas bursting with flavors that dance in your mouth. The theme of both menu and decor is Latin American and Caribbean melange: the wild folk art is vaguely Guatemalan, the Santería altars are Haitian, and the miserable wait is straight out of communist Cuba. Some people actually order the entrees, but most regulars fill the table with little signature plates containing a variety of dazzling taste treats. The best tapas include pan-fried breaded trout with grilled asparagus and caper remoulade; crisp, fried calamari with lemon aioli; chicken pailliard; Cajun shrimp, served in a miniature iron skillet; and barbecued pork quesadillas topped with salsa and guacamole. Get plenty of bread to sop up all the extra sauces.

Cha Cha Cha's newer branch in the Mission (2327 Mission St; tel. 415/648-0504), offers the same spicy menu but in more subdued surroundings.

Ebisu

1283 Ninth Ave (btw Lincoln/Irving). Tel. 415/566-1770. Reservations not accepted. Kitchen open Sun-Wed 1130am-10pm, Thurs-Sat 1130am-midnight. Main courses $11-$16. MC, V.

Huge sushi, great combinations. That could be the motto of this top-rated fish bar that's always packed to the gills with knowledgeable locals. Tuna, yellowtail, salmon... all the standards

are here, along with occasional seasonal delicacies like Kumamoto oysters, abalone and soft-shell crab. Over two-dozen varieties of rolls include several outstanding and unique combinations. The Japanese decor is just standard, and seating is not the most comfortable. Big cuts mean big lines, so get there early and go solo or in pairs. One more thing: insiders never go on Sunday, the one day the fish market fails to deliver.

Harris'

2100 Van Ness Ave (at Sacramento). Tel. 415/673-1888. Reservations recommended. Kitchen open Mon-Thurs 530-930pm, Fri 530-1030pm, Sat 5pm-1030pm, Sun 5pm-930pm Main courses $26-$35. AE, MC, V.

Every American city has at least one great steakhouse, and in San Francisco Harris' is it. The restaurant's beautifully-marbled, dry-aged steaks are cut thick and proudly showcased in the window. They're served in an Old World dining room with large chandeliers, tall palms and commodious, well-spaced booths. You've got to love a place that lists a martini under "appetizers," and patently ignores any existence of vegetarianism. The king of the menu is T-bone steak, an amazing piece of meat that arrives perfectly charred on the outside and deliciously tender within. Spoon on some of Harris' special brandy-laced sauce and you have a steak that's worthy of one's last meal. Other cuts, along with some chicken and fish dishes are also available, but why? Forget the dreary starters, limit side dishes to potatoes and creamed spinach, and resign yourself to a wine list that is unremarkable, at best.

Indian Oven

233 Fillmore St (btw Haight/Waller). Tel. 415/626-1628. Reservations recommended. Kitchen open daily 5pm-11pm. Main courses $8-$15. AE, MC, V.
Though competition is scarce, Indian Oven is one of the best restaurants of its kind in San Francisco. This downscale, Lower Haight tandoori room cooks North Indian cuisine with spectacular results. All the curry house traditionals are here, including excellent Saag Paneer, made with homemade cheese and fresh spinach, and dynamite chicken tikka masala—tender tandoori chicken bathed in a spicy, rich cream sauce. The breads are great, and the slightly edgy crowd is a hoot.

Lichee Garden

1416 Powell St (btw Broadway/Vallejo). Tel. 415/397-2290. Reservations not accepted. Open daily 7am- 915pm. Main courses $7-$10. MC, V.
Of all the divvy joints in and around Chinatown, Lichee Garden is tops for terrific Cantonese food at exceedingly decent prices. Barbecued duck, pork and spare ribs, all served at room temperature, are fantastic, as is the terrific variety of dim sum, which many consider to be the best in town. Other recommendables include deep fried squab, prawns with honey and walnuts, and oysters with fresh ginger root and onion. Absolutely packed at lunch, this linoleum cafe is one of the city's best finds.

PJs Oyster Bed

737 Irving St (btw Eighth/Ninth). Tel. 415/566-7775. Reservations not accepted. Kitchen open Mon-Thurs 1130am-3pm and 5pm-10pm, Fri 1130am-3pm and 5pm-11pm, Sat 1130am-3pm and 4pm-11pm, Sun 1130am-3pm and 4pm-10pm. Main courses $17-$22. AE, MC, V.
　　Easily the most popular seafood bar in the Sunset district, PJs is an

upbeat, happy place with an extensive menu of fresh fish, most of which is prepared with bold flavors reminiscent of the Louisiana Bayou. The fact that so many of the regulars at this neighborhood restaurant don't even live in the neighborhood is a testament to PJs excellence. The best of a long list of Creole-style tapas are blue crab cakes, baked oysters with spicy barbecue sauce, fried calamari, and *mariscos a la plancha*, a medley of prawns, scallops, and squid in a tangy marinade. Entrees are equally as enticing, especially the locally-caught rex sole, which is prepared whole and filleted tableside; rainbow trout, charred in a cast iron skillet and topped with gulf shrimp and fried onion strings; and the "shellfeast roast" of gulf shrimp, squid, clams, mussels and cod in a spicy garlic sauce. The jambalaya is good too, providing you don't expect the exact flavors of New Orleans.

Thirsty Bear Brewing Company

661 Howard St (btw Hawthorne/ Third). Tel. 415/974-0905. Reservations recommended. Kitchen open Mon-Thurs 1130am-1030pm, Fri-Sat 1130am-midnight, Sun 5-10pm. Main courses $10-$16. AE, MC, V.

It's rare that we would ever recommend a brew-pub as one of a city's best restaurants, but Thirsty Bear's kitchen dishes-out terrific Spanish and Catalan meals that go from strength to strength. The restaurant's Paella Valenciana, the region's trademark meal, is one of the very best we've eaten, and a long list of tapas includes several outstanding selections—fish cheeks sautéed with garlic and sherry; and grilled fennel sausage, to name but two. Its South of Market location, a half-block from the Moscone Center, means a good mix of office workers, conventioneers, frat boys and foodies. The atmosphere is contemporary and somewhat industrial, with the best seats on the ground floor, close to the main bar and most of the action. Upstairs tables share a gaming room with pool tables and dart boards. Oh yah, the beer's great too.

Scoma's

Pier 47 (Jones/Jefferson). Tel. 415/
771-4383. Reservations not accepted.
Kitchen open Sun-Thurs 1130am-
1030pm, Fri-Sat 1130am-11pm. Main
courses $13-$22. AE, MC, V.

As a rule Fisherman's Wharf restaurants
are touristy and overpriced and Scoma's
is no exception. But if you're hankering
for a classic, fishy eatery right in the
heart of the hustle this is the very best
place to go. It's a sprawling place with
lots of snug little dining areas and an
anti-avant family atmosphere. There's
nothing courageous about the menu
either; just straightforward seafood
dishes created with morning-fresh fish.
The simplest preparations are the best:
broiled and fried fruits of the sea served
with lemon and butter. Lobster, crab and
shellfish are specialties, as is that local
favorite, cioppino, which is brimming
with meat and served with thick slices
of broiled buttered toast. Expect crowds
throughout the week and, on Saturdays
and Sundays, be prepared to wait in
line.

Ton Kiang

5821 Geary Blvd (btw 22nd/23rd).
Tel. 415/387-8273. Reservations
recommended. Kitchen open Sun-
Thurs 1130am-10pm, Fri-Sat
1130am-11pm. Main courses $7-$17.
AE, MC, V.

Great entrees and fantastically delicious
dim sum served in excruciatingly plain
surroundings pretty much sums up this
Richmond District Chinese. Ton Kiang
consistently wows diners with fair prices,
friendly service and some of the best
Hakka cooking in the Bay Area. Once
seated in the sparse, two-story dining
room, waiters will walk you through a
menu of Chinese hits that sound
familiar but taste far better than the
glutinous rice toppers dished out by
most other places. All of the sauces,
wines, pickles and stuffings are made
from scratch in their own kitchens.
Chicken in rock salt and chili peppers,
braised oxtail with carrots and celery,
and spicy Szechwan oysters with red chili
peppers consistently get raves. The dim
sum are numerous and to die for,
regularly winning "the best of" awards
in city magazines.

Yank Sing

427 Battery St (btw Clay/Washington).
Tel. 415/781-1111. Reservations
accepted. Kitchen open Mon-Fri
11am-3pm, Sat-Sun 10am-4pm. Dim
sum $3-$5. AE, MC, V.

People come here for the great selection
of dim sum. Pure and simple. Hidden
in a corner of the Financial District,
Yank Sing is one of those exotic and
wonderful Hong Kong-style hideaways
(translation: crowded, noisy, bullet
service, and lazy susans in the middle
of big round tables) that you would have
a hard time finding on your own. A huge
variety of dim sum, piled high on carts,
is piloted around the dining room by
middle-aged, no-nonsense waitresses.
Hail one, and start pointing to the little
treats you want: Steamed meat-filled
dumplings, sautéed soft-shell crab,
bacon-wrapped shrimp, rice-noodle
rolls, Peking duck, savory pork triangles
and much more. Other items are available
from a vast Cantonese menu, but they
somehow seem superfluous. Yank Sing
is only open for lunch.

Preparations range in complexity from simple linguine pomodoro to "firecracker" fusilli, tossed with ginger-braised pork, habañero pesto and sour cream. Also recommended is the Japanese-style udon, swimming in sweet broth with tons of fresh vegetables. Meals are delicious, and few top $7. It's no wonder Fuzio is branching-out all over town.

Branches: 1548 Stockton St (at Columbus; tel. 415/392-7601); and 69 Castro St (btw 18th/Market; tel. 415/863-1400).

Caffe Greco

423 Columbus Ave (btw Green/Vallejo). Tel. 415/397-6261. Reservations not accepted. Kitchen open Sun-Thurs 7am-midnight, Fri-Sat 7am-1am. Main Courses $5-$7. No cards.

Nothing in San Francisco is more contentious than naming "the best" cafe in North Beach, but there can be no doubt that this is one is a contender. Despite it's name, Greco is Italian through and through. Built with tall ceilings and huge plate-glass windows overlooking the street, there are few better spots to grab a newspaper or Nietzche and wile the day away. They've got a great espresso machine and baristas who know how to use it, as well as focaccia sandwiches, and excellent cheese cake, fruit tarts and tiramisu.

Fuzio

2175 Chestnut St (at Pierce). Tel. 415/673-8804. Reservations not accepted. Kitchen open Sun-Thurs 1130am-1030pm, Fri-Sat 1130am-1130pm. Main courses $5-$8. MC, V.

Perpetually packed, and for good reason, Fuzio may be the best-value dining experience the city has to offer. The frenetically-paced dining room is narrow as a bowling alley and tighter than a gnat's chuff, and service is so fast your meal is practically at your table before you order it. But there's no need to rush. Begin with a cocktail from the bar, which is likely to arrive in one of the restaurant's trademark zigzag martini glasses. Then move on to the appetizers: noodle salad with sweet chili-glazed prawns, perhaps? Or maybe organic baby greens with fresh tomatoes and tangy roasted garlic vinaigrette. Food is delicious across the board and portions are substantial. Pastas are the best main courses and there are at least ten varieties to choose from.

La Cumbre Taqueria

515 Valencia St (btw 16th/17th). Tel. 415/863-8205. Reservations not accepted. Kitchen open Mon-Sat 11am-10pm, Sun noon-9pm. Main courses $4-$6. No cards.

When your wallet is crying "uncle" and your stomach is not far behind, La Cumbre Taqueria comes to the rescue with delicious tacos and burritos that consistently win raves from locals who know. Be it beef, chicken or veggie, the contents hold no surprises, but the barbecuing of meats and use of whole pinto beans are the secrets that put this place far ahead of the (substantial) competition. In a word, yummy.

Mario's Bohemian Cigar Store

566 Columbus Ave (at Union). Tel. 415/362-0536. Reservations not accepted. Kitchen open Mon-Sat 11am-midnight, Sun 11am-11pm. Main courses $5-$8. No cards.

Mario's window-wrapped corner at Union and Columbus is the perfect place to install yourself and watch the world walk by. Order a glass of house-made

Campari, and an eggplant sandwich on the cafe's trademark focaccia bread, and you'll soon discover North Beach's definition of Heaven.

Branch: Polk St (btw Green/Vallejo; tel. 415/776-8226).

Sweet Heat

3324 Steiner St (btw Chestnut/Lombard). Tel. 415/474-9191. Reservations not accepted. Kitchen open Sun-Thurs 11am-11pm, Fri-Sat 11am-midnight. Main courses $5-$7. No cards.

The best burrito joint in the Marina delivers terrific vegetarian, chicken, beef and fish wrappers, sauced with sizzlingly hot salsa. The restaurant's most unique recipes are its best, including dungeness crab quesadillas with chili chutney ginger sauce; steak and wild mushroom enchiladas; and burritos filled with jerked chicken, red snapper, or calamari. A simple dining room, bullet service, and generous opening hours are the *menage a trois* of success.

Branches: 2141 Polk St (btw Broadway/Vallejo; tel. 415/775-1055); 1725 Haight St (btw Cole/Shrader; tel. 415/387-8845).

Ti Couz

3108 16th St (btw Guerrero/Valencia). Tel. 415/252-7373. Reservations not accepted. Kitchen open Mon-Fri 11am-11pm, Sat 10am-11pm, Sun 10am-10pm. Main courses $6-$9. MC, V.

Specialization is the name of the game at Ti Couz, where the single menu items—perfectly made crepes—are cooked to perfection. Far better than most found in Breton, these thin and crispy buckwheat pancakes are wrapped around your choice of ingredients, chief of which are sautéed vegetables, ham, ratatouille and Gruyere cheese. The bright cafe atmosphere is also a pleasing place to linger over dessert crepes, filled with the likes of fresh fruit and ice cream. And the prices can't be beat.

MEALS AfteR MidNiGhT

There are surprisingly few places in San Francisco that serve late into the night. Some of the restaurants listed above keep their kitchens open an hour or two past midnight, especially on weekends. Check-out **Globe**, **Rose Pistola** and **Caffe Greco**. The best late-closing restaurants are listed below.

Black Cat

501 Broadway (at Kearny). Tel. 415/981-2233. Reservations recommended. Kitchen open daily 1130am-2am. Main courses $15-$22. AE, MC, V.

This trendy and sleek dining room with red booths, and cream-and-black floor tiles, is one of the brightest late-night bites in North Beach. The *Chat Noir* menu is all over the culinary map with items such as lobster in black bean sauce, grilled squab, and linguine with white clam sauce; and diners are encouraged to share most dishes, family style. Several favorites from owner Reed Hearon's other restaurants appear on this menu as well, including figs and prosciutto (from Rose Pistola) and the addictive roasted mussels (*a la* Lulu). There's a price premium for late hours ($9 martinis!), but at 1am, these are the best meals in town.

Hamburger Mary's

1582 Folsom St (at 12th). Tel. 415/626-1985. Reservations not accepted. Kitchen open Mon-Fri 1130am-2am, Sat 10am-2am, Sun 10am-1am. Main courses $8-$11. AE, MC, V.

Located deep in the heart of SoMa and open most nights until 2am, this funky bar and burger joint has been serving the city's early-to-bed clubbers for almost 30 years. Nothing's cheap and the menu is banal—burgers, sandwiches, and breakfast served anytime. But food and service are decent, and after midnight there's little else open in the vicinity anyway. The restaurant doesn't stay open late enough to really become a late-night scene, which makes us sorry to report that this place is the best of its kind in the neighborhood.

Mel's Drive-In

3355 Geary Blvd. (btw Parker/Stanyan). Tel. 415/387-2255. Reservations not accepted. Kitchen open Sun-Thurs 6am-1am, Fri-Sat 6am-3am. Main courses $6-$10. No cards.

Despite the fact that Mel's is a 1950s-theme diner, they get high marks for excellent, juicy burgers, meaty sandwiches, and a strong list of specials ranging from chicken pot pie and meat loaf, to fish & chips and chicken fried steak. It's a bright, lively place, with Formica tables, leatherette booths, and table-side jukeboxes stocked with plenty of discs from the Elvis-era. The Drive-In becomes something of a scene on weekends, after 2am, when post-club partiers are feeding their munchies.

Branches: 2165 Lombard St (at Steiner; tel. 415/921-2867); 1050 Van Ness Ave (at Geary; tel. 415/292-6357).

Yuet Lee

1300 Stockton St (at Broadway). Tel. 415/982-6020. Reservations not accepted. Kitchen open Wed-Mon 11am-3am. Main courses $6-$11. MC, V.

There's no getting around it, Yuet Lee is a divvy Chinese diner with anti-decor that begins with a reflexive green exterior and only gets worse inside. But the food! This is one late-niter that we're happy to eat in even during scheduled mealtimes. Much ink has been spilled about the restaurant's fabulous clams sautéed with pepper and black-bean sauce, and indeed, seafood is what Yuet Lee knows best. Other outstanding dishes include braised catfish, pork with sweet-and-sour plumb sauce, and chicken liver and kidneys with cashew nuts. The menu is exhaustive, encompassing all the Cantonese traditionals, and prices are well within this world.

Doidge's Kitchen

2217 Union St (btw Fillmore/Steiner). Tel. 415/921-2149. Reservations not accepted. Main courses $7-$10. MC, V.

Doidge's is one of those classic morning meal spots: an institution with home cooking, perfect surroundings, and decent prices. Weekends here are social events, even in the impossibly long line of wannabe diners that spills out the door. Once seated, most insiders head straight for the eggs Benedict—the state of the art, or the buttermilk pancakes that share their plate with fresh fruit and designer sausages. There's omelets too, along with homemade granola, and steel cut oats served with brown sugar, currants and walnuts.

Dottie's True Blue Cafe

522 Jones St (btw Geary/O'Farell). Tel. 415/885-2767. Reservations not accepted. Kitchen open Wed-Mon 730am-2pm. Main courses $5-$9. No cards.

Frankly, we'd never wait in line for breakfast. But if you're ever inclined to do so, set out for Dottie's on a weekend morning and you can plow through half the Sunday paper well before you're seated. Kitschy Americana decor is the perfect surrounding in which to chow down gargantuan portions of eggs, pancakes, or both. Whatever you order, include bread, muffins or scones, all of which are made on the premises. With just ten tables and a few counter stools, you'd be wise to arrive either on a weekday, or alone.

Garden Court

Sheraton Palace Hotel, 2 New Montgomery St (at Market). Tel 415/512-1111. Reservations recommended. Kitchen open Sun-Mon 630-10am, 1130am-130pm; Tues 630-10am, 1130am-130pm, 6-10pm; Wed-Sat 630-10am, 1130am-130pm, 2-430pm, 6-10pm. Set brunch $25. AE, MC, V.

It's hard to beat this grand hotel's fantastic glass-roofed Garden Court, especially during Sunday brunches, when changing sunlight and moody clouds turn the room into a dramatic light show. The Old World room was built at the turn of the last century, with marvelous fin de siécle elements that include glittering crystal chandeliers, gilded marble columns, mirrored doorways and the most amazing skylight dome you've ever seen.

Sunday brunch is a beloved tradition here and, unless you're a guest of the hotel, you'll need reservations well in advance. The meal is an enormous all-you-can-eat buffet that includes everything from roast beef and shrimp salad to poached eggs and chicken apple sausages. Have a dollop of the hotel's trademark Green Goddess salad dressing (a blend of anchovy, green onion, parsley, tarragon, vinegar, chives and mayonnaise), invented here in 1915 at the request of actor George Arliss, then starring in William Archer's play, "Green Goddess."

The Terrace Restaurant

Ritz-Carlton Hotel, 600 Stockton St (btw California/Pine). Tel. 415/296-7465. Reservations recommended. Kitchen open daily 630am-1030pm; brunch served Sundays 1130am-230pm. Set brunch $26. AE, MC, V.

Ah, The Terrace Restaurant at the Ritz-Carlton... if you're ever lucky enough to be in San Francisco on a Sunday morning when that rare combination of sun and warmth strikes, run, do not walk, to this best outdoor dining experience the city has to offer. It's a huge space with a terrific menu that's served indoors year-round. But al fresco Sundays, when the live jazz is brought into the open air, creates an insiderish, indulgent vibe that's not replicated anywhere else. The meal, a sumptuous buffet that includes everything from eggs to oysters, is sure not to disappoint.

Sears Fine Foods

439 Powell St (btw Post/Sutter). Tel. 415/986-1160. Reservations not accepted. Kitchen open daily 630am-330pm. Main courses $7-$10. MC, V.

This ultimate breakfast spot is packed each morning with a mix of tourists and locals who are drawn by the restaurant's authentic old-fashioned diner atmosphere and big reputation for little pancakes that are served a dozen-and-a-half at a time. The fluffy little "silver dollar" griddle cakes are mounded onto a plate with a big scoop of butter and a quartet of syrups. From French toast to eggs, all the other calorie-unconscious American classics are here too. Only the prices, which are raised to match Sears' ground-zero Union Square location, will keep you mindful of the fact that you're entering the 21st century.

ENTERTAINING NIGHTLIFE

bARS & LOUNGES

Contemporary San Francisco nightlife is as bizarre and dynamic as it has always been, just a whole lot safer and more expensive. That's not to say that things haven't changed. Mega-clubs are fewer than they were a dozen years ago, as contemporary cognoscenti refuse to wait in line at Neanderthal-manned velvet ropes, pay eight bucks for a badly made drink, and sardine into an earsplitting space where conversation is impossible. Meanwhile, the late-night underground scene is flourishing. And swing dancing and cocktail lounges are thriving. There seems to be no limit to the number of relaxed places with comfy couches, low tables, and colorful drinks served in Y-shaped glasses. Often attached to a kitchen, lounges blur the line between restaurant and bar. They are places where you are meant to install yourself and imbibe expensive retro cocktails—martinis, Manhattans, negronis and cosmopolitans.

When it comes to "serious" music and culture, San Francisco is the best in the West. The San Francisco Opera is one of the world's finest, the Symphony is top flight, and the Ballet, er, well... did we mention how great the Opera is?

YUPSCALE bARS & dESiGNER SCENES

Bubble Lounge

714 Montgomery St (btw Washington/Jackson). Tel. 415/434-4204. Open daily 4pm-2am.

Deep in the heart of the Financial District, there's a place where local traders and land-owners can toast each other's success over endless glasses of fine champagne and mountains of Petrossian caviar. There are literally hundreds of sparklers to choose from—including 20 by the glass—but it will cost a long-bond to get obfuscated. The appealing rich decor includes overstuffed chairs and sofas, crystal chandeliers, and occasional live jazz—a comfortable environment that improves after 10pm, when the Dow crowd is just tucking itself into bed.

Harry Denton's Bar & Grill

161 Steuart St (btw Howard/Mission). Tel. 415/882-1333. Open daily 730am-2am.

Sizzling with as much energy as any room full of bankers can bring to a party, Harry Denton's is an ever-popular, after-work hang for thirtysomething suits, and the twenty-something office workers who want to meet them. It's a stylish place, with velvet curtains, deco tiles, a wooden bar and beautiful staff. Food is served, but only for people who don't have anywhere better to go. In the right mood, Harry Denton's is a lot of fun, especially after the crowd gets drunk enough to dance.

Backflip

in the Phoenix Hotel, 601 Eddy St (at Larkin).
Tel. 415/771-3547. Open daily 5pm-2am.

A little bit of Los Angeles in San Francisco, Backflip is the city's bastion of young liposucked beauty. Designed to feel like an aquatic utopia, the lounge is immersed in shimmering hues of blue, and filled with playful elements which include a bank of prancing Liberace-style fountains and a mirror-tiled fireplace. The watery theme is enhanced with intense tropical lighting, pool tile walls and Atlantis-meets-Jetsons chrome and plastic furnishings. Perfectly coifed barflies include mostly straight stockbrokers, post-lesson swing teachers, would-be AMWs (actress-model-whatever), and the occasional touring musician just up from LA. Wednesdays are best, especially in warm weather, when the party extends to the poolside patio. A small grazing menu is served until late.

Johnny Love's

1500 Broadway (at Polk). Tel. 415/931-8021. Open daily 5pm-2am.

The next-best place, after an airplane, to pick up a flight attendant? Look no further than Johnny Love's, the ultimate watering hole for Bebe-wearing Ally McBeals in search of a J. Crew-clad guy they can bring home to their parents. The ever-popular bar was begun by bartender Johnny Metheney, who's infamous for his ability to remember the name of every girl who ever leaned over the central horseshoe bar. Because everyone thinks that Johnny Love's is the city's premier meet market, it has become a self-fulfilling prophesy. The bar is basically one large room with great sightlines and occasional live music. Johnny Loves is best on weekends when it's a packed party.

Moose's
1652 Stockton St (btw Filbert/Union). Tel. 415/989-7800. Open daily 11am-2am.
The legendary Ed Moose's stylish Washington Square fishbowl is a sophisticated and energetic hotspot that has miraculously remained fiery for a decade. Both the restaurant and bar are known for their mover-and-shaker magnetics. And the head bartender, Matt McCambridge, mixes some of the wickedest drinks in town. Dress for success.

Royal Oak
2201 Polk St (at Vallejo). Tel. 415/928-2303. Open daily noon-2am.
Designed with Tiffany-style lamps, beveled glass mirrors, Victorian-style couches and plenty of plants, Royal Oak is the last of the great 1970s fern bars. The crowd is also somewhat of a throwback: upscale, untrendy and hetero. It's a casual place, designed for comfort, with a great-looking all-female staff serving from a well-stocked bar.

StREEt-SMARt SCENES

Beauty Bar
2299 Mission St (at 19th). Tel. 415/285-0323. Open daily 4pm-2am.
This West Coast outpost New York's coif-theme bar attracts one of the city's most diverse crowds. It's enviable borderland location (between the heterosexual Mission and the flaming Castro) pulls in straight boys, glamour queens, fag hags, lonesome ladies and even the occasional lesbian. The clientele is uniform in their shimmery good-looks and partiality towards manicurists, hair dryers and the Mermaids soundtrack. The unfortunate few who are less-than-beautiful tend to stick out like a cheap dye job.

Casanova
527 Valencia St (btw 16th/17th). Tel. 415/863-9328. Open daily 4pm-2am.
The archetypal Mission District bar, Casanova feels post everything: post grunge, post rave and post collegiate. It's even post-ironic, attracting an honest crowd of bike messengers, coffee shop barristas, office workers and freelance designers. The result is a great bar, built with thrift store couches, low red lighting and a pool table that accepts quarters. Cocktails are frowned upon in favor of low balls like gin-and-tonic, screwdrivers, and Jack-and-Coke.

Kate O'Brien's

579 Howard St (btw First/Second). Tel. 415/882-7240. Open daily 10am-2am. KO'Bs is a classic woody Irish bar most days; but come Thursday, you'll be dancing with the pierced, dressed-to-sweat drum 'n bass kids who mob the party Eklektic. Hugely respected underground DJs from all over the world come to work the decks at this small, but internationally famous bash run by a trio of hip women who are almost religious about junglism. The music tends towards furious and hardcore (the soundtrack to some gritty, dystopian, millennial megatropolis), and the place reaches capacity almost as soon as the doors open. The crowd is fresh, young and unselfconsciously beautiful. They dance with their eyes closed, or with their faces tightened into masks of rapturous concentration. And dancing with them, with the beats rearranging the neurons in your brain, you'll swear you're on the cusp of something big.... Really big.

Lucky 13

2140 Market St (btw Church/Sanchez). Tel. 415/487-1313. Open Mon-Fri 4pm-2am, Sat-Sun 2pm-2am.
If punk were dead, Lucky 13 would be just a theme bar. As it happens, punk's second wave is centered in the Bay Area (think Green Day and Rancid) and this happening jukeboxed bar is very much in vogue. Black-dyed hair is the badge of regulars, amongst whom slumming yupsters can be regularly spotted. Seats on the upper level are tailor-made for seeing without being seen. Forget cocktails for gnarlier libations: two dozen beers on tap and shots are the drinks of choice.

The Make-Out Room

3225 22nd St (btw Mission/Valencia). Tel. 415/647-2888. Open daily 6pm-2am. Despite its self-consciously hip name, this decidedly unsexy Mission bar has the look of a minimalist garage sale. There's a bar and booths up front, and cocktail tables and a spacious stage in back, where live bands occasionally perform. There's always plenty of eye-candy. The Room's bar-meets-club ambiance attracts local womanizers (and manizers) throughout the week, reaching a sensuously steamy crescendo by Saturday.

The Mint

1942 Market St (btw Duboce/Laguna). Tel. 415/626-4726. Open daily 11am-2am. Scoff if you will, but nightly karaoke sessions make The Mint one of San Francisco's favorite spots. The occasional off-key interloper notwithstanding, talent is serious here, and often seriously good. Customers are mostly gay, and well-acquainted with camp and irony. Video dramatizations, featuring youthful Japanese actors, accompany most songs on a big screen behind the singers. Donna Summer and Patsy Cline are in heavy rotation. The atmosphere is fun, upbeat and far from cruisy. The Mint is a great night out.

Noc Noc

557 Haight St
(btw Fillmore/Steiner). Tel. 415/861-5811. Open daily 5pm-2am.

If Sartre or Beckett had focused less on religion and more on club land, they might have had a hand in designing this wacky industrial/ stone age chill-out space. The bar's vibe is very much like a perennial after-party, where the Fluevogged flock to come down from a rave that never happened. It's dark and ambient, set with copper barstools and pillowy floor cushions on which would-be club kids marinate with doses of trip hop and home-spun electronica. It's liveliest on Monday nights, when the best-looking crowd of day-sleepers come in to strike a pose over a microbrew (no cocktails are served) and wait for their own private Godot.

The Orbit Room

1900 Market St (at Laguna). Tel. 415/252-9525. Open Sun-Thurs 730am-1am, Fri-Sat 730am-2am.

Cafe by day, the Orbit room transforms into a funky neighborhood bar by night, when Teddy boy alcoholics and post-Jetsons clubbers mingle with all manner of un-chic hoi-polloi in this small, but first rate deco cocktail bar. Stone furnishings and high ceilings are warmed by low lighting and a good jukebox, which sometimes goes silent in favor of the odd live performance. The window-wrapped space is a popular neighborhood spot, known for making definitive Lemon Drops and Manhattans with frighteningly unpretentious finesse.

Place Pigalle

520 Hayes St (btw Octavia/Laguna). Tel. 415/552-2671. Open Sun-Thurs 4pm-midnight, Fri-Sat 4pm-2am.

A wine bar with a trip hop DJ? How very San Francisco. French in name and wine list only, Place Pigalle has found the intersection between slumming Marina girls and upwardly-mobile Mission boys; a place where customers are equally at home ordering a 1995 Rabbit Ridge Zinfandel, a pint of beer, or cider.

The Red Room

827 Sutter St (btw Leavenworth/ Jones). Tel. 415/346-7666. Open daily 5pm-2am.
True to its hellish name, everything in this grungy cocktail bar is crimson, cherry and carmine. The room is small, dark and alcoholic, with a couple of leather banquettes (maroon) and a dozen backless bar stools (scarlet) surrounding a semi-circular bar (red). Intentionally rough around the edges, the vibe is young, hip and slightly dangerous. From the creators of the ever-hip Backflip (see below), the bar is best late at night, when the monster martinis have taken their toll.

Tosca Cafe

242 Columbus St (btw Broadway/Pacific). Tel. 415/221-0773. Open daily 5pm-145am.
While Tosca has been around for decades, its current reputation is as a film-star bar for the likes of Sean Penn, Johnny Depp, Michael Douglas and Nicholas Cage, all of whom have been spotted in the Cafe's cozy, wood-paneled VIP room. Physically it's relaxed and unpretentious, built with arched ceilings, oversized red leather booths, Formica tables and a long wooden bar. Operatic arias resound from the jukebox. In short, little has changed since opening day in 1919, except the show-biz crowd and the drink list, which now includes the infamous brandy-based "cappuccino." It's an elegant place, said to have inspired the bar in Dublin's U2-owned Clarence Hotel.

Zeitgeist

199 Valencia St (at Duboce). Tel. 415/255-7505. Open daily 9am-2am.
Part Deliverance part Easy Rider, Zeitgeist is a blue-collar Harley bar for keg bellied bikers which rates high on our pig-o-meter. Despite it's Hell's Angels tone (beer by the pitcher, pitbull friendly and plenty of swearing), Zeitgeist attracts a crazy mix of everybody to its expansive urban patio, directly beneath a freeway. Go with bullet-proof confidence and don't even think about ordering a Fuzzy Navel. A true San Francisco experience.

Carnelian Room

Bank of America Ctr., 555 California St., 52nd fl. (btw Kearny/Montgomery). Tel. 415/433-7500. Open for cocktails daily 3-6pm.

It's all about the view at this stuffy, Financial District skyroom. Named for the marble with which this city's tallest building is clad, the Carnelian Room serves up the most sumptuous bridge-to-bridge panorama. The effect is so dramatic you can almost reach out, pluck up the Transamerica Pyramid, and stir your martini with it. Arrive early and don't forget to bring a date.

Cliff House Bar

1090 Point Lobos Ave (at Great Hwy). Tel. 415/386-3330. Open Mon-Thurs 11am-130am, Fri-Sat 9am-130am.

The Ben Butler Bar, as the cocktail lounge at the Cliff House is officially called, is one of the most spectacular places in the city for a sunset cocktail. Although the Victorian-style room is nothing special, its stunning views of Ocean Beach and Seal Rocks is a lush's definition of romance. A small list of appetizers compliments the booze.

Julius' Castle

1541 Montgomery St (at Union). Tel. 415/392-2222. Open daily 6pm-midnight.

In-the-know locals join Wisconsin tourists for hardy drinks, at Herculean prices, in this thoroughly romantic Telegraph Hill bar and restaurant. The view over North Beach and the city beyond is spectacular, and the only reason for coming here. Forget about the kitchen.

Harry Denton's Starlight Room

in the Sir Francis Drake Hotel, 450 Powell St (btw Post/Sutter). Tel. 415/395-8595. Open Mon 430pm-1230am, Tues-Sat 430pm-130am.

Twenty-one floors above the city a cherubic-faced Harry Denton dons his velvet smoking jacket and welcomes the evening's parade of society brats, nouveau Silicon Valley investors and well-heeled international types, with the same grace that his pillow-lipped bar girls welcome American Express and a generous tip. Blessed with sweeping city views and plush burgundy booths, the burnished gold and velvet room is the perfect place for oysters and champagne, a bottle of which can usually be spotted at every other table. Wednesday's Indulgence party is the best night of the week, when men in black-tie and skinny young things in strappy dresses boogie to generic funkadelic and tired eighties remixes.

Top of the Mark

in the Mark Hopkins Hotel, 1 Nob Hill (at California/Mason), 19th Fl. Tel. 415/616-6916. Open Sun-Thurs 3pm-1230am, Fri-Sat 3pm-130am.

The glass-wrapped Top of the Mark restaurant and lounge is one of the most sensational spots in San Francisco. An elegant interior and awesome 360-degree views made it the choice of World War II servicemen who stopped in for a last drink with loved ones before heading off to the Pacific, and it remains one of the city's most romantic rooms. It's the best place to wow out-of-towners with the sparkling lights of the city below. A pianist entertains until about 8pm, after which swing bands perform in front of a raised central dance floor. Reservations suggested.

CULtiVAtEd CLASSiCS

Maxfield's

In the Palace Hotel, 2 New Montgomery St (at Market). Tel. 415/392-3600. Open daily 11am-2am.

What is it with painter Maxfield Parrish and fancy hotel bars? The two seem to go together like martinis and olives. This Maxfield bar dates from 1909 and contains one of the artist's largest works, a mural said to be worth in excess of $3 million. Indeed, the martini is the drink of choice for in-the-know lawyers and other locals who mingle with hotel guests in this very clubby room.

The Redwood Room

In the Clift Hotel, 495 Geary St (at Taylor). Tel. 415/775-4700. Open daily 11am-2am.

Honest Old World swank is what the Redwood Room is all about. It's an exquisite place with original deco lighting, beveled glass, brass railings, full-scale Klimt prints, high ceilings and remarkably beautiful walls, sheathed in luminous redwood that is said to have come from a single tree. The Union Square location guarantees there will be plenty of tourists, but even they can't diminish this room's elegance.

Tonga Room

In the Fairmont Hotel, 950 Mason St (at California). Tel. 415/772-5278. Open Sun-Thurs 5pm-midnight, Fri-Sat 5pm-1am.

Like Trader Vic's before it, the Tonga Room is a totally kitschy flashback to the early '60s fascination with all things Polynesian, which includes bamboo-hut tables, an indoor thunderstorm, and a horrible cover band on a stage that floats out into the middle of a centerpiece lake. The South Seas drinks are small, poorly-executed and pricey, but even that doesn't deter the crowds of middle-aged conventioneers, playful hipsters, partying city workers and even a few PoDs (people on dates). Down enough mai-tais and you too might hula onto the wooden raft-like dance floor.

Edinburgh Castle

950 Geary St (btw Polk/Larkin). Tel. 415/885-4074. Open daily 4pm–2am.
Looking more like a Roman fortress than Scottish palace, Edinburgh Castle is an cavernous beer hall with an enormous bar and wooden seating on two levels. Despite a Brit-heavy clientele, plenty of stylish locals brave the seedy Tenderloin location for two-dozen beers on tap, an excellent single-malt selection, and perfect fish-and-chips served in traditional newspaper cones. Wednesday nights are best, due to the excellent experimental-music series that gives a stage to everything, from alt-rock to avant-jazz. Check-out the large picture windows that give unobstructed views of the neighborhood's johns and streetwalkers.

Gino & Carlo

548 Green St (btw Stockton/Grant). Tel. 415/421-0896. Open daily 6pm–2am.

An institution since the 1940s, G&C is a neighborhood classic that attracts a good cross-section of the area's gene pool. The place is best at 6am sharp, when post-rave metal-heads rub shoulders with pre-work metal workers who've come in for a morning cap. The bar is also known for serious pool playing; so serious in fact, that one of their tables is almost always reserved for San Francisco Skinny and other members of the National Pool Association.

Li Po Cocktail Lounge

916 Grant Ave (btw Washington/Jackson). Tel. 415/982-0072. Open daily 2pm–2am.

Li Po is the quintessential Chinatown dive. Its cave-like entrance gives way to a cluttered Ming-American interior decked out with cheap leather booths, a dusty jukebox, enormous ricepaper lantern and a glittery golden Buddha behind the bar. Stiff shots, chased by long neck beers, are the drinks of choice. Go in the afternoon.

Persian Aub Zam Zam

1633 Haight St (btw Clayton/Belvedere). Tel. 415/861-2545. Open whenever Bruno feels like it.

Bruno, the tyrannical owner of this singular institution, is the most feared man on Haight Street. A cushioned stool at his decades-old Casablanca theme bar (a changeless anomaly on the strip that gave birth to a revolution) is highly coveted real estate. There are no regulars. People come here to see if all the rumors are true. Is it true that the bartender is so surly? Is it true that Bruno regularly stares would-be patrons in the eye and says "some people don't belong in here?" Is it true that, although the bar is well stocked, you can only order a gin martini? Is it true that the empty tables are always "closed?" Yet, there is something strangely fetching about such a well-kept bar that time forgot; where women are always served first and given napkins, and the barkeep never fails to entertain.

BREW-PUBS / MICRO-BREWERIES

Seeing how there are so many upwardly mobile young white people in San Francisco, it's perhaps not surprising that the city leads the nation in micro-brew culture. Bar owners know that to make it in this town they better stock a good variety of specialty beers, and preferably on draught. They say that the reason American beer is served cold is so that you can tell it apart from piss. Not so at the city's breweries, where full-flavored barley pop is created under near-perfect conditions. Here's the scoop:

Anchor Brewing Company

1705 Mariposa St (at DeHaro). Tel. 415/863-8350). Telephone for tour times/reservations.

Established during the gold rush, Anchor is the Bay Area's oldest brewery. Revived in the 1970s by washing-machine heir Fritz Maytag, the brewery offers irregular tours to those who make reservations (up to two weeks in advance). Tours are free and, of course, tastings are included.

Beach Chalet Brewery

1000 Great Hwy (btw Fulton/Lincoln), Tel. 415/386-8439. Open daily 1130am-midnight.

It's all about location at this upbeat beer/brasserie situated directly on Ocean Beach at the edge of Golden Gate Park. The crowd is just a few years out of college and, when the sun sets, pitchers are poured and the place can get as loud as a frat party. A half-dozen homemade brews are always on tap (including house-made root beer) along with forgettable food that is little more than beer ballast.

Gordon Biersch Brewery

2 Harrison St (at The Embarcadero), Tel. 415/243-8246. Open daily 1130am-1am.

The city's best-known brew-pub is an enormous place, occupying the former Hills Brothers coffee building. The beer is excellent, the setting is stunning and the crowd is a good-looking mix of Financial District suits, Nob Hill slummers and marketers from Gap who work across the street. The food's pretty good too.

San Francisco Brewing Company

155 Columbus Ave (at Pacific). Tel. 415/434-3344. Open Mon-Fri 1130am-130am, Sat-Sun noon-130am.

San Francisco's best microbrews are crafted in this beautiful Victorian-style North Beach bar. There's live jazz most nights and outdoor tables in summer.

Twenty Tank Brewery

316 11th St (btw Folsom/Harrison). Tel. 415/255-9455. Open Sun-Thurs 1130am-1am, Fri-Sat 1130am-130am.

This stunning SoMa brewpub is as enormous as it is popular. It's jumping most nights with a lively crowd getting "tanked" before heading out to nearby clubs. A half-dozen beers are usually on tap, along with a long list of glorified diner food.

Of course the Castro has more gay bars than you can shake a stick at, but the queer city has long since expanded beyond the borders of its most famous ghetto. Likewise, the scene has developed to encompass all manner of club and pub; the rainbow-flag set is no longer limited to the stereotypical leathermen and Lite-beer-drinking girls with bi-level haircuts. As in most cities, the environment is decidedly less exciting for San Francisco's notoriously homebound lesbians. There are only a small handful of girl clubs; and during the week, most are only a heartbeat away from dead.

Some of the best events are one-off parties at various venues around town. Check the listings magazines for the latest.

Alta Plaza

2301 Fillmore St (at Clay). Tel. 415/922-1444. Open Mon-Sat 4pm-2am, Sun 530-10pm.
Alta Plaza is for civilized men in French cuffs and cashmere sweaters who find the Castro a little too brazen. This wood-and-brass restaurant and bar is tailor-made for older professionals cruising for trophy companions who, hopefully, won't steal the Deco napkin rings. Drink prices are steep (draft beer tops four dollars), but if you're on the avant side of the age break, it'll be easy enough to find some Telly Savalas to pick up the tab.

The Cafe

2367 Market St (at Castro). Tel. 415/861-3846. Open daily 1230pm-2am.
Once charged with discrimination for its "no straight kissing" policy, The Cafe hasn't toned down one bit. Metrosexual by day, the nights are almost exclusively populated by gay men and boys: under-aged bridge-and-tunnel types who funk it up to remixed anthems, mainstream house, and techno. The Cafe has three big draws: it's free, has a huge balcony overlooking Market Street, and is one of the few places in the neighborhood where dancing is legal. Hanging out on the balcony and catcalling to passers-by is practically a gay right-of-passage. By 9pm there's usually a line to get in, so get out your Lycra and get there early.

Detour

2348 Market St (btw Noe/Castro) Tel. 415/861-6053. Open daily 2pm-2am.
Seemingly always crowded, Detour is a neighborhood fixture for phallocentric locals. It's not a pretty place; chain link fencing is the primary decorative device, though even that's hard to see in the dark. Techno DJs keep the dance floor throbbing, especially on Saturdays, when there's hardly any room for an erection. Sure, one can play coy, but boys here are upfront in their desires and not shy about expressing them.

Club Townsend

177 Townsend St (btw 2nd/3rd). Tel. 415/974-1156. Open Sat 930pm-7am, Sun 9pm-6am.
When Townsend's massive, tiered space transforms into Club Universe on Saturday nights, it's definitely where the boys are. Throngs of beautiful, shirtless gym queens undulate to deep house and cruise each other madly (and that's just the bartenders). It's best after 2am, when the amateurs go home, the poppers and GHB come out, and the real frenzy begins. A warning to girls: even the most dedicated fag hags will likely feel out of place here (as will most guys without a gym membership).

Esta Noche

3079 16th St (btw Mission/Valencia). Tel. 415/ 861-5757. Open Sun-Thurs 1pm-2am, Fri-Sat 1pm-3am.
Somewhere between Wigstock and Tijuana lies the province of Esta Noche. The Mission's synagogue of high camp is also the best gay bar in the hood. A great sound system pumps out the latest salsa beats for Latino men, and the men who love them. Every Friday and Saturday night the bar hosts a terrific drag show in which sexual dissidents lip-synch to Toni Braxton and Selena. And with so many characters in the audience, it's often hard to distinguish spectators from performers.

Hole In the Wall

289 Eighth St (btw Folsom/Harrison). Tel. 415/431-4695. Open Tues-Thurs noon-2am, Fri-Sun 6am-2am.
The standard by which all other sleazy gay bars are measured, Hole in the Wall is infamous for its raunch, even in this seen-it-all city. In short, this bar lays claim to the sweatiest, seediest and nakedest clientele in town. From the front room, where men play pool in jockstraps, to the back of the bar, where you risk spilling your beer due to an accidental bump from someone's one hour stand, Hole in the Wall ain't the prettiest sight, but it's always a guaranteed eyeful.

The Lexington Club

3464 19th St (btw Mission/Valencia). Tel. 415/863-2052. Open daily 3pm-2am.

The Lexington is one of the best lesbian bars in the city. Granted the competition is thin; grrrls just aren't much for going out, we guess. The scene is both lipstick and leather, with butch bikers and leopard-skinned chanteuses mixing with flannel-clad dog walkers, and the occasional sailoress on-leave. Gender aside, it's one of the most interesting blend of patrons in the city. From working-class to co-ed collegy, the atmosphere is communal and cruisey. Many other places have women-oriented evenings once or twice a week, but the Lexington Club is tops for seven-day-a-week girl-on-girl action.

Martuni's

4 Valencia St (at Market). Tel. 415/241-0205. Open 2pm-2am.

One of the few boy bars in the city completely devoid of any element of sleaze, Martuni's is a thoroughly upscale and sophisticated lounge for the most stylish members of the pink triangle set. This beautifully-designed and candlelit blond-wood cocktail bar attracts a democratically mixed crowd after work, and an avalanche of good-looking guys on weekends. It's a fashionable place, right down to the piano bar, where professional ivory-ticklers seem to know every Noel Coward tune.

Motherlode

1002 Post St (at Larkin). Tel. 415/928-6006. Open daily 6am-2am.

Your reward for braving the mean streets of the Tenderloin is to be a part of one of the most sordid, sexually charged scenes in the city. Catering primarily to drag queens, pre-op transsexuals and the men who lust after them, Motherlode is eons away from the cheerful theme-park atmosphere of the Castro district. The first floor is the most crowded and cruisiest; one floor above a few desultory strippers gyrate on a small stage, while still higher is a lounge where patrons can get acquainted on plush couches that surround a big TV screen flickering with lite-rock videos. Sleazy, and a little intimidating, the Motherlode is one of the few places in this rapidly gentrifying city in which you can still go slumming.

The Pendulum

4146 18th St (at Collingswood). Tel. 415/863-4441. Open daily 6am-2am.

The Pendulum has been the city's premier spot for black men and their white friends for nearly three decades. It's a popular, upbeat place that closes for only four hours each day.

AVANt
SAN fRANCiSCO
dRiNkS

Every lizard knows that you don't have to lindy to look like a swinger. Lounges are on the ins and colorful drinks in Y-shaped glasses are an inextricable part of the scene.

Vodka Gimlet

2 oz. Vodka
.5 oz. Roses Lime Juice
Shake with ice and strain into a chilled cocktail glass. Garnish with a lime wedge.

Manhattan

2 oz. Bourbon or Whiskey
.75 oz. Sweet Vermouth
3 dashes Angostura Bitters
Shake with ice and strain into a chilled cocktail glass. Garnish with a Maraschino cherry.

Cosmopolitan

1.5 oz. Vodka
.5 oz. Cointreau
.5 oz. Roses Lime Juice
.5 oz Cranberry Juice
Stir with ice and strain into a chilled cocktail glass. Garnish with a lime wedge or twist.

Lemon Drop

2 oz. Vodka
.5 oz. Cointreau
1.5 oz Sour Mix
juice of 1 lemon
2 tsp. sugar
Stir with ice and strain into a chilled cocktail glass with sugar around the rim. Garnish with a lemon wedge.

dANCE CLUbS

d espite
California's draconian alcohol laws
which mandate a 2am last-call, San
Francisco's nightlife is thriving and intense, with
dozens of passionate subcultures: experimental
turntablism, hardcore jungle, decadent cabaret, artistic
"happenings," post-ironic raves... devotees of each are
thoroughly convinced that their unique clique is at the
epicenter of the local scene. In a way, each is right. Spend
a night partying with any of them, and you'll quickly start to feel
like you're experiencing something wonderfully powerful, and
destined to be remembered.
        The clubs below are San Francisco's current crop of hot spots.
Often, however, the best parties in town are one-offs, not weekly
events. The *SFStation* Web site (www.SFStation.com) has up-to-
the-minute club information, as does *Late Train* (www.
latetrain.com/clubs). The *Be-At Line* (tel. 415/626-4087) is a
recorded telephone line that's updated daily, with some of the
night's best bets. **San Francisco Metropolitan**, a free bi-
weekly arts and nightlife magazine, is the best place to
look for club listings throughout the week and is
available at restaurants and cafes around town.
Creampuff, also free, is the place to find
everything you need to know about
the gay club scene.

111 Minna

111 Minna St (btw 2nd/New Montgomery). Tel. 415/974-1719. Hours vary
by event.

"Eclectic" is the key word at this edgy art gallery-cum-nightclub, where electronic
and jazz-hybrid bands trade off with talented DJs. Each night brings a new scene:
live music, performance art, films, drum-and-bass turntablists; only the youth
factor remains constant. The company varies from baby-faced ravers to the post-
collegiate, chunky-black-glasses-and-vintage-clothes art crowd, and things
rarely roar before 11pm. The space is laid-out like one gigantic dance floor.
The bar is awkward and drinks pricey; and if no one in the crowd grabs your
attention, there's always something great to look at on the walls.

 **Coco Club**

139 8th St (btw Mission/Howard). Tel. 415/626-2337. Open Wed-Sat 9pm-2am.

Dark, red and sexy, Coco is a former speakeasy turned stylish girl club that attracts more lipstick lesbians than Macy's MAC counter. The underground club features lots of feminist-oriented entertainment, from live jazz, pop, punk and alt rock to spoken word, cabaret, and deep house DJs. The second and fourth Fridays of each month host the enormously popular "In Bed With Fairy Butch," a campy erotic cabaret that's consistently one of the city's best bets. The performance on the last Friday of the month is strictly for women, but everyone is welcome at the mid-month show. Men are welcome almost every other night too, and if they want to see what America's best lesbian club looks like, they should stop by. The entrance is on Minna Street.

The End Up

401 6th St (at Harrison). Tel. 415/357-0827. Open Mon and Wed 10pm-4am, Thurs 10pm-430am, Fri 10pm-3pm, Sat 9pm-3am, Sun 5am-10pm. Even after a full night underground, you haven't even approached the soul of San Francisco nightlife unless you make it to The End Up, the city's most legendary late club. Although the most fabulous people do indeed end up here, the vibe remains exceedingly welcoming and radically inclusive; even the most imperial drag queen can't pull attitude after a night of sweaty SF revelry, when her beehive is tilting and her stockings are running faster than her mascara. Inside is shadowy and intimate (ie. dark enough to hide wrecked appearances, and protect the eyes of vampires coming off a crystal meth binge). It's just perfect for post-gig DJs, giddy girls with a little more flirt left in them, and the odd supermodel or big-ticket actor reveling in relative anonymity. Sunday mornings are best. The party starts at 5am and segues right into an afternoon T-dance. Boys looking for action don't want to miss Fag Fridays, while girls can get lucky at Saturday's G-Spot.

Justice League

628 Divisadero St (at Hayes). Tel. 415/289-2038. Open daily 9pm-2am. The city's premier venue for cutting edge hip-hop, drum and bass, and world music, Justice League attracts those who are serious about sound. Just listen as the crowd cheers a particularly expert series of scratches or breaks, and almost everyone dances solo, facing the DJ. Recent live acts have included Fatboy Slim, De La Soul, DJ Spooky, the Jungle Brothers and Photek, all of whom are revered by boys in big pants and expensive sneakers, and girls wearing tiny, shiny tank tops. The League is particularly colorful on Thursdays at The Box, an exuberant and inclusive long-running club where multiculti partiers bounce to smooth, sexy soul, garage and house.

Liquid

2925 16th St (btw South Van Ness/ Mission). Tel. 415/431-8889. Open Mon-Wed and Fri 8pm-2am, Sat 9pm-2am.

Behind a barely visible sign, on a desolate block deep in the Mission, sits one of the hottest places in town. Devotees aren't fazed by the sketchy neighborhood and occasional line, or even by the cramped dance floor, because the music is so luscious and deep, and the crowd is so local, gorgeous and laid-back. There's not much to the minimalist decor: the car seats along one wall are lined with a jumble of lithe, woozy bodies, while the dance floor overflows with sweaty ecstatics. Monday's Joy party is particularly good. If you go (and you must go) wear as little as possible, because it gets so hot by 1am that even the walls are sweating.

Six

60 6th St (btw Market/Mission). Tel. 415/863-1221. Open Fri-Sat 9pm-2am.

The latest venture from the folks who brought us Liquid, Six has evolved into one of the hippest spots around. The upstairs teems with comfy chairs and couches that are perfect for intimate conversations and smooching cute strangers, while the sprawling basement boasts what may be the best sound system in the city. If the club is successful in getting its after-hours permits in place, Six is poised to be legendary. Go now, and in a few years you'll be bragging about being there before it was famous.

Storyville

1751 Fulton St (at Masonic). Tel. 415/441-1751. Mon-Thurs 5pm-1am, Fri-Sun 5pm-2am.

Once a traditional jazz club, Storyville morphed into one of the city's most important venues for soul-stirring Latin, funk and experimental electronica. Plush and cozy, with red brick and soft lighting, the club boasts both a large dance floor and a comforting fireplace that's perfect for a chill out. It's the music that's the big draw here. Friday night's Pyrotechnics party features turntablists that have racked up accolades all over the world; and Tuesday's swinging Jive Samba incorporates an intoxicating blend of sultry Latin jazz and hip-hop beats. Storyville is a good choice for clubbing any night of the week.

The Stud

399 9th St (at Harrison). Tel. 415/252-7883. Open daily 5pm-2am (occasionally open until 4am on weekends).

Rivaled only by The End Up for it's place in San Francisco nightclubbing lore, The Stud is one of the oldest gay clubs in town, and remains one of the best. Liberally doused with a celebratory mix of high energy house music, the crowd encompasses everyone from the lavishly painted drag queens to anti-fashion flannel dykes. It's exceedingly breeder friendly, too. Although the club is good most every night of the week, it's best on Tuesdays when the Trannyshack party attracts the hysteric glamour of the most fabulous drag queens in town. The non-stop, carnival-like atmosphere includes fat, old showtune queens, bare-assed boys in Tina Turner wigs, and towering transsexuals decked out like peacocks, angels and Martian supermodels (surely it doesn't get anymore San Francisco than this!).

Ten 15

1015 Folsom St (between 6th/7th). Tel. 415/431-1200. Open first Wed of each month 10pm-430am, Thurs 9pm-4am, Fri 10pm-6am, Sat 10pm-7am, Sun 10pm-530am.

The largest nightclub in San Francisco is a multilevel disco theme park, with a trio of dance floors, a chest-thumping sound system, and a laser show that would make a Vegas hotel proud. From reggae and rock to acid-jazz, hip-hop and techno, there's usually something for everyone. On any given night, the club attracts the entire spectrum of clubbers, from frat boys to homeboys. If you're not "on the list" forget weekends before 2am, unless you enjoy standing behind velvet ropes with the bridge-and-tunnel crowd. Hardcore club kids flock here after-hours. The best night at Ten 15 is Spundae, an incredibly friendly Sunday night party where blissed-out scenesters, buff muscle boys, winsome fashion plates, and a hundred other varieties of beautiful people, work hard to extend their weekend by one more day.

Up and Down Club

1151 Folsom St (btw 7th/8th). Tel. 415/626-2388. Open Mon-Tues 9pm-2am, Wed-Thurs 8pm-2am, Fri-Sat 930pm-2am.

The Up and Down Club is where earnest young professionals, of the Ally McBeal variety, retreat after a melodramatic day at the office. Downstairs you'll find soothing jazz that's both polished and unthreatening. Upstairs is a bit more rambunctious, with yuppies and buppies grinding to classic R&B and radio-friendly hip-hop. It's actually a pretty good place to dance, with a friendly, unpretentious atmosphere that's just the ticket for those weary of hipster attitude. Tuesday's are the exception, when the Texture parties pull in the black-clad electronica connoisseurs.

VSF

278 11th St (at Folsom). Tel. 415/621-4863. Open Mon-Thurs 9pm-2am, Fri-Sat 9pm-4am, Sun 9pm-6am.

True to its cheesy name (an acronym for "Very San Francisco"), this whitebread nightclub features danceable mainstream house that's largely appreciated by aging frat boys and the midriff-baring chicks who love them. It gets mention here for its Wednesday night's Bondage-a-Go-Go fetish party, which appeals to leather and latex voyeurs who crave a bit of naughtiness, but are too shy for the city's more hardcore venues. The crowd is mostly straight and latex is required for entry.

Swing dancing is so red-hot in San Francisco that it's hard not to believe it's just another fad revisited. Whatever the future may hold, there's no question that plenty of cool cats and kittens are rocketing into the third millennium with a partner in one hand and a drink in the other. The heppest hoppers are dead serious about their swing, and dress to the nines in retro duds and two-tone steppers. Every night of the week there's a jump-swing party at any number of city clubs. Check the listing magazines for swing nights at **Bimbo's** (1025 Columbus Ave; tel. 415/474-0365), **Top of the Mark** (in the Mark Hopkins Hotel, 1 Nob Hill; tel. 415/616-6916), **DNA** (375 11th St; tel. 415/626-1409), **Skylark** (3089 16th St; tel. 415/621-9294) and the **Great American Music Hall** (859 O'Farrell St; tel. 415/885-0750). The clubs below are usually Swing City several nights a week:

Cafe Du Nord

2170 Market St (btw Church/Sanchez). Tel. 415/861-5061. Open Sun-Tues 6pm-2am, Wed-Sat 4pm-2am.

One of the most swelegant, shabby-chic clubs in the city, Cafe Du Nord still feels like the swank speakeasy it once was. Bordello red, with lush lighting that makes everyone look that much more beautiful, it's a favorite with swing kids and salsa dancers. The club boasts a carved mahogany bar, sizable dance floor, a performance stage and separate cozy cafe. The crowd is all over the generational map, and entertainment varies widely, from cool jazz and vaudeville-style shows to downbeat DJs and live local heroes, like the Folk-Ups, and Lavay Smith and Her Red Hot Skillet Lickers. Swing lessons are usually offered on Sundays from 8 to 9pm. Dinner is served until 11pm (Peking-style pork ribs, gourmet pizzas, Jack-stuffed chicken breast), but food is definitely not the main draw.

Club Deluxe

1511 Haight St (btw Ashbury/Clayton). Tel. 415/552-6949. Open Mon-Sat 4pm-2am, Sun 11am-2am.

It's not all swing all the time, but when it is, you can be sure that everyone's cutting the rug. Club Deluxe is a hopping cocktail lounge for younger lizards in search of good cocktails and live 1940s grooves. The club is especially rocking on Sunday afternoons, and when owner Jay Johnson is fronting his band with a bang-on impression of the Chairman of the Board.

Hi-Ball Lounge

473 Broadway (btw Montgomery/Kearny). Tel. 415/39-SWING. Open Sat-Thurs 7pm-2am, Fri 5pm-2am.

A San Francisco standard far longer than Gap Khaki's and Pottery Barn, the Hi-Ball is ground zero for the Swing Nation. Cramped like a speakeasy and wrapped in red velvet, the lounge is lindy hop central most nights of the week. Lessons are offered on Sundays, Tuesdays and Wednesdays from 7 to 9pm, followed by top local bands like Lee Press-On and The Nails, and Steve Lucky and the Rhumba Bums. Jeans and sneakers are banned in favor of baggy retro rags, suspenders, and skirts that really move.

Metronome Ballroom

1830 17th St (at DeHaro). Tel. 415/252-9000. Open Fri-Sat 730pm-midnight. A dance school during the week, the Metronome transforms into a top weekend club every Friday, Saturday and Sunday. Each night begins with a group lesson followed by the city's most serious swinging. The music's great, but no booze is served.

LiVE ROCk

Having nurtured seminal rockers like the Grateful Dead, Jimi Hendrix and Jefferson Airplane, San Francisco can be counted among the cradles of rock civilization. The scene is still dynamic: latter-day musicians from the hood include Counting Crows, Metallica, Tracy Chapmen and Green Day. Sure, corporate rock has pulled most serious contenders down to LA, but there are still plenty of places to hear great live music. Check the clubs below and the listings magazines for up-to-date info on what's on.

Bottom of the Hill

1235 17th St (at Texas). Tel. 415/621-4455. Open Tues-Thurs 6pm-1am, Fri-Sat 6pm-2am. Cover $3-$8.
Indie rockers love to jam into this edgy, live music venue where punk, thrash and ska bands are served up by the half-dozen. It's a laid-back spot with a cool staff, ass-kicking sound system and twin patios for letting off smoke and steam. We love the all-you-can-eat rock 'n roll barbecue, held most Sunday afternoons.

Chameleon

853 Valencia St (btw 19th/20th). Tel. 415/821-1891. Cover free-$5. Spewing garage rock five nights a week, Chameleon is a small post-punk dive with no-name thrasher bands, college-radio artists, and occasional lounge acts. It's a good place to hear up-and-comers, along with an occasional came-and-wenter debuting a new project. The sound system is dubious, admission is low, and there's a rec room in the basement furnished with a couch and ping-pong table.

Club Teuffel

3246 17th St. No phone. Open Sat 9pm-2am. Cover $3-$5.
Parking structure by day, Club Teuffel transforms most weekends into one of the grungiest punk places known to bandkind. It's the ultimate garage-band venue where few audience members stay an entire night, unless they're "with the band."

Kilowatt

3160 16th St (btw Valencia/Guerrero). Tel. 415/861-2595. Open Mon-Fri 5pm-2am, Sat-Sun 1pm-2am. Cover free-$7.
Still looking very much like the fire station it once was (wooden floors, high ceilings, and spiral stairs where the pole used to be), Kilowatt is a great space with an adventurous booking policy that fills the bills with the best local bands. The venue even has cheep beer, pool tables that cost two bits, and earplugs for sale behind the bar.

Paradise Lounge

1501 Folsom St (at 11th). Tel. 415/861-6906. Open daily 9pm-2am. Cover $3-$8.
Lounge only in name, the Paradise is something of a rock 'n roll megastore offering a trio of stages and a myriad of additional rooms in which several events are staged simultaneously. Thrash and trash is the club's main stock in trade, but that's regularly augmented by singer-songwriters, avant-jazz, and even the occasional performer slamming poetic. There's a chill-out loft and pool tables for letting off steam.

COUNTRY MUSIC

Rawhide II

280 Seventh St (btw Howard/Folsom). Tel. 415/621-1197. Open Mon-Thurs 4pm-2am, Fri-Sun noon-2am.

A meager C&W scene is proof positive that San Franciscans see themselves as being spiritually closer to New York City than Dallas. Rawhide is the lone club in the city for urban cowboys and girls. And it's a gay club at that. Same-sex couples, many of whom are in chaps, two-step to achy-breaky beats. Thursdays is especially for gals, though they are welcome here every night of the week.

LIVE JAZZ & BLUES

While San Francisco's traditional jazz and blues scenes barely have a pulse, the city has been one of the country's main proponents of acid-jazz and live swing, both of which can be found in abundance any night of the week (see Dance Clubs and Swinging, above).

LATIN, CARIBBEAN & WORLD BEAT

Bahia Cabana

1600 Market St (at Franklin). Tel. 415/626-3306. Open Thurs-Sun 6pm-2am.

Bahia Cabana has carried on through the decades with a tropical-motif and Carmen Miranda atmosphere, dishing out regular doses of contemporary African, Caribbean and World Beat music that traverses the Southern Hemisphere. Thursdays are exclusively salsa nights, and the price of admission includes a group dance lesson at 9pm.

Esta Noche

3079 16th St (btw Mission/Valencia). Tel. 415/861-5757. Open Sun-Thurs 1pm-2am, Fri-Sat 1pm-3am.

Esta Noche jumps every night of the week with Latin lovers who make this the hottest salsa club north of the Rio Grande. It's so male oriented that even the few women who find their way here are usually men just below the surface. Weekends bring a raucous drag show, followed by more shaking into the night.

Blue Lamp

561 Geary St (btw Taylor/Jones). Tel. 415/885-1464. Open daily 8pm-2am.

One of the few clubs in the city featuring regular blues jams, this Tenderloin blooze bar is best on electric Sundays and acoustic Mondays, when the finest no-name players are invited to work out their chops in public. It's a miniature dive, on a hardscrable block, that attracts an older music-loving crowd.

Bruno's

2389 Mission St (btw 19th/20th). Tel. 415/550-7455. Open daily 3pm-2am.

A well-regarded mainstay for decades, Bruno's revamp in the mid-nineties ushered-in the birth of two eras: the Cocktail Nation and the gentrification of the Mission. Half the place is a good restaurant, with round vinyl booths and bachelor pad atmosphere. The other half contains a long bar, and a colorful lounge where perfect Manhattans, flattering lighting, and the best live local jazz bands attract the neighbors: bike messengers, writers and computer programmers, all of whom float over here in equal numbers.

Elbo Room

647 Valencia St (btw 17th/18th). Tel. 415/552-7788.
Open daily 5pm-2am.
This Mission area clubroom was one of the city's first proponents of the acid-jazz scene, giving a stage to some of the genre's most seminal acts. It's a beautiful club on two levels, set with cocktail tables, and a room-length bar serving the usual selection of micro-brews and single-malts. Live jazz and funk are regular features upstairs, where a diverse crowd of beat locals and Marina slummers come to dance.

CLASSICAL MUSIC, OPERA & dANCE

San Francisco Symphony

Louise M Davies Symphony Hall, 201 Van Ness Ave (btw Hayes/Grove). Tel. 415/431-5400. Box office open Mon-Fri 10am-6pm, Sat-Sun noon-6pm. Tickets $15-$90.

Considered to be something of a rock star in the classical world, the Symphony's flamboyant conductor, Michael Tilson Thomas, has built a progressive orchestra that plays to both neophytes and aficionados. Davies Hall, a soaring, clean-lined performance space, offers good sightlines, great acoustics, and comfortable seating throughout. Seats up in the nosebleed section are far away indeed. If you're looking for a deal, wait until the day of the show when terrace seating, located next to the side loge and orchestra, goes for half price. Also, a few dozen of their best seats are usually on sale two hours before showtime. The cheapest seats, at center terrace, are actually behind the orchestra, where you can practically read the music. The Symphony's season runs from September through May.

San Francisco Conservatory of Music

1201 Ortega St (at 19th). Tel. 415/759-3475 (recording); Tel. 415/759-3477 (box office). Box office open Mon-Fri 9am-5pm. Tickets $7-$11.
The Conservatory holds a series of concerts throughout the year ranging from solo and chamber performances, to organ recitals and full orchestra arrangements.

With religion on the outs and tourism in full-swing, several churches have turned to classical music as a way of attracting crowds, and money. The repertoire is usually the best-known Baroque and Classical hits by Bach, Handel, Beethoven and Mozart. **Old St. Mary's Cathedral** (660 California St) offers concerts Tuesdays and Thursdays at 1230pm; and at **St. Patrick's Church** (756 Mission St) on Wednesdays at 1230pm. Concerts at both churches last about 90 minutes and are free ($3 donation requested). Call 415/288-3840 for program information.

Grace Cathedral (1100 California St; Tel. 415/749-6300), at the top of Nob Hill, is well-known for it's excellent music and top acoustics. Phone for current schedules and prices.

OPERA

San Francisco Opera

War Memorial Opera House, 301 Van Ness Ave (btw Grove/McAllister). Tel. 415/864-3330. Box office open Mon-Sat 10am-6pm. Tickets $25-$150; Standing Room Only $10-$12 on day of show. The SF Opera has evolved into a fantastic company, second only to New York City's Met in quality, size and budget. The Opera is known for daring productions of such attention-getting vehicles as The Death of Klinghoffer, Dangerous Liaisons, Harvely Milk and A Streetcar Named Desire. For the 2000-2001 season, Terrence McNally will write the libretto for a production based on the Academy Award-winning film, Dead Man Walking. The 3,200-seat rococo building has excellent acoustics everywhere, except beneath the balcony. Likewise, sightlines are compromised on both "ends" of the house, and the cheapest seats are too far away from the action for those without 20/20 vision. SROs should dash to the rear of the first-balcony for top acoustics, or to the rear of the orchestra for the best views. The season runs from May to early June; and September to early December. Dress is anything from casual to conformist, except at the annual opening, which is one of the swankiest social events of the year.

dANCE

San Francisco has long been a thriving Mecca for dance. From George Balanchine and Martha Graham to Mikhail Baryshnikov and Jerome Robbins, almost all the big names from the classical and modern schools have played here. And lots of small companies (of all styles) are based in the Bay Area. There's always something interesting happening on local stages. Check-out the listings magazines for the latest.

San Francisco Ballet

War Memorial Opera House, 301 Van Ness Ave (at Grove). Tel. 415/865-200. Box office open Mon-Sat 10am-6pm. Tickets $25-$150. Standing Room Only $7 on day of show.

The country's oldest professional ballet company was founded in 1933 and, with some outrageously avant exceptions, generally sticks to its traditional roots. The season includes both self-commissioned works and recognized standards, all performed in repertory. The season opens with the Christmas spectacular, "Nutcracker Suite," which runs each year from November through January.

MAJOR CONCERT AND THEATER VENUES

Each Theater's own box office is usually the best bet for tickets. The much hated BASS agency (tel. 415/776-1999 or 510/762-2277) sells tickets by phone to most theaters in the city, for which they collect a hefty surcharge. If you're desperate for seats to a sold-out show, a scalper might be your last-best chance.

Ticket agencies sell the best seats in the house at premium prices—sometimes as much as fifty percent above face value. Try **Best Seats** (tel. 800/984-2538); **Mr. Ticket** (tel. 415/292-7328); and **Murray's** (tel. 415/441-1900).

Bill Graham Civic Auditorium

99 Grove St (btw Polk/Larkin). Tel. 415/974-4000.

Named for the city's best-loved rock music impresario, this mini-arena hosts everything from B-list pop concerts to big-scale operas.

Cow Palace

Geneva Ave (at Santos), Daly City. Tel. 415/469-6065.

Cow Palace is a great-looking arena that's bad for concerts but great for rodeos, hockey games, and monster truck derbies.

Fillmore Auditorium

1805 Geary Blvd (at Fillmore). Tel. 415/346-6000.

An institution made famous by the Grateful Dead, the Allman Brothers, and promoter Bill Graham in the 1960s, the Fillmore is a terrific old ballroom that, once again, is attracting big names. A limited number of tickets are usually released an hour before showtime.

Great American Music Hall

859 O'Farrell St (btw Larkin/Polk). Tel. 415/885-0750.

A former bordello turned concert space, GAMH is one of the best-loved showrooms in the city. The decor is extravagant and the sound is decent; in short, an enjoyable place to catch a risen star.

213

Maritime Hall

450 Harrison St (btw First/Fremont). Tel. 415/974-0634.

One of the city's newest concert halls often attracts acts that the other venues miss; namely world-beat, big-name jazz and reggae. In addition to a main stage, there are several smaller rooms where various events are held. All-in-all, a welcome addition to the city's music scene.

StAGE: ThEAtER & PERfORMANCE ARt

San Francisco has a lively theater culture. Dozens of shows are scheduled at any one time, including international musicals like Chicago, Phantom of the Opera and Miss Saigon, and lots of smaller productions by local and international playwrights. Each Theater's own box office is usually the best bet for tickets since the BASS agency (tel. 415/776-1999 or 510/762-2277) collects a hefty surcharge for their phone-in services.

TIX Bay Area (tel. 415/433-7827), a small kiosk on the Stockton Street side of Union Square, sells half-price tickets on the day of the show to more than 80 performing arts venues, including the San Francisco Opera, the Symphony, and a number of top theaters. They won't tell you over the phone what they have for sale; you'll have to show up in person and read their board. And they only accept cash. However, they do accept credit cards for full-price advance tickets. They're open Tues-Thurs 11am-6pm, Fri-Sat 11am-7pm.

Slim's

333 11th St (btw Folsom/Harrison). Tel. 415/522-0333.

Bozz Scaggs' big-time venue books a lot of big names for limited engagements at this South of Market venue. Sightlines are compromised by a pair of columns, and sound is hampered by the high ceiling. Skip this show if you can.

The Warfield

982 Market St (btw Fifth/Sixth). Tel. 415/775-7722.

Great views, terrific sound, and three full bars have long made the Warfield a favorite of local rockers. Snag seats in one of the rear VIP booths, and it's sure to be a concert to remember.

Audium

1616 Bush St (at Franklin). Tel. 415/771-1616. Shows Fri-Sat at 830pm. Admission $10. Box office open 30 minutes prior to showtime.

The lights are dimmed, and a collage of sound moves through the audience. Audium is a thoroughly unique sound-in-space show that we've never heard of anywhere else. It's the brainchild of composer Stan Shaff, realized with a grant from the National Endowment for the Arts. There are 136 speakers embedded in sloping walls, a suspended ceiling and floating floor, all of which make Audium the ultimate sound studio. Music and disembodied effects are "sculpted" by Shaff, who directs the show using playback equipment and a custom console. The result is everything from the abstract to the everyday; otherworldly wails mix with the disquiet of children laughing, waves crashing, clocks ticking... it's sound you can practically taste and feel, very New-Agey and avantly excellent.

Beach Blanket Babylon

Club Fugazi, 678 Green St (btw Columbus/Powell). Tel. 415/421-4222. Box office open Mon-Sat 10am-6pm., Sun noon-6pm. Showtimes Wed-Thurs 8pm, Fri-Sat 7pm and 10pm, Sun 3pm and 7pm.

Creator Steve Silver is gone, but it seems his kitchy cartoon-bright review will live on forever. Singer Val Diamond plays Snow White in drag, looking for love in all the wrong places. The show is a nonstop barrage of visual puns and popculture references that have kept audiences applauding for over 20 years.

ThE MOSt RESPECtEd tHEATER COMPANiES

The Curran Theater (445 Geary St; tel. 415/551-2000), **Golden Gate Theater** (1 Taylor St; tel. 415/551-2000), and the **Orpheum Theater** (1192 Market St; tel. 415/551-2000) are beautifully-restored playhouses that exclusively feature Broadway-scale productions. We always skip these in favor of the city's smaller spaces, where excellent original productions are mounted by local artists. The best companies are listed below:

450 Geary Studio Theater, 450 Geary St (btw Mason/Taylor). Tel. 415/673-1172.

American Conservatory Theater (ACT), 415 Geary St (btw Mason/Taylor). Tel. 415/749-2228.

Climate Theater, 252 Ninth St (btw Folsom/Howard). Tel. 415/262-2169.

Eureka Theater Company, Tel. 415/243-9899.

Exit Theater, 156 Eddy St (btw Mason/Taylor). Tel. 415/931-1049.

Lorraine Hansberry Theater, 620 Sutter St (btw Mason/Powell). Tel. 415/474-8800.

Magic Theater, Building D, Fort Mason Center (btw Laguna/Buchanan). Tel. 415/441-8822.

The Marsh, 1062 Valencia St (at 22nd). Tel. 415/641-0235.

Theater Artaud, 450 Florida St (at 17th). Tel. 415/621-7797.

COMEdy ANd CAbAREt

It seems that every comedy club advertises theirs is the place where Whoopi Goldberg, Robin Williams and every other home-grown funny bone got their start. None of them is lying: When you're a struggling comedian, you play *everywhere*. It's a far cry from the 1980s heydays though, when San Francisco supported a half-dozen or more comedy clubs; now there are only two full-time laugh factories: **Cobb's Comedy Club**, 2801 Leavenworth St (tel. 415/928-4320), and **Punchline Comedy Club**, 444 Battery St (tel. 415/397-7573). Both offer essentially the same acts. Comedians are served-up by the half-dozen and, aside from the occasional sarcastrophe, quality is tops. The clubs charge about $10 on weeknights and $20 on weekends, and there's usually a two-drink minimum. Phone for show times and reservations.

Josie's Cabaret and Juice Joint

3583 16th St (btw Market/Pond). Tel. 415/861-7933. Open Mon-Thurs, Fri-Sat 715-1130pm, Sun 715-10pm. Admission $6-$12.

Sometimes campy, sometime serious, Josie's is one of the Castro's most beloved club rooms. Intimate plays are interspersed with off-the-wall comedy, cabaret, and open mikes every Monday night. Quality is usually excellent, but the same can't be said for the balcony seating, from which views are severely obstructed. Arrive early to snag a premium seat.

Kimo's

1351 Polk St (btw Post/Sutter). Tel. 415/885-4535. Open Fri-Sat 9pm-2am. La Cage aux Folles meets Showgirls at this extraordinarily fun and raunchy cabaret. Forget Cher and Tina Turner; the faux-girls here go way beyond the standard camp classics and create their own hilarious characters. These hilarious shows have both trendy locals and adventurous middle-American tourists clamoring to go to one of the seediest neighborhoods in San Francisco. Phone for reservations.

Plush Room Cabaret

in the York Hotel, 940 Sutter St (btw Leavenworth/Hyde). Tel. 415/885-2800. Admission $12-$20.

This classic cabaret room gives a regular stage to velvety voiced torch-song vocalists, and plenty of campy songsters. There's almost always something good going on here.

fiLM

San Francisco is a city of cinemanics. Big films often open on local screens before they're unveiled anywhere else, and even when ticket prices approach $10, evening shows are constantly sold-out. Most theaters show Hollywood flash and trash exclusively, but there are still a handful of alternative houses.

All the listings magazines and most newspapers have comprehensive movie listings. MoviePhone (tel. 415/777-3456) is the number to call for automated information on what's playing at every major cinema in the city. The line doesn't cost any money, but you pay for the service by having to listen to horrible film advertisements. You can purchase tickets by phone, using your credit card, for a $1.50 service charge per ticket.

Castro Theater

429 Castro St (at Market). Tel. 415/621-6210.

The Castro is the city's premier movie palace. Built in 1922, the ornate Spanish Renaissance movie house is a neighborhood landmark specializing in international and American classics. The movie-going experience begins with a preamble by the house organist, who hydraulically rises onto the stage before selected screenings.

San Francisco Public Library

100 Larkin St (at Grove). Tel. 415/557-4515.

The city's main library offers weekly screenings of alt-features and top documentaries, based on a different theme each month (i.e., architecture, automobiles, war and the like). All films are free; phone for the latest.

Sony Metreon IMAX
150 Fourth St. Tel. 415/537-3400.

In addition to 15 regular movie theaters, this new entertainment complex contains retail shops from Sony, the Discovery Channel and Microsoft, and a 600-seat IMAX theater. Programs on the 8-story-high screen change every few months.

Yerba Buena Center for the Arts
701 Mission St (at Third). Tel. 415/978-ARTS. Admission $3-$10.

Yerba Buena's Media Screening Room is the venue for a spirited series of films, shown almost every day of the week, that are some of the most avant in the city. Daytime shows included admission to the gallery (see Chapter 5/SoMa); evening screenings have separate admissions.

ALTERNATiVE/REPERtORY CiNEMAS
Lumiere, 1572 California St (btw Polk/Larkin). Tel. 415/352-0810.
Bridge, 3010 Geary Blvd (at Blake). Tel. 415/352-0810.
Opera Plaza, 601 Van Ness Ave (btw Golden Gate/Turk). Tel. 415/352-0810.
Clay, 2261 Fillmore St (at Clay). Tel. 415/352-0810.
Embarcadero Center Cinemas, Battery St (btw Sacramento/Clay). Tel. 415/352-0810.
The Red Vic, 1727 Haight St (at Cole). Tel. 415/668-3994.
The Roxie, 3117 16th St (at Valencia). Tel. 415/863-1087.

SEX

Obviously AIDS has devastated the San Francisco sex scene, but consentual non-monogamy is far from dead. A quick dip into almost any bar in the Castro is proof positive that the city still leads the way when it comes to tolerance toward sexual expression and diversity. To be sure, most of the city's existing sex clubs are musky, manly affairs, but there are also plenty of opportunities for hetero ones. Serious sexoholics should check out *Little Black Book* (www.lovings.com) for the full picture of the Bay Area's scene. The Web site contains honest info on prostitution, spas and shops, with plenty of advertisements catering to all predilections. The San Francisco *Yellow Pages* contains 30 pages of ads and listings for personal companions under the heading "Escort" (most are open nonstop and accept credit cards). There are several venues in which to wank, from table-top strippers to peep-booth cleavage-wielders. The best are listed below.

The Gold Club
650 Ho··ard St (btw 2nd/3rd).
Tel. 415/536-0300. Open daily noon–
2am. Cover $20.

If you're looking for them, you'll spot this strip club's billboards and posters all over town. Strategically located only a half-block from the Moscone Convention Center, The Gold Club is San Francisco's own Silicon Valley, with lots of beautiful bottle-blondness doing the shake and bake on laps and poles.

The Lusty Lady
1033 Kearny St (btw Pacific/ Broadway). Tel. 415/391-3126. Open nonstop. No cover.

The Lusty Lady's claim to fame is that it's a humane shop managed by women, where all the dancers are unionized (Service Employees International Union Local 790). Most of the gals are "real" 10s (without silicone), and are so popular that we have actually spotted lines outside the peep booths. On the wall are portraits of the strippers inside, tissue dispensers, and signs sternly forbidding same-sex couples from sharing a booth. Once inside, have a roll of quarters at the ready, then watch the strippers wave to repeat offenders whose windows keep opening.

Mitchell Brothers' O'Farrell Theatre
895 O'Farrell St (at Polk). Tel. 415/776-6686. Open Mon-Sat 1130am-2am, Sun 430pm-2am. Cover $35.

Open since 1969, Mitchell Brothers is the cream of old San Francisco sleaze. They claim to have at least 50 girls per shift; which is a lot, unless you're counting ones that you actually want to see with their clothes off. One ticket is good all day, and they'll even stamp your hand for re-entry! There are six rooms, each with a different show or theme including "two-girl action," lap dances, and "Kopenhagen Live," in which patrons are furnished with flashlights so they can spotlight their favorite parts. First-run smut is screened in a small theater, and private video booths are available for those looking for a more secret five-finger shuffle.

Nob Hill Adult Theatre
729 Bush St (btw Powell/Mason). Tel. 415/781-9468. Open daily noon-2am. Cover $25.

Strip club meets showplace at this unusually bright and clean man-on-man raunch pad. In addition to the usual on-stage antics, patrons can pay-to-play with the staff (so to speak); dancers are happy to pose in various positions for a negotiated fee. At the weekend "safe-sex orgy," more than a half-dozen guys perform at once. And the private video booths here conveniently seat three.

¶¶
#10

TRiPPiNG: dAY tRiPS & SLEEP-AWAYS

Northern California is one of the world's greatest playgrounds. There are tons of great things to see and do within two hours of San Francisco, which is one of the main reasons that people love to live here. Just a short drive and you can climb a mountain, bike through vineyards, sunsoak on a beach, swing on a premier golf course, lap it up at a spa or ski at a top resort. And that's just Day One. We could write a whole book on the great things to do and see in Northern California (and in fact, we are in the process of doing just that). In the meantime, we present the highlights.

Getting Around

For information on renting a car, see Chapter 11/Cars & Driving.

By Bicycle

Peddling around is one of the best ways to explore the Bay Area—especially Marin County, and the Wine Country north of the city. Almost a half-dozen bike-rental companies offer high-end mountain bikes for about $25 to $35 per day. The best are **Adventure Bicycle Company**, 968 Columbus Ave (tel. 415/771-8735); **Holiday Adventures**, 1937 Lombard St (tel. 415/567-1192); **Blazing Saddles**, Pier 41-Fisherman's Wharf (tel. 415/202-8888); and **American Rentals**, 2715 Hyde St (tel. 415/931-0234). All the companies include maps and directions for itineraries that range from an easy 10-mile trek to Sausalito (and back by ferry) to the strenuous, legendary 38-mile loop across the trails of Mt. Tam, where the mountain bike was invented.

Tours

As you probably already know, the Avant-Guide philosophy is diametrically opposed to most standard tours; there's not many things worse than listening to dry tour patter while watching the world fly by from the back of a smog-belching bus. That said, we highly recommend **Tom Martell's Nature Walks** (tel. 415/381-5106) through the nearby Muir Woods and Marin Headlands. An experienced Sierra Club guide and world traveler, Tom knows Marin's trails and trees better than anyone we've ever met. His walks are involved, heartfelt and intimate, as they are limited to 6 people. They cover two to four miles, include door-to-door transportation and cost $40 to $50.

THE EAST BAY

Oakland and Berkeley are the two most interesting and important cities on the Bay, just east of San Francisco.

Although it is much larger than San Francisco, **Oakland** has long played poor cousin and bedroom community to its far more famous neighbor. Neighborhoods here are diverse, from upscale hilltop communities to downtown gangland dumps. The city is also the focus of Northern California's lesbian community, populated by women who can't afford the exorbitant rents across the Bay. Only the most patriotic Oaklanders would argue that their city isn't something of a pit, and a dangerous one at that. If you are visiting San Francisco for a few days there is really no reason to check-out Oakland, except to visit a luckless friend or to see how the other half lives.

Getting There
• **By Car** From San Francisco, take the Bay Bridge to I-580 East to downtown Oakland. For Berkeley, take I-80 along the bay and follow signs to the University. The trip takes about 30 minutes, depending on traffic.
• **By BART** Bay Area Rapid Transit (BART) connects San Francisco with Downtown Berkeley and Oakland City Center. Trains run beneath Market Street at the Embarcadero, Montgomery Street, Powell Street and the Civic Center. Service is provided Monday through Friday from 4am to midnight, Saturday from 6am to midnight and Sunday from 8am to midnight. Fares range between $2.20 and $4.50, depending on how far you go.

BERKELEY
on the other hand, is definitely worth a visit. Justifiably famous as an intellectual and counter-cultural center of Northern California, the town at once offers a glimpse of the past and a peek at the future, should the Birkenstock generation ever rule the world. The life of Berkeley is inextricably related to its **University of California** campus, reputed to be one of the best in the West. Both town and gown came into their own in the 1960s, when Berkeley was transformed into a leftist battleground. In late 1967, the University demolished an entire block of dilapidated buildings north of Telegraph Avenue to rid the neighborhood of hippies and other "undesirables." But after the lot lay vacant for almost two years, a group of local radicals, a list of whom reads like a Who's Who of 1960s Leftists—Jerry Rubin, Bobby Seale, Tom Hayden et al.—decided to seize the land for "the people." On April 29th, 1969, hundreds of activists stormed the vacant lot armed with gardening tools and transformed the muddy ground into a park. One month later the city's Republican mayor dispatched 250 police officers to reclaim the property, and 4,000 demonstrators materialized to challenge them. A riot ensued; and the police fired buckshot at the crowd killing one rioter and blinding another. Governor Ronald Reagan escalated the violence by sending in the National Guard, and for the next seventeen days innocent students, faculty and passersby were repeatedly gassed and harassed. Ultimately, sensing no happy end to this public-relations disaster, the University capitulated and "Peoples Park" was born. UC-Berkeley is a lot tamer these days; the quest for cash has long since replaced battling for one's convictions. The university's 30,000 students who command Telegraph Avenue can still be found idling their days away in hole-in-the wall cafes, except lattes are now the joe of choice. Although the adjacent campus is not particularly

beautiful, it's interesting to see. The **University Visitor Information Center,** 2200 University Avenue (tel. 510/642-5215) is a good place to begin your exploration and pick-up a free self-guided tour map. It's open Mon-Fri 830am-430pm, Sat 10am-4pm.

Chez Panisse, 1517 Shattuck Ave., Berkeley (tel. 510/548-5525) is the other good reason to visit Berkeley. Chef/Owner Alice Waters is considered the mother of California cuisine, and her top-of-the-line restaurant continues to be one of the hardest reservations to get in the Bay Area. Each course of the nightly fixed-price menu is a revelation. Meals might include pan-seared scallops, roast garlic sausages and baked pears with mascapone. **Chez Panisse Cafe,** next door, is far less formal and serves a delicious range of salads, pizzas, and pastas together with an extensive wine list.

MARiN COUNtY

The Golden Gate Bridge has one foot in San Francisco and the other firmly planted in Marin County. A land of milk and money, Marin has become the de facto old-age home for the bleeding-ponytail set; former hippies who have traded their Birkenstocks for Volvos, tie dies for hot tubs and splifs for million dollar homes. Well, maybe they haven't gotten rid of their splifs.... For the visitor, Marin offers a glimpse of the good life—Northern California style; and an even clearer view of the City of San Francisco across the bay.

Getting There
• **By Car**   Highway 101 over the Golden Gate Bridge is the way to go. Once on the other side take the first exit, Alexander Avenue, to Sausalito. For Tiburon, take Hwy 101 to Tiburon Boulevard East. A small lot at the end of the road is the best place to park your car. To reach the Marin Headlands, exit onto Alexander Avenue, turn left under the highway and follow Conzelman Road up the hill.

• **By Bicycle**   You can safely peddle over the Golden Gate Bridge, exiting onto Alexander Avenue to Sausalito or the Marin Headlands. A pretty bike path beginning along Bridgeway in Sausalito runs north along the bay to Tiburon Boulevard to downtown Tiburon. *See* Chapter 6/Fitness & Sports for bike rental information.

• **By Ferry**   **Blue & Gold Fleet Ferries** (tel. 415/773-1188) run regular boat service between San Francisco's Fisherman's Wharf and downtown Sausalito and Tiburon. There are frequent daily departures. The journey takes about thirty minutes each way and costs around $6.

TIBURON

If you only have time for a single stop in Marin head straight for Tiburon, a large, fin-shaped peninsula jutting into the bay directly across from San Francisco. Unrivaled views and unclogged streets make it a perfect brunchtime destination; there's not much else to do. In the summer **Sam's Anchor Cafe** (27 Main St.; tel. 415/435-4527) is heaving with locals. The food is indifferent, but it's always packed due to unrivaled Bloody Mary's and the unobstructed panoramic vistas from the enormous back deck. According to local lore, there's a trap door leading to the bay which was used during Prohibition to gain access to boats bringing in whiskey. **Guaymas** (5 Main St.; tel. 415/435-6300), an upscale Mexican place, is the best restaurant in the neighborhood. They're well-known for ceviche and salsa, as well as mesquite-grilled meats. In warm weather snag a table on the patio where the in-crowd comes for stunning views of the bay, and each other.

SAUSALITO

Sausalito, a cloying coastal town close to the Golden Gate Bridge is home to a mere 7,500 residents. Originally a fishing village-turned-artists' retreat, the village now swarms with tourists, deposited here by the busload to cruise the waterfront, eat forgettable food and shop for trap-crap in a myriad of "art" galleries and T-shirt shacks. In summer, you can hardly get down the street for all the slow-walking "Meanderthals" looking to go nowhere fast. Off-season is a lot friendlier, but the Marin Headlands keep the hamlet in shadows throughout the afternoon. It's worth a stroll to see the houseboats floating just north of town, and the nearby **San Francisco Bay Model** (2100 Bridgeway; tel. 415/332-3870), a working facsimile built by the Army Corps of Engineers to study the tides of the bay. The lively **Mikayla at Casa Madrona**, 801 Bridgeway (tel. 415/332-0502) is the best restaurant in town (which is not saying a lot), serving the usual California/Continental creations in a romantic setting with spectacular views of the Bay.

MARIN HEADLANDS

The Marin Headlands are spectacular. A vast expanse of wildflower-blanketed hills and valleys just north of the Golden Gate Bridge, the Headlands offer amazing views and hiking opportunities just minutes away from the city. The trails are especially popular with local hard-core stoner mountain bikers. But you don't have to be huffing and puffing in order to appreciate the vistas. You can also climb into World War II canon battlements that are still hiding in the hills. Just off Conzelman Road, at the end of a dirt road, you'll find **Kirby Cove**, a secluded beach concealed almost directly beneath the Golden Gate Bridge. **Hawk Hill**, at the top of Conzelman Road, is where you'll find that famous picture-postcard view of the bridge in the foreground, and the city in the distance. **Point Reyes National Seashore** extends up the coast and beyond, opening up the great outdoors for seemingly endless miles.

ThE WiNE COUNtRY

Wine Country delivers a one-two punch of beauty and booze that's hard to top. A joyride through Napa or Sonoma (or both) is one of the best days out we can imagine. It's a great way to learn about wine, or merely an epic excuse to get drunk in the country. Either way, it's an excursion that should be experienced by everyone at least once in their lives.

The terrain is the bombshell: beautiful to look at and exciting to explore, with curves in all the right places. Winding roads dip into lush valleys, then deposit you into the heart of yet another historic town. Along the way dozens of wineries beckon you to stop and taste the fruits of their labor.

California's 700 wineries produce about 90% of the wine made in the US. There are growing regions up and down the state, but the relatively cool and dry valleys just north of San Francisco are the most celebrated. Unlike France, where wines are named for the region in which they are grown, California wines are named after the grapes used to produce them. Chardonnay, the predominant varietal in Burgundy, is the most popular Wine Country white. Cabernet Sauvignon, used in French Bordeaux wines, is Northern California's top red wine grape.

The Lay Of The Land

Napa and Sonoma lie in adjacent valleys about one hour by car north of San Francisco. Although the two regions are divided by less than 20 miles, their separation by Mount St. Helena makes them feel a world apart. It's possible to travel up one valley and down the other in a single day, but that's only for windshield tourists and other masochists.

Napa is the rich and famous sister of the two valleys; the gaudy and gregarious one who relishes publicity, loves the limelight and works hard wooing the fans who obligingly arrive by the busload. Napa's flashy big-business wineries fall all over themselves in endless games of one-upmanship for the attentions of tourists. The result is multi-million dollar architecture and Disneyesque attractions that include tram rides and entertaining tours. No matter that many of these corporate pop shops are also known for producing dismal grapes of wrath. Most of Napa's wineries are concentrated along Highway 29, the Rodeo Drive of Wine Country, that runs the entire 25-mile length of Napa Valley from the town of Napa to Calistoga. It becomes something of a parking lot in summer, when the views you came here for may be continuously obscured by RVs and buses. The off-season (November through March) is better, but even then we recommend you travel the Silverado Trail instead, which runs parallel to Highway 29, and leave behind the tourists in their swerving rentals. It's a lot prettier too. As a rule, the wineries in Napa charge a $3 to $10 fee for tastings.

Sonoma by contrast, is a little bit country to Napa's rock and roll. For those in the know, this is the real wine country, where nobody dresses up to be noticed. It's naturally beautiful and locals fight hard to keep it that way. Corporate winemaking is discouraged here, and natives are quick to wax beat-poetish about the virgin beauty that called them here in the first place. If Napa is sleight-of-hand, than Sonoma is real magic. The wineries are intimate and have an honest quality about them; reinforced by the fact that, unlike Napa, few charge for tastings—that's just not done here. Best of all, Sonoma attracts far fewer crowds. And because it's more spread-out, you can take a back route and feel like you're the only car on the road. Each of the three main parts of Sonoma County is known for a particular kind of wine: the warm hills of Dry Creek are ideal for Zinfandel; the cool climate of the Russian River produces top Pinot Noir, Chardonnay and Sauvignon Blanc; and the coastal influences of the Alexander Valley are ideally suited for Cabernet Sauvignon and Sauvignon Blanc. Happy drinking!

Getting There And Around

Drink and drive—there's really no other choice. Of course we can't endorse such behavior, we're just telling you what most people do. Wine Country is an autopia, especially on summer weekends when it feels as though the entire Bay Area is here.

From San Francisco, cross the Golden Gate Bridge and take 101 north to Highway 37 (Vallejo). For Napa, follow signs to Highway 29; for Sonoma take Highway 121 to Highway 12 which will take you right into the town of Sonoma.

If you're with a group of four or more, a chauffeur-driven limo is a fun alternative that will allow you to get as stewed as you like. **Strawberry Limousine** (tel. 415/381-8016 or 888/891-9533) and **Majestic Limousine** (tel. 415/239-7155 or 888/606-5166) offer Wine Country tours in the $150/day range.

• The **Napa Valley Wine Train** (tel. 800/522-4142) is an off-beat, if slightly vanilla way to tour the Wine Country. The three-hour round-trip runs 36 miles, from Napa to St. Helena and back. It stops at several wineries along the way where some passengers disembark while others stay aboard for a "gourmet-style" meal. Fares are $25/$50 per person (with/without food), and reservations are required.

Ballooning/Gliding

Almost any morning in the Wine Country you can see hot-air balloons floating overhead. The skies above Napa are now replete with companies taking passengers on eagle-eye tours 500 feet above the vineyards. At about $150 a pop flights aren't cheap, but if you've never ballooned before this is a great place to do it. Reliable companies include **Bonaventure Balloon Company** (tel. 800/359-6272); **Balloons Above the Valley** (tel. 800/464-6824); and **Sonoma Thunder** (tel. 415/238-6359).

      Calistoga Gliders, 1546 Lincoln Ave., Calistoga (tel. 707/942-5000) soars their one- and two-passenger sailplanes high above the Napa Valley. Thirty-minute flights cost about $120 for one person and $180 for two. Flights are scheduled daily, on the half hour, weather permitting. Reservations are recommended.

229

THE BEST WINERIES

The Hess Collection
4411 Redwood Rd., Napa.
Tel. 707/255-1144. Open daily
10am–4pm.
Don't miss this cool ivy-covered stone winery, so swellegantly restored it rates high on our Cool-O-Meter. The "collection" refers not just to the ensemble of good wines, but to an impressive assemblage of contemporary European and American art that makes this spot something of a mini-museum. After a few glasses of the home-made hooch, visitors are invited to float through the galleries, many of which have huge windows showcasing the winery-works and ginormous steel wine tanks.

Domaine Carneros
1240 Duhig Rd., Napa.
Tel. 707/257-0101. Open:
Summer, daily 1030am-6pm;
winter, daily 1030am-5pm.
Domaine Carneros is a sparkling winery, both literally and figuratively. The sprawling estate is amazing—built to resemble the 18th Century Chateau de la Marquetterie, residence of the Tattinger family in Champagne—and the winery is one of the few in the area producing sparkling varietals: Brut Cuvee, Blanc de Blancs and Brut Rose. The huge Frenchish mansion is a grandiose eyeful. It's so out of place in the Napa hillside that you half expect Mel Brooks to jump out of the bushes in a pair of tights, singing a number from History of the World. Like most Napa wineries, DC charges a small tasting fee but light snacks are served gratis.

Stag's Leap Wine Cellars
5766 Silverado Trail, Napa.
Tel. 707/944-2020. Open daily
10am-4pm.
Physically Stag's Leap is one of the least pretentious places in the Valley; a modest factory that belies the grand reputation of their wines. But there is nothing unassuming about the winery's 1973 Cabernet Sauvignon, which took first place in a prestigious tasting in Paris. Younger Cab Savs are also world class (Cask 23 is among the most coveted and expensive in California), though they're rarely poured for day-trippers. Detractors criticize management whose pomposity has grown in proportion to the success of their overrated plonk. That said, Stag's one hour tour is one of the best in the neighborhood, covering the wine-making process from grape to glass.

Pine Ridge Winery
5901 Silverado Trail, Napa.
Tel. 707/252-9777. Open daily 11am-5pm.
Away from the well-trodden tourist circuit, Pine Ridge offers a glimpse of the old Napa, before tour buses began herding-in their windshield-tourist passengers. Hidden at the base of a hill wrapped with grapevines, pines and a tangle of rose bushes, the winery is comfort-addicting and perfect for picnicking. The floribundance sprawls into the Demonstration Vineyard, where trellising is explained with a collection of contraptions. Insiders advice: Chenin Blanc.

Domaine Chandon

1 California Dr., Yountville. Tel. 707/944-8844. Open Wed-Sun 11am-6pm.

Founded in 1973 by the French-based Moet et Chandon champagne house, Domaine Chandon is the region's leading producer of *methode champenoise* sparkling wines. The product is outstanding and their breezy French-country salon is the ultimate place in Napa to eat, drink and be very. The adjacent French-California dining room is one of the best restaurants in the Bay Area. It's pricey, but for a better meal you'd have to fly to France. (Reservations are required; tel. 707/944-2892).

Silver Oak Wine Cellars

915 Oakville Cross Road, Oakville. Tel. 707/944-8808. Open Mon-Sat 9am-4pm.

Definitely one to check out, this Mediterranean-style winery is a Napa Valley gem, known for its great wines in general, and outstanding Cabernet Sauvignon in particular. Full-bodied to the point of being Rubenesque, the 100-percent Cabernet Silver Oak routinely sells-out before it's even bottled. The elegant tasting room is inside an imposing masonry building where a knowledgeable and dedicated staff effusively gush their respect for winemaker Justin Meyer.

Opus One

7900 St. Helena Hwy., Oakville. Tel. 707/944-9442. Open daily 1030am-330pm.

Ostentatiously flamboastful, Opus One is the wine world's equivalent to fake breasts and bottle-blondness. There's something so repulsive about its flagrant artificiality that we can't keep from having a look. The architecture's the thing—a shocking stone-and-metal edifice designed by the team who created San Francisco's scandalous Transamerica Pyramid. The result is a marketers' wet dream that has furthered the fame and fortunes of owners Robert Mondavi and Baron Phillipe de Rothschild. Their slick, state-of-the-art operation produces only 30,000 cases of a single wine—a velvety rich cabernet that goes for $15/glass or $150/bottle.

St. Supery Vineyards & Winery

8440 St. Helena Hwy., Rutherford. Tel. 707/963-4507. Open: Summer, daily 930am-6pm; winter, daily 930am-5pm.

OK, here's the plan: swoop through here to really learn something about winemaking, then quickly hit the road. This place is excellent for easy-to-follow instructions on the grape-brewing process. Wander through the Display Vineyard, then check-out the scratch-and-sniff exhibit that helps you differentiate between oaks and tannins. St. Supery is a brainy charmer, but unless you're partial to Silicon Valley business parks or cheap mediocre drinks, skip the tasting, wave good-bye to the tourist herds and move on to greener pastures.

Peju Province Winery

8466 St. Helena Hwy., Rutherford. Tel. 707/963-3600. Open daily 10am-6pm.

As surely as Opus One (above) looks like it's straight out of Architectural Digest, Peju Province seems perfectly cast for House & Garden. It's coffee-table-book beautiful, built in French Provincial-style with luscious gardens, modern statuary and exquisite flower beds. With a total production of less than 10,000 cases per year, their wines are some of the best you've never heard of, and are available exclusively at this winery. Their Cabernets have won numerous awards, as has their massively sweet late-harvest Chardonnay.

Niebaum-Coppola Estate Winery

1991 St. Helena Hwy., Rutherford. Tel. 707/963-9099. Open daily 10am-4pm.

Filmmaker Francis Ford Coppola sunk his profits from Bram Stoker's Dracula into this winery and brought Northern California a bit closer to Planet Hollywood. Coppola's film memorabilia and souvenir shop are tourist trappings, and wine tastings cost as much as a movie ticket. But even we have to acknowledge that the estate's Rubicon—a Cabernet Sauvignon-Merlot-Cabernet Franc blend—is a truly great wine; the mini movie museum is interesting and the beautiful 19th-century, ivy-draped stone chateau is absolutely divine.

Robert Mondavi

7801 St. Helena Highway, Oakville. Tel. 800/666-3284. Open: Summer, daily 930am-530pm; winter daily 930am-430pm.

A pioneer in the Valley, Mondavi is credited by many for putting the Wine Country on the map in the mid-1960s. While he remains a respected name in wine making, Mondavi's newest reputation is as an innovator of mass production. This goes for both the wines and the Mission-style winery, which has become one of the most popular in the Valley for inexperienced grape gulpers. It's actually a great stop for first-time tasters: tours are informative and tastings are free, though in summer it's something of a zoo.

Beringer Vineyards

2000 Main Street, St. Helena. Tel. 707/963-7115. Open: Summer, daily 930am-6pm; winter, daily 930am-5pm.

Boasting one of the biggest names in the Valley, Beringer pulls in crowds by the busload. Its imposing Victorian mansion is the oldest continuously-operating winery in Napa Valley. We would bypass this place entirely but for the decent tour, which highlights some unusual storage caves that were tunneled into the hillside by the same Chinese laborers who built America's Trans-Continental Railroad. When it comes to tasting time, grape nuts praise the vineyard's Chardonnay and Reserve Cabernet. Beringer's Zinfandel, on the other hand, is made for the masses.

RESTAURANTS

French Laundry

6640 Washington St., Yountville. Tel. 707/944-2380. Kitchen open Jun-Oct, Mon-Thurs 530-930pm, Fri-Sun noon-130pm and 530-930pm. Closed Nov-May. Reservations required. Main courses $25-$35. AE, MC, V.

French Laundry is more than a restaurant, it's a veritable institution that's heralded by foodies world-over as one of the best places to eat in the United States. Executive Chef Thomas Keller presides over an intimate country chalet in which every dinner smacks of an exclusive event. What more can we say about a place *The New York Times* called "the most exciting restaurant in America," and in which a food editor at Gourmet magazine said she had one of the best meals on her life? The Frenchish freestyle cuisine (ie. free-range squab with celery root purée, and herb encrusted New England codfish) is best negotiated via multi-course tasting menus; studies in gastronomic gluttony that begin at $85 per head, without wine. Reservations are essential, up to two months (to the day) in advance.

Mustards Grill

7399 St. Helena Highway, Yountville. Tel. 707/944-2424. Kitchen open daily 1130am-10pm. Reservations recommended. Main courses $12-$17. AE, MC, V.

An up-market, friendly-to-the-masses dining room with 1980s written all over it, Mustard's has long been a safe and happy destination for Napa dining. Blessed with a nonstop buzz, it's a bright and happy place that offers something for everyone. Indeed, it's rare that the wait for a table is less than 30 minutes, but few diners seem to mind relaxing by the bar. Entrees are all over the map, from California salads and char-broiled burgers to grilled rabbit and Chinese chicken. Regulars order the deep-fried onion threads with everything.

Pinot Blanc

641 Main Street, St. Helen. Tel. 707/963-6191. Kitchen ope 1130am-10pm. Reservations recommended. Main courses $15-$22. AE, MC, V.

This exceptional French bistro is the brainchild of Joachim Splichel, one of Los Angeles's top chefs. Meals here are faultless rustic/urban combinations that fit perfectly with Napa's vibe. The continually evolving menu might include roast beet and hazelnut salad, ricotta cheese gnocchi with veal and artichokes, or roasted monkfish with white asparagus and purple mustard. Two distinctly different dining areas also define city chic and country adventurousness: Inside it's all snappy wood, leather, and white table cloths, and feels lik a Parisian gentleman's club. Th outside courtyard, shaded by mulber trees and rambling vines, whisks ye away to the French countryside.

Terra

1345 Railroad Ave., St. Helen Tel. 707/963-8931. Kitchen ope Wed-Sun 6-9pm. Reservation Recommended. Main courses $17 $24. AE, MC, V.

Chef/owner Hiro Sone comes to Terra k way of that legendary L.A. institution Spago. The result is one of the Valley' favorite restaurants. An elegant, diml lit dining room is the perfect backdro for adventurous eclectic dishes that include everything from tripe stew and soft goat cheese wantons, to grilled salmon with Thai red-curry sauce. Nothing's cheap, but unforgettable meals often come at a price.

TRiED ANd tRUE WINE-tASTiNg TiPs fROM ThE AVANt*GUidiANS:

* Eat breakfast.
* Plan on a picnic lunch; bring a corkscrew and a sharp knife.
* Six wineries in one day is a lot.
* Don't let newly-bought wine roast in the back seat.
* After one swallow, it's perfectly OK to dump.
* Hold the glass by the stem, extending your pinkie as high as it'll go.

Wine connoisseur vs. Freeloading Swiller

"Full-bodied" =	"Wow, That's Strong"
"Crisp and fruity" =	"Kind of like sucking on a lemon"
"Tannic" =	"Chalky"
"Intensely flavored" =	"My mouth is tingling"
"Noble, with a velvet caress" =	"Regal, yet unpretentious"
"Slightly smoky finish" =	"I can still taste it"
"Woody, over-oaked" =	"Tastes like a barrel"

CHEESE AND WINE SHOPS

Dean & DeLuca
607 South Street, St. Helena. Tel. 707/967-9980. Open Mon-Sat 10am-7pm, Sun 10am-6pm.
As big and bright as a SoHo art gallery, this New York transplant is the ultimate specialty gourmet grocery. Exotic deli items from around the world are especially long on cheese, chocolates and produce, at stratospheric prices.

Oakville Grocery
7845 St. Helena Hwy., Oakville. Tel. 707/977-8802. Open daily 8am-7pm.
Marinites who come up to Napa for the weekend swear by this gourmet picnic supplier for top-of-the-line lunches to go. With a simple phone call one day in advance, the Grocery will pack you a hamper of goodies. The "Epicure" includes paté, salami, brie, olives, cornichons, bread, fresh fruit and homemade cookies. They also do superb sandwiches and a terrific salad nicoise, and offer an extensive wine selection. The adjacent cafe serves light lunches on a sunny outdoor patio.

V. Sattui
1111 White Lane (at Hwy. 29), St. Helena. Tel. 707/799-2357. Open: Summer, daily 9am-6pm; winter, daily 9am-5pm.
This winery-cum-grocery is usually heaving with customers, some of whom are buying lunch and wine, and others who are grazing on the generous free nibbles that are always on offer. This place has such a great selection of cheeses, meats, breads, salads and deserts (including white chocolate cheesecake) that we can almost overlook the crowds. Very good wines too, many of which are sold here exclusively.

HOTELS

Auberge du Soleil

180 Rutherford Hill Road, Rutherford. Tel. 707/
963-1211 or 800/348-5406. Fax 707/963-8764.
aubergdusolei@aol.com; www.aubergedusoleil.com.
$350-$475 single/double. From $500 suite. AE, MC, V.

Time and again the Auberge makes most every list as one of
the finest hotels in the world. This intimate 52 room inn is
the quintessence in self indulgence. All the earthly pleasures are
here, including bedside fireplaces, Jacuzzis, tennis courts and
33 mountainous acres planted with olive trees and crossed
with nature trails. Each of the hotel's twelve suites comes with
a private deck offering heavenly views over the Valley. Prices
are also in the stratosphere, soaring up to $2,000 per night
for the cottage suite. Auberge du Soleil is a member of Relais
& Chateau, a small organization of some of the finest places
to stay in the entire world.

Maison Fleurie

6529 Yount Street, Yountville. Tel. 707/944-2056.
$115-245 single/double. AE, MC, V.

Recently voted one of the "best places to kiss in Napa
Valley" may sound cheesy, but once you step foot
inside this extraordinarily romantic B&B, you too will
want to pucker up. Rooms are housed in three 1873
ivy-covered brick buildings. Each is small and cozy,
and some have fireplaces, private balconies and hot
tubs. Although Yountville is not as charming as
some of the other towns in the Valley, it is
centrally located and within easy reach of a
handful of wineries. When dinnertime rolls
around, borrow a bicycle and peddle to any
number of nearby restaurants.

Deer Run Bed & Breakfast

995 Spring Mountain Road, St. Helena.
Tel. 707/963-3794. $135-160 single/double.
AE, MC, V.

Secluded in the woods, ten minutes from
St. Helena, this four-unit B&B is the one of the
Valley's best known secrets. Far from being a
pampering spa, Deer Run is for individualists
looking to unwind far away from it all. Each
accommodation comes equipped with a feather
bed, a fireplace and a decanter of brandy.

THE BEST WINERIES

Gloria Ferrer Champagne Caves

23555 Arnold Drive, Sonoma. Tel. 707/996-7256. Open daily 1030am-530pm.

Gloria Ferrer wins high praise for its majestic Spanish-style winery built with stucco walls and arched doorways overlooking the rolling Carneros hills. They offer free tapas with tastings—on the terrace in summer, and in front of the fire in winter. Catalan oils and vinegars, olives, anchovies and other gourmet Spanish successories are available in the winery's store.

Cline Cellars

24737 Arnold Drive, Sonoma. Tel. 707/935-4310. Open daily 10am-6pm.

Cline is one of our all time favorites, and not just because it's owned by the descendants of the inventor of the Jacuzzi. Every single wine we've tasted here is outstanding, especially the Zinfandels where for about $8 you can always find something great. The best Zins come from old-growth vines that have been producing grapes for over 130 years. Tastings are laid-back affairs inside a wonderfully-restored green-and-white 1850s farmhouse. There are great views of the Sonoma Valley from well-manicured grounds that are ideal for picnicking. Perhaps we should keep this one to ourselves....

Gundlach-Bundschu Winery

2000 Denmark St., Sonoma. Tel. 707/938-5277. Open daily 11am-430pm.

This winery, on a road less traveled, is also one of the best in Sonoma. Linda Trotta, one of the region's rare female winemakers, is often praised for her Zinfandels, Pinot Noirs, Chardonnays and Rieslings. The staff is great too. Their light-hearted appreciation of the wine-making process combined with serious dedication to the product is a double-barreled pleasurable experience. The old stone winery itself is yet another great place in the hood for a picnic; and a small outdoor theater hosts Shakespearean plays in summer. As the posters in the tasting rooms say, "If you can't say 'Gundlach-Bundschu Gewurztraminer' you shouldn't be driving."

Buena Vista Winery

18000 Old Winery Road, Sonoma. Tel. 707/938-1266 or 800/926-1266. Open: Summer, daily 1030am-5pm; winter, daily, 1030am-4pm.

"Charm" is the operative word at this righteously beautiful old stone winery. The 19th-century historic-landmark is draped in ivy, surrounded by flower gardens, creekside picnic areas and numerous cats. Tastings are offered in the Press House, which also contains a small collection of locally-made art. The second-floor Heritage Bar serves-up rarer, intensely-flavored vintages from the Carneros region.

Kunde Estate Winery

10155 Sonoma Hwy., Kenwood. Tel. 707/833-5501. Open daily 11am-5pm.

Established in 1904, The Kunde's grow such excellent Chardonnays and Zinfandels that they supply grapes to about 30 other wineries in Napa and Sonoma. The wines produced here are exceptional, especially the 1990 Sonoma Valley Chardonnay. Tastings take place in a new winery, built close to the original structure, which stands alongside a duck pond and estuary. You can come just to taste, but the tour is a worthy one and includes awesome aging-caves.

Chateau St. Jean

8555 Sonoma Hwy., Kenwood. Tel. 707/833-4134. Open daily 10am-430pm.

Sizzling views of Sugarloaf Ridge and sweeping vistas of the valley are reasons enough to come here; they will knock your socks off. The drive up is awestriking too. The winery's 1920s chateau and faux-medieval tower are less inspiring, but the wine they pour proves that true beauty is within. Chardonnays and Rieslings are excellent and their 1991 Sonoma Country Reserve Cabernet is something of a one-glass fiesta.

Canyon Road

19950 Geyersville Ave., Geyersville. Tel. 707/857-3417. Open daily 10am-5pm.

One of the newer additions to the Alexander Valley, Canyon Road is definitely worth exploring. It's a pretty place with fascinating cellars and old railroad tracks out back. Daryl Groom and Mick Schroeter create some excellent wines. Excellent values, too. And

while most casual visitors go for the main Canyon Road label, insiders know that their second label, Venezia, is often better tasting and better priced. If you're lucky enough to be in the neighborhood in late fall, Canyon Road invites you to help harvest, then crush this year's grapes.

Chateau Souverain

Independence Lane (at Hwy. 101), Geyserville. Tel. 707/433-8281. Open daily 10am-5pm.

Souverain is an imposing French chateau owned by the Beringers, one of the worlds most powerful winemaking families. Situated on a hill overlooking the Alexander Valley, the view's the thing here: breath-taking Sonoma vistas extend to the distant profile of Mount St. Helena (which is said to look like a local girl, Sarah Date, lying on her back). Chardonnay is the drink of choice, either on the lawn with a picnic or on the balcony of the Chateau Restaurant, which serves good, upscale bistro food from Friday to Sunday.

Pezzi King Vineyards

3805 Lambert Ridge Rd., Healdsburg. Tel. 707/433-3305. Open daily 10am-430pm.

Pezzi King is a small, comfortable winery that, despite its relative newness, has quickly established itself as a favorite of locals. The winery's peaceful tree-hugging anarchitecture fits the Valley to a tee, and is the direct opposite of the future schlock that's overtaken Napa. Try their 1994 Estate Dry Creek Valley Zinfandel, or any Zin or Cab for that matter. There are views galore and picnickers are welcome.

Lambert Bridge Vineyards

4085 West Dry Creek Rd., Healdsburg. Tel. 707/431-9600. Open daily 1030am-430pm.

In 1920 C.L. Lambert built the steel trestle that spans Dry Creek; and today he is honored with two low-key Healdsburg landmarks: Lambert Bridge and the nearby Vineyards that take its name. The redwood winery is a contemporary California beauty, fronted by wisteria-covered trellises and surrounded by towering trees and rolling vineyards. The unique tasting room doubles as a cellar, and behind an enormous floor-to-ceiling glass wall are hundreds of barrels of aging wine. While the winery is especially known for their Merlots and Petite Sirah (our favorite), the Chardonnays are also impressive.

RESTAURANTS & DELIS

Babette's

464 First St., Sonoma. Tel. 707/939-8921. Reservations recommended. Kitchen open daily 11am-930pm. Main courses $16-$24. AE, MC, V.

Once a secret known only to local foodies, Babette's reputation has widened to San Francisco, and beyond. It's an enchanting place, with great food and a phunky atmosphere that perfectly reflects the feeling of Sonoma in general. Set in a cobblestoned alley just off the town square, this intimate French restaurant has the feel of a Left Bank living room. Presided over by chef Daniel Pattern (formerly of Napa's Domaine Chandon and Mustards Grill), the kitchen turns-out equally informal fare from soups, salads and sandwiches to caviar and goat cheese salad, roasted monkfish with leeks, and pan-roasted veal with mushrooms.

Della Santina's

133 East Napa St., Sonoma. Tel. 707/935-0576. Reservations recommended. Kitchen open daily 11am-930pm. Main courses $13-$20. AE, MC, V.

Locals in search of authentico food, moderate prices and an unpretentious atmosphere, often end up at this intimate trattoria. Casual indoor and outdoor seating contrasts with top-notch Italian cuisine, including some of the best roasted meats anywhere. Pastas are great, too, including tender gnocchi and chicken-filled cannelloni. Top it all off with a killer tiramisu.

Bistro Ralph

109 Plaza St., Healdsburg. Tel. 707/433-1380. Reservations recommended Kitchen open daily 11am-930pm. Main courses $13-$18. AE, MC, V.

Ralph Tingle's wonderful restaurant is almost like a private dining room for local winemakers. Like most good eateries, Ralph offers a short menu done right. The Californian bistro fare includes fresh grilled fish, roasted poultry, and the chef's signature Caesar's salad. Insiders order shoestring potatoes with everything. They also do a knock-out creme brulee. We also recommend Ralph's spin-off restaurant, Felix & Louie (106 Matheson St., Healdsburg; tel. 707/433-6966), which serves excellent pasta and pizza.

The Girl and The Fig

13690 Arnold Dr., Glen Ellen. Tel. 707/938-3634. Reservations Recommended. Kitchen open daily 11am-10pm. Main courses $17-$24. AE, MC, V.

This delightfully low-key bohemian cafe is quickly winning fans with creative meals and offbeat surroundings. True to its name, figs are the featured ingredient, both fresh and dried, in arugula and goat cheese salads, with rack of lamb, on pork tenderloin and baked with fish. Fittingly, the wine selection focuses on Rhone-style selections, many of which are available by the glass. The restaurant has become something of a locals' scene, and is thoroughly recommended as an experience that is replicated nowhere else.

Sonoma Cheese Factory

2 Spain Street, Sonoma. Tel. 707/996-1000. Open Mon.-Fri 830am-530pm, Sat-Sun 830am-6pm.

Located on the Plaza, this shop offers more home-made jack cheeses than we've seen outside Wisconsin. A wedge of something aged and sharp, along with crackers, fresh cold cuts and marinated olives makes the perfect Sonoma picnic.

HOTELS

Sonoma Mission Inn & Spa

18140 Highway 12, Boyes Hot Springs. Tel. 707/938-9000 or 800/862-4945. Fax 707/996-5358. smi@smispa.com; www.sonomamissioninn.com. $160-$275 single/double. Suites from $295. AE, MC, V.

Sonoma Mission Inn is the best spa in the Bay Area. It's a place for pampering, with a huge number of Gumby-inducing treatments from Swedish massage, reflexology and shiatsu, to aromatherapy, sports rubs, body scrubs, wraps and facials. And because it's in California, they even have tarot-card readings and personal meditation consultations. Hollywood types, including Barbra and Sly have been spotted racing through these hallways in their robes.

El Dorado Inn

405 First Street West, Sonoma. Tel. 707/996-3030 or 800/289-3031. Fax 707/996-3148. $110-$175 single/double. AE, MC, V.

From the outside, El Dorado looks like it dropped out of the Wild West. But the inside has all the lux of a deluxe hotel, complete with concierge and bellmen. This is a great choice for those who wish to stay in the Wine Country, but don't need all the bells and whistles of a full-on resort. Rooms are upscale and casual, and come with continental breakfast and a split of wine.

¶
¶
#11

PLANNiNG:
BEfORE yOU GO
ESSENTiALS

The www.avantguide.com *CyberSupplement*™ is the best source for happenings in San Francisco during your stay. Visit us for book updates and links to info on cultural events and other happenings.

For specific questions, contact the **San Francisco Convention & Visitors Bureau**, P.O.Box 429097, San Francisco, CA 94102 (tel. 415/974-6900; www.sfvisitor.org). Drop them a postcard and the Bureau will send you a free package containing information about the city, and discount coupons to stores, attractions, sightseeing companies and more.

Weather

Situated as it is on a peninsula, San Francisco is susceptible to a wide variety of climactic changes: sunshine, rain, heat, cold, calm, windy—sometimes all in a single day. Locals know that sticking their head out the window in the morning will provide little help in determining what to wear. Especially if you're planning to move around a lot. Often the city is sunny and warm in the Mission District while at the same time chilling under that famous foggy "Marine Layer" in the Marina District (where Mark Twain is supposed to have said "The coldest winter I ever spent was a summer in San Francisco"). The best advice: prepare for every eventuality.

San Francisco Weather Averages

Month:	Temperature Ranges
January:	46-56°F / 08-13°C
February:	48-59°F \ 09-15°C
March:	49-60°F / 09-16°C
April:	49-61°F \ 09-16°C
May:	51-63°F / 11-17°C
June:	53-64°F \ 12-18°C
July:	53-64°F / 12-18°C
August:	54-65°F \ 12-19°C
September:	56-69°F / 13-21°C
October:	55-68°F \ 13-20°C
November:	52-63°F / 11-17°C
December:	47-57°F \ 08-14°C

For Travelers with Disabilities
Steep hills notwithstanding, San Francisco is very hospitable to wheelchair-bound and other disabled travelers. Buses kneel, sidewalks are smooth and every curb and public building is ramped.

For information on the city's disabled access, contact the San Francisco Convention & Visitors Bureau (see above). They maintain a TDD/TTY information line at 415/392-0328.

SAVING MONEY GETTING THERE

Frankly, we don't trust most travel agents to really dig for the lowest fares. They get paid a small percentage of the price of each ticket, so it doesn't benefit them to spend *more* time trying to make *less* money. We usually make reservations ourselves, directly with the airlines, then visit our travel agent for ticketing. Here's the secret to getting the best deal: If you don't know airline jargon, don't use it. Just ask for the lowest fare. If you're flexible with dates and times, tell the sales agent. Ask him or her to hunt a bit.

******* THE MAJOR AIRLINES *******

Air Canada (US tel. 800/776-3000; UK tel. 0990/247266)
Air France (US tel. 800/237-2747; UK tel. 0181/742 6600)
Air India (US tel. 800/442-4455; UK tel. 0171/495 7950)
Air New Zealand (US tel. 800/262-1234)
Alaska Airlines (US tel. 800/426-0333)
American Airlines (US tel. 800/433-7300; UK tel. 0345/789789)
Austrian Airlines (US tel. 800/843 0002; UK tel. 0171/434 7350)
British Airways (US tel. 800/247 9297; UK tel. 0345/222 111)
Continental Airlines (US tel. 800/525-0280; UK tel. 0800/776 464)
Delta Air Lines (US tel. 800/221-1212; UK tel. 0800/414 767)
KLM (US tel. 800/777-5553; UK tel. 0990/074074)
Lufthansa (US tel. 800/645-3880; UK tel. 0345/737747)
Northwest Airlines (US tel. 800/225-2525; UK tel. 01293/543511)
Quantas (US tel. 800/227-4500; UK tel. 0345/747767)
SAS (US tel. 800/221-2350; UK tel. 0171/734 6777)
Southwest Airlines (US tel. 800/435-9792; UK tel. 01293/596677)
Swissair (US tel. 800/221-4750; UK tel. 0171/434 7300)
Trans World Airlines (US tel. 800/221-2000; UK tel. 0345/333333)
United Airlines (US tel. 800/241-6522; UK tel. 0845/8444777)
US Airways (US tel. 800/428-4322; UK tel. 0800/7835556)
Virgin Atlantic (US tel. 800/862-8621; UK tel. 01293/747 747)

Budget Airlines & Consolidators

Recently, we have been buying airplane tickets almost exclusively from consolidators. Also known as "bucket shops," consolidators are travel agents that buy airline seats in bulk in return for deep discounts. This business has become so sophisticated that most bucket shops now buy their tickets from even larger wholesalers. To find the best fare at any given time, check the travel sections of *The New York Times*, the *Los Angeles Times* or Time Out magazine in London. Bucket shop ads are usually very small and list a lot of destinations. The consolidators we use to get to San Francisco are:

USA: Cheap Tickets, 115 East 57th St., (tel. 212/570-1179 or 800/377-1000).

Britain: European Travel Center, 216 Earls Court Rd., London SW5 (tel. 0171/373 80)

Packages vs. Tours

When it comes to travel lingo, most people confuse packages and tours. In the industry, a tour usually refers to a group that travels together, follows a flag-toting leader and is herded on and off buses. Obviously, we seldom recommend this kind of tourism.

A package, on the other hand, is a travel deal in which several components of a trip—transportation, accommodation, airport transfers and the like—are bundled together for sale to independent, unescorted travelers. Many independent travelers purchase complete vacations from travel agents without ever knowing that they're buying a package. That's O.K.—packages can offer great values. Package companies buy in bulk, and are often able to sell complete vacations for less than you'd pay when buying each component individually.

Independent packages to San Francisco are offered by most US airlines, including **American Airlines Fly AAway Vacations** (tel. 800/634-5555), **Delta Dream Vacations** (tel. 800/872-7786), **TWA Getaway Vacations** (tel. 800/438-2929), and **United Airlines' Vacation Planning Center** (tel. 800/328-6877).

CARS & dRiViNG

You don't need a car in San Francisco, but it's nice to have one. Parking is difficult and expensive (at least $20/day) and public transport and taxis can get you everywhere. But if money is no object, by all means get behind the wheel. The city is bigger then it initially looks and flying over the hills is a gas—especially in a rental car. If you're planning a trip to Wine Country or elsewhere outside the peninsula, then a car is almost mandatory.

Auto Rentals

As usual, the big international car-rental firms are the most expensive. Rates vary, but expect to pay about $50 per day and $300 per week, including unlimited mileage, for a two-door tin can. Competition is sometimes fierce, and we've seen deals as low as $150 per week. Compare **Alamo** (tel. 800/327-9633), **Avis** (tel. 800/331-1212), **Budget** (tel. 800/527-0700), **Dollar** (tel. 800/800-4000), **Enterprise** (tel. 800/325-8007), **Hertz** (tel. 800/654-3131) and **National** (tel. 800/227-7368).

Local rental firms are cheaper, but their cars are decidedly worse. Try **A-1 Rent-a-Car** (320 O'Farrell St; tel. 415/292-1000) or **Reliable Rent-a-Car** (349 Mason St; tel. 415/928-4414).

At the other end of the spectrum there's **Specialty Car Rental** (tel. 415/433-6500) offering Jaguars, Porsches, Ferraris and other luxury cars by the day or week. They deliver to your hotel. **Service in Style** (tel. 415/677-8953; www.serviceinstyle.com) offers 24-hour professional limousine service.

iN-SEASON: tHE bEST ANNUAL hAPPENiNGS

Weatherwise, the best time to visit San Francisco (or almost anyplace, actually) is in late spring and early fall. When it comes to crowds, summer is the cruelest season. General city information and detailed calendars of performing arts events, museum exhibitions and sporting events for the next 12 months are available online at no charge via the *San Francisco Convention & Visitors Bureau Website* (www.sfvisitor.org) or through their FastFax system (tel. 617/960-9216 or 800/220-5747).

Public Holidays

January 1	New Year's Day
January (3rd Monday)	Martin Luther King's Birthday (observed)
February (3rd Monday)	Presidents' Day
May (last Monday)	Memorial Day (observed)
July 4	Independence Day
September (1st Monday)	Labor Day
October (2nd Monday)	Columbus Day
November 11	Veterans Day
November (4th Thursday)	Thanksgiving
December 25	Christmas Day

JANUARY: MacWorld Expo, one of the biggest geek events of the year takes over the Moscone Center (Tel. 310/455-2886).

fEbRUARY: **Chinese New Year** is celebrated in SFs Chinatown later in the month. Dragon dancers snake through streets crammed with crowds, decorations and food stalls (tel. 415/982-3000).

MARCh: **St. Patrick's Day Parade** staggers down Market Street, from Fifth Street to the Embarcadero on the Sunday before March 17th (tel. 415/661-2700).

APRiL: Cherry Blossom Festival, in Japantown
during the first two weekends of the month, includes traditional crafts and excellent drumming performances (tel. 415/563-2313).

MAY: Bay to Breakers Footrace, a wacky *San Francisco Examiner*-sponsored 7.5-mile (12k) event that's more about how silly you look then how fast you run. On the 3rd Sunday of the month (tel. 415/808-5000).
Carnival San Francisco takes over the Mission District on Memorial Day Weekend with a huge parade, music and food. (tel. 415/826-1401).

jUNE: Haight Street Fair, on one weekend day early in the month, is all the excuse thousands of people need to wear tie-dye and pop hallucinogens. (tel. 415/661-8025).
North Beach Festival, in Washington Square is a more laid-back affair with lots of arts and crafts and plenty of Italian street food. (tel. 415/989-6426).
KQED International Beer and Food Festival, the city's premiere event for foodies, attracts star chefs who cook for charity. In the middle of the month at the Concourse Exhibition Center (tel. 510/762-BASS).
Lesbian/Gay/Bisexual/Transgender Pride Celebration Party, better known at the Gay Pride Parade, is one of the city's best parties attracting royalty from both the government and the Castro. Held at the end of the month. (tel. 415/864-FREE; www.sf.pride.org).

jULY: San Francisco Marathon takes over the city early in the month (tel. 415/296-7111).
July Fourth Festivities are held along the waterfront near Fisherman's Wharf. We go for the fog-shrouded fireworks.

AUGUSt: Comedy Celebration Day is a free, outdoor comedy marathon held in Golden Gate Park's Sharon Meadow in the middle of the month. It's great. (tel. 415/777-8498).
Nihon Machi Street Fair, in the middle of the month, is a celebration of Japanese culture in Japantown and the Japan Center (tel. 415/771-9861).

SEPTEMbER: Sidewalk Painting Festival, atFisherman's Wharf's Anchorage Shopping Center, is one of the few events worth fighting the tourists for. At the beginning of the month (tel. 415/382-9293).

Blues & Art on Polk, at the beginning of the month, is a fun street fair that lives up to its name (tel. 415/346-9162).

Sausalito Art Festival, a major juried exhibit accompanied by music, food and wine is one of the season's most anticipated events. Held on Labor Day Weekend (tel. 415/332-3555).

Festival De Las Americas, formerly known as Mexican Independence Day, is yet another excuse for a Mission District street party. Held in the middle of the month (tel. 415/826-1401).

San Francisco Blues Festival, a weekend-long fest of the best blues west of the Mississippi. Held the third or fourth weekend of the month at Fort Mason Center. Tickets $25 per day (tel. 415/979-5588).

The Folsom Street Fair, the last Sunday in September is an adults-only party that rivals the Gay Pride Parade and Halloween for fun and debauchery (tel. 415/861-3247).

OCtObER: Open Studios, a two-decade tradition in which local artists open their studios to the public each weekend of the month. Tickets costs about $15 (tel. 415/861-9838).

Fleet Week, a celebration by the US Navy brings thousands of sailors, dozens of warships and amazing displays by the low-flying Blue Angels.

Reggae in the Park, yet another great Golden Gate Park music festival. The two-day affair is becoming one of the city's hottest annual tickets. Held early in the month; admission $15. (tel. 415/458-1988).

Castro Street Fair, Castro St. Tel. 415/467-3354. One of the city's very best annual festivals. Held in the middle of the month.

Great Pumpkin Weigh-Off, at the Ferry Plaza Farmer's Market attracts monstrous and abnormal orange gourds from around the country. Held in the middle of the month (tel. 415/346-9162).

Halloween Celebrations, moved from the Castro to the Civic Center and became less intense in the process. There's still plenty of fun to be had if you dress for participation (tel. 415/777-5500).

NOVEMbER: San Francisco Bay Area Book Festival, at the Concourse Exhibition Center, is the West Coast's premiere book fair. Admission $3 (tel. 415/908-2833).

FOR FOREIGN VISITORS

Document Regulations

Brits, Kiwis, South Africans and most Euros don't need a visa to enter the US for less than 90 days. A passport with an expiration date at least six months later than the scheduled end of your visit to the United States, and a roundtrip (return) ticket are usually required for entry, along with proof of sufficient funds.

Citizens of most other countries, including those of Australia, must also obtain a tourist visa, available from US embassies and consulates.

Canadians can enter the US without passports or visas, and need only proof of residence.

Medical Requirements

Inoculations are not normally required to enter the United States.

Customs Requirements

Each adult visitor may bring into the US free of duty: one liter of wine or hard liquor; 200 cigarettes or 100 cigars or three pounds of smoking tobacco; and $100 worth of gifts. No goods are allowed in from Cuba, North Korea, Libya and other enemies of the US. It's also *verboten* to bring foodstuffs (particularly cheese, fruit, cooked meats, and canned goods) and plants (including vegetables and seeds). Foreign visitors may import up to $10,000 in US or foreign currency with no formalities; you're allowed to move larger sums, but they must be declared to Customs upon entering.

Insurance

Because there is no national health system in the United States and medical care is extremely expensive, we strongly advise you to wait until you return home before you fall ill. Failing that, you might wish to take out a travel insurance policy that covers sickness or injury costs. Travel insurance is often available through automobile clubs and travel agencies.

Dollars & Dont's

The almighty dollar is the coin of the realm, and is divided into 100 cents. Greenbacks come in $1, $5, $10, $20, $50, and $100 denominations. If you encounter a $2 bill, think about keeping it as a souvenir—everyone else does.

Coins are minted in 1¢ (one cent or "penny"), 5¢ (five cents or "nickel"), 10¢ (ten cents or "dime") and 25¢ (twenty-five cents or "quarter") denominations. Although they exist, you will rarely encounter 50¢ (fifty cents or "half dollar") or $1 ("buck") coins.

"Foreign Exchange Bureaus" that are common in Europe and Asia are rare in the US—they don't even exist at many airports in the United States. Don't even think of trying to exchange foreign currency outside most major US cities.

Traveler's Cheques

Traveler's cheques denominated in US dollars are accepted at most hotels and restaurants, as well as in larger stores. Do not bring traveler's cheques denominated in other currencies as nobody will know what to do with them.

You'll find the best exchange rates at **American Express** (tel. 800/528-4800 for the nearest location), where checks from all issuers are exchanged commission-free. Some restaurants and many hotels will exchange traveler's checks, but their rates are always much worse than banks.

Credit & Charge Cards

The US practically runs on credit. The federal government is overextended, and so are most of the country's citizens. Yes, credit cards are accepted virtually everywhere. MasterCard (EuroCard in Europe, Access in Britain, Chargex in Canada), Visa (Barclaycard in Britain), American Express, Diners Club, Discover and Carte Blanche are not only accepted in most hotels, restaurants and retail stores, but are increasingly the payment of choice in food and liquor stores as well. Most ATMs accept credit cards for cash advances (be sure to have a Personal Identification Number).

Essentials for Foreigners

✳ Business Hours   Most **offices** are open Monday through Friday from 9am to 5pm. **Stores** are usually open daily, including Sunday. **Banks** are usually open Monday through Friday from 9am to 3 or 4pm; 24-hour automated teller machines (ATMs) are installed at most banks and many other places as well.

✳ Climate   Average monthly temperatures are listed above. Check avantguide.com. for this week's weather conditions.

✳ Computers/Internet   If you have trouble jacking-in, visit **The CoffeeNet**, 774 Harrison St (btw Third/Fourth Sts; tel. 415/495-7447; www.coffeenet.net) a cyber spot with Web access that's the choice of SFs digerati. **Internet Alfredo**, 790A Brannan St (at Seventh St; tel. 415/437-3140) has 18 terminals and is usually open nonstop.

✳ Currency Exchange   In San Francisco visit **American Express**, 455 Market St (tel. 415/778-5420 or 800/528-4800 for the nearest location). They exchange foreign currency commission-free, and offer competitive rates.

✳ Drinking Laws   In the US you can be drafted into the military at age 18, but 21 to legally purchase alcohol. Go figure. Beware that San Francisco enforces an open container law which prohibits drinking alcohol in parks and other public places.

✳ Electricity   110-120 volts AC, 60 cycles. European appliances need to be plugged into converters.

✳ Embassies/Consulates   In addition to embassies, all of which are located in Washington, D.C., many countries maintain consulates in major US cities. The embassy of **Canada** is at 501 Pennsylvania Ave. NW, Washington, DC 20001 (tel. 202/6821740). There are Canadian consulates in New York, Los Angeles, Atlanta, Buffalo (NY), Chicago, Dallas, Detroit, Miami, Minneapolis, San Francisco, and Seattle. The embassy of the **United Kingdom** is at 3100 Massachusetts Ave. NW, Washington, D.C. 20008 (tel. 202/4621340). British consulates are located in New York, Los Angeles, Atlanta, Boston, Chicago, Houston, Miami and San Francisco. The embassy of the **Republic of Ireland** is at 2234 Massachusetts Ave. NW,

Washington, D.C. 20008
(tel. 202/4623939). There are Irish
consulates in New York, San Francisco,
Boston and Chicago. The embassy of
Australia is at 1601 Massachusetts Ave.
NW, Washington, D.C. 20036
(tel. 202/7973000). Australian consulates
are located in New York, Los Angeles,
Honolulu, Houston and San Francisco.
The embassy of New Zealand is at 37
Observatory Circle NW, Washington, D.C.
20008 (tel. 202/3284848). There is a New
Zealand consulate in Los Angeles.

* Emergencies 911 is the number
to call to report a fire, to call the police,
or get an ambulance. From public
telephones no coins are required for
a 911 call.

* Gasoline (Petrol) One US gallon
equals 3.8 liters or .85 Imperial gallons.
Most gas stations offer lower priced
"self-service" gas pumps and several
grades of gas; fill your rental with the
cheapest.

* Holidays Banks, government
offices, post offices, and many stores,
restaurants, and museums are closed on
the following legal national holidays:
January 1 (New Year's Day), the third
Monday in January (Martin Luther King
Day), the third Monday in February
(Presidents' Day, Washington's Birthday),
the last Monday in May (Memorial Day),
July 4 (Independence Day), the first
Monday in September (Labor Day), the
second Monday in October (Columbus
Day), November 11 (Veterans
Day/Armistice Day), the last Thursday in
November (Thanksgiving Day), and
December 25 (Christmas). Also, the
Tuesday following the first Monday in
November is Election Day, and is a legal
holiday in presidential election years.

* Information (*see* Chapter
2/Information).

* Taxes There is no
VAT or any other national sales tax in the
US. Instead, each state and municipality
is entitled to levy its own tariff on
purchases, and these range from 0% to
about 9%. Hotel "bed" taxes can be 15%
or more. Taxes are already figured-in for
some services, including transportation,
telephone calls, and gasoline, otherwise
they are tacked on at the register.

In San Francisco, the combined city
and state sales taxes amount to 8.5%. The
local hotel occupancy tax is 13%.

* Telephone/Fax The cost of a phone
call varies widely in the US, depending on
which private carrier you are using. Local
calls made from public pay phones cost
between 20¢ and 35¢. In San Francisco
its 35¢ for the first three minutes.

Long distance and international calls
can be dialed directly from almost any
phone. Because most American pay
phones don't accept "smart" cards, it can
be both expensive and unwieldy to call long
distance on a roll of quarters. Pre-paid
phone cards are the cheapest way to go.
These are usually sold in denominations
of $10 and $20, and are available at
grocery and drug stores throughout San
Francisco.

When calling from the US to other
parts of the United States or Canada, dial
1 followed by the area code and the
seven digit number. For international
calls, dial 011 followed by the country
code (Australia, 61; Republic of Ireland,
353; New Zealand, 64; United Kingdom,
44), the city code, and the telephone
number of the person you wish to call.

Be forewarned that hotel surcharges
on both long distance and local calls can
be astronomical. Think about using
a public pay phone in the lobby.

For local **directory assistance** (a.k.a. "information" or "directory inquiries") dial 411; for long distance information dial 1, then the appropriate area code and 555-1212.

For **Cellular Phone Rental** contact **Action Cellular Rent A Phone**, 99 Osgood Place (tel. 415/929-0400; www.rentaphone.com; hello@rentaphone.com). They deliver rentals on a daily or weekly basis.

* Time   The contiguous United States is divided into four time zones. From west to east, these are: pacific standard time (PST), mountain standard time (MST), central standard time (CST) and eastern standard time (EST).

San Francisco is usually eight hours behind Greenwich mean time. Daylight saving time, which moves the clock one hour ahead of standard time, is in effect from the last Sunday in April through the last Saturday in October .

* Tipping   Hourly wages in the service industry are very low as waiters, bartenders and the like are expected to make the bulk of their money from tips. That's the reason why service in America is so good compared to Europe. Here are the rules of thumb: Restaurants, bars, and nightclubs: 15% of the check to waiters; $1 per drink to bartenders; $1 per garment to check-room attendants; $1 to parking valets when retrieving your car. Cab drivers: 15% of the fare. hotels: $1 per piece to bellhops; $10 per service to the concierge, especially if you plan on staying there again. Airports: $1 per piece to redcaps. Hairdressers: 15 to 20 percent, provided they didn't scalp you.

* Video System   NTSC

AMERiCAN SYStEM Of MEASUREMENtS

Length

1 inch (in.) = 2.54cm
1 foot (ft.) = 12 in. = 30.48cm = .305m
1 yard = 3 ft. = .915m
1 mile (mi.) = 5,280 ft. = 1.609km
MILES TO KILOMETERS
multiply the number of miles by 1.61 (100 miles x 1.61 = 161km).
KILOMETERS TO MILES
multiply the number of kilometers by .62 (100km x .62 = 62 miles).

Liquid Volume

1 fluid ounce (fl. oz.) = .03 liter
1 pint = 16 fl. oz. = .47 liter
1 quart = 2 pints = .94 liter
1 gallon (gal.) = 4 quarts = 3.79 liter = .83 Imperial gal.
US GALLONS TO LITERS
multiply the number of gallons by 3.79 (10 gal. x 3.79 = 37.9 liters).
US GALLONS TO IMPERIAL GALLONS
multiply the number of US gallons by .83 (10 US gal. x .83 = 8.3 Imperial gal.).
IMPERIAL GALLONS TO US GALLONS
multiply the number of Imperial gallons by 1.2 (10 Imp. gal. x 1.2 = 12 US gal.).
LITERS TO US GALLONS
multiply the number of liters by .26 (10 liters x .26 = 2.6 US gal.).

Weight

1 ounce (oz.) = 28.35 grams
1 pound (lb.) = 16 oz. = 453.6 grams = .45 kilograms (kg)
1 ton = 2.000 lb. = 907 kg = .91 metric ton

POUNDS TO KILOGRAMS
multiply the number of pounds by .45 (10 lb. x .45 = 4.5kg).

KILOGRAMS TO POUNDS
multiply the number of kilograms by 2.2 (10kg x 2.2 = 22 lb.).

Area

1 acre = .41 hectare
1 square mile (sq. mi.) = 640 acres = 2.59 hectares = 2.6km

ACRES TO HECTARES
multiply the number of acres by .41 (10 acres x .41 = 4.1ha).

SQUARE MILES TO SQUARE KILOMETERS
multiply the number of square miles by 2.6 (10 sq. mi. x 2.6 = 26km2)

HECTARES TO ACRES
multiply the number of hectares by 2.47 (10ha x 2.47 = 24.7 acres).

SQUARE KILOMETERS TO SQUARE MILES
multiply the number of square kilometers by .39 (100km2 x .39 = 39 sq. mi.).

Temperature

DEGREES FAHRENHEIT TO DEGREES CELSIUS
subtract 32 from —F, multiply by 5, then divide by 9 (85—F - 32 x 5 ÷ 9 = 29.4—C).

DEGREES CELSIUS TO DEGREES FAHRENHEIT
multiply —C by 9, divide by 5, and add 32 (20—C x 9 ÷ 5 + 32 = 68—F).

Clothing Conversion Chart

WOMEN'S CLOTHES					
UK:	08	10	12	14	16
US:	06	08	10	12	14
Euro:	38	40	42	44	46

WOMEN'S SHOES							
UK:	03	04	05	06	07	08	09
US:	05	06	07	08	09	10	11
Euro:	36	37	38	39	40	41	42

MEN'S CLOTHES					
UK:	38	40	42	44	46
US:	38	40	42	44	46
Euro:	48	50/52	54	56	58/60

MEN'S SHOES					
UK:	8	09	10	11	12
US:	9	10	11	12	13
Euro:	42	43	44	45	46

iNDEXES